Immigrant Prince

Florida Government and Politics

UNIVERSITY PRESS OF FLORIDA

Florida A&M University, Tallahassee
Florida Atlantic University, Boca Raton
Florida Gulf Coast University, Ft. Myers
Florida International University, Miami
Florida State University, Tallahassee
New College of Florida, Sarasota
University of Central Florida, Orlando
University of Florida, Gainesville
University of North Florida, Jacksonville
University of South Florida, Tampa
University of West Florida, Pensacola

IMMIGRANT PRINCE

Mel Martinez and the American Dream

RICHARD E. FOGLESONG

Foreword by David Colburn and Susan MacManus

University Press of Florida

Gainesville · Tallahassee · Tampa · Boca Raton

Pensacola · Orlando · Miami · Jacksonville · Ft. Myers · Sarasota

16   15   14   13   12   11   6   5   4   3   2   1

Library of Congress Cataloging-in-Publication Data
Foglesong, Richard E., 1948–
Immigrant prince : Mel Martinez and the American dream / Richard E. Foglesong;
foreword by David Colburn and Susan MacManus.
p. cm.
Includes bibliographical references and index.
ISBN 978-0-8130-3579-6 (alk. paper)
1. Martinez, Mel (Melquiades Rafael), 1946– 2. Legislators—United States—
Biography. 3. United States. Congress. Senate—Biography. 4. United States.
Dept. of Housing and Urban Development—Officials and employees—
Biography. 5. Cabinet officers—United States—Biography. 6. Politicians—
Florida—Biography. 7. Cuban Americans—Biography. 8. Immigrants—
United States—Biography. I. Title.
E901.1.M37F64   2011
328.73'0929–dc22 [B]   2010042229

The University Press of Florida is the scholarly publishing agency for the State
University System of Florida, comprising Florida A&M University, Florida
Atlantic University, Florida Gulf Coast University, Florida International
University, Florida State University, New College of Florida, University
of Central Florida, University of Florida, University of North Florida,
University of South Florida, and University of West Florida.

University Press of Florida
15 Northwest 15th Street
Gainesville, FL 32611-2079
http://www.upf.com

To Jeri

A man who wishes to make a profession of goodness in everything must come to grief among so many who are not good. Therefore it is necessary for a prince, who wishes to maintain himself, to learn how not to be good, and to use this knowledge and not use it, according to the necessity of the case.

NICCOLÒ MACHIAVELLI, *THE PRINCE*

CONTENTS

FOREWORD

Florida has held a unique place in the American mind for more than six decades. For many retirees, its environment has been like a healthy elixir that has allowed them to live longer and more robust lives; for others, Florida is a place of renewal, where all things are possible; and for immigrants, it represents a place of political freedom and opportunity. Florida has been described by one leading state historian as a "powerful symbol of renewal and regeneration." Those who relocated into the state observed that, if Florida had not existed in the post–World War II era, they and many others would have been much the poorer for it. Others who watched the results of the 2000 presidential election wondered if that were so.

During World War II, Americans from all walks of life discovered Florida through military service, and it opened their eyes to the postwar possibilities. When the war ended in August 1945, Florida veterans returned home, where they were soon joined by hundreds and then thousands of Americans who were anxious to pursue a new life in the Sunshine State. By the end of the century the population had grown almost tenfold, to 18 million.

Florida's population growth, the settlement patterns of new residents, and their ethnic and racial diversity had a profound effect on the state's place in the nation as well as the image Floridians had of themselves. Prior to 1940, Florida was the least populous state in the South and one of the poorest in the nation. Its society and economy were rural and agricultural, biracial and segregated, and most residents lived within forty miles of the Georgia border. These demographics and the state's history shaped the public's racial and cultural mindset and its politics. Florida was a one-party state, controlled by the Democratic Party since the end of Reconstruction in 1876.

All that changed in the fifty-five years following World War II. By 2000, in less than an average life span today, Florida became the most populous state in the region and fourth in the nation, a senior haven, and a dynamic multiracial and multiethnic state. Most Floridians now reside closer to the Caribbean than they do to Georgia, and their image of themselves and their state has been significantly influenced by this new geographic orientation. By the twenty-first century, demographers viewed Florida as a microcosm of the nation because of its size and population complexity.

As Florida changed, so too did its politics. In 1968, voters threw out the Constitution of 1885 in favor of a new document that spoke to the needs of a modern state with a diverse population. In the two decades that followed, "Blue Dog" Democrats, Republican retirees, Cuban immigrants, and religious conservatives threw their support to the national Republican Party and more gradually to the state Republican Party. Florida Republicans relied on their expanding constituency to assert control over the districting process in 1992. While heavily Democratic majority-minority districts were carved out of densely populated urban areas, the state's high-growth suburban districts were designed to favor Republicans. Within three years, the Republican Party took control of the state legislature and the congressional delegation. These were remarkable political developments and reflected the dramatic population shifts and social changes occurring in Florida.

Despite the Republican ascendancy, Democrats have continued to compete successfully in statewide races for governor, the U.S. Senate, and elected cabinet positions, as well as in presidential contests. Registered Democrats outnumber Republicans by 6 percentage points (42 percent to 36 percent), but the tendency for "Blue Dog" Democrats to vote Republican, together with the dramatic expansion of registered Independent voters, has made the outcome of state elections uncertain in the extreme. Of the four most populous states in the nation—California, Texas, New York, and Florida—far and away the most competitive is Florida, and it has become the political battleground in presidential elections.

The political competitiveness and complexity of Florida have led political analysts to observe that "as Florida goes, so goes the nation." It is a state to which people throughout the country and, indeed, the world are connected through relatives, retirement, vacations, space exploration, or the 2000 presidential election. As a result, Florida politics are often imported from other countries and other regions of the United States.

The fact that two-thirds of Florida's residents in 2005 came from other states or other nations suggests the volatility of its politics. As one political scientist commented, if a politician counts on "last election year's demographics to win this year's election, he/she might very well lose."

With such a politically and demographically complex and diverse population, Florida today cannot be regarded as a unified whole. The political maxim "All politics is local" has been truer of Florida than of most other states. For example, those who reside in North Florida have little in common with those living in Central or South Florida. Residents of southeastern Florida see themselves as part of the "new America," while those in North Florida view the southeast region as a foreign country. Even within the Hispanic community, profound political differences exist between Cubans and other Hispanics. The political divide in the state is magnified by large and diverse media markets (ten in all), which appeal to the uniqueness of the state's regions and its residents. Not surprisingly given this political diversity, microtargeting was first utilized and perfected in Florida, and national parties and candidates routinely go to Florida to test national political messages with polls and focus groups.

The demographic changes in the state have made Florida something other than a southern state. But there is little agreement about what it has become. Ask a resident what it means to be a Floridian and few, if any, can answer the question. Ask a Floridian about the state's history, and even fewer can tell you that it has operated under five different flags, or that its colonial period is much older than that of New England or Virginia. Perhaps one in ten or twenty residents can tell you who LeRoy Collins was, despite Republican Jeb Bush's recognition of this Democratic governor as the model for all who followed. It is literally a state unknown and indefinable to its people. Such historical ignorance and regional alienation have become significant obstacles for state political leaders who seek to find consensus among voters and solutions that address the needs of all citizens.

An essential purpose of this series is to put Floridians in touch with their rich and diverse political history and to enhance their understanding of the political developments that have reshaped the state, the region, and the nation. This series focuses on the Sunshine State's unique and dynamic political history since 1900 and on public policy issues that have influenced the state and the nation. The University Press of Florida is dedicated to publishing high-quality works on these subjects. It welcomes book-length manuscripts and is also committed to including in this series shorter essays of 25 to 50 pages that address some of the immediately pressing public policy issues confronting Florida.

This particular volume, *Immigrant Prince: Mel Martinez and the American Dream*, by noted Florida political scientist Richard Foglesong, gives the reader remarkable insights into how Martinez reluctantly got into politics and ultimately became the nation's first Cuban-born U.S. senator. What makes the biography particularly intriguing is the author's acknowledgment up front that his politics are quite opposite to those of Martinez.

By the end of the book, the reader will have a deep appreciation for the role that culture, language, religion, family, school-based friendships, sports, historical events, and his own personality played in the meteoric rise of Martinez onto the national stage—and in his decision to exit it before the end of his first term in the U.S. Senate. Along the way we learn a lot about how being an outsider, an immigrant, made him more determined to build coalitions among divergent populations even within the broader Hispanic community and affected his issue priorities, especially on immigration reform. We gain a better understanding of just how strong a pull was his belief in the American (and Florida) dream and, as a consequence, his deep commitment to giving something back to his new country. We also learn how profoundly his experience in a foster home in Orlando, as opposed to one in Miami, shaped his political career. That experience accelerated his assimilation into the predominantly Anglo world, while allowing him to proudly keep his Hispanic identity. As the author notes: "For Mel, not finding an ethnic support group in Orlando . . . gave him a burning desire to fit in, to be liked, to win approval and esteem—as well he did."

Foglesong relies on a wide variety of sources to tell the Martinez story: (1) extensive interviews with Martinez, his family, schoolmates, former business associates, key players in the political arenas in which Martinez has served, (2) newspaper articles detailing his political successes and failures, and (3) major academic works focusing on the role of leadership (Weber, Machiavelli), the influx of Cubans into Florida across two decades, the rise of the Republican Party in Florida, the growing role of religion in politics, and the role of Hispanics in the presidential elections of 2000 and 2004. The multiplicity of sources gives the story a rich context well beyond that of most political biographies. What piqued Foglesong's interest in writing about Martinez "was more than just his storybook

American Dream saga, from his emigration from Cuba by himself at age fifteen through his rapid ascent from county chairman to [U.S.] secretary of Housing and Urban Development to U.S. senator in barely four years . . . it was emblematic of broader changes taking place in Florida and the nation—namely, the rise of Hispanic political power, pitched battles over religion, and heightened concern over terrorism in the post-9/11 environment."

The biography begins with a story of the persecution Martinez experienced as a high school student in Cuba, where he was a rather vocal opponent of the new Castro regime. When someone in the crowd at a basketball game yelled out, "Kill the Catholic," meaning Mel, his parents became extremely frightened and made the agonizing decision to send their son to the United States as part of the Pedro Pan operation. Thus, from the beginning, we gain an understanding of the powerful role that family, his Cuban identity, and Catholicism would play throughout Martinez's life—how they would pull him into politics at the highest levels, then lead him to exit the political world prematurely. Even leaders of his own party acknowledged that the reasons he departed early were genuine. Senate minority leader Mitch McConnell told Martinez: "Most of the time when people say they're resigning for personal reasons"—in Martinez's case an ill mother and cousin, a high-school-aged son involved in his beloved pastime of baseball, deep disappointment in the GOP's willingness to enact immigrant-friendly immigration reform—"it's BS. In your case it happens to be true."

In summary, this book covers the rise of Hispanic political power in Florida, describes the struggles immigrants experience in "fitting in," details the powerful impact of family, religion, and ethnic identity on issue selection (for Mel, Cuba, abortion, and immigration), and explains why many, including the author, judge Martinez's legacy to be his life story as a trailblazer rather than his policy successes. This biography puts Martinez's personal and political dimensions in perspective and should be read by serious students of Florida politics and history as well as by those who enjoy well-written, highly informative biographies.

David Colburn and Susan MacManus
Series editors

PREFACE

In her brilliant book *Team of Rivals*, Doris Kearns Goodwin explains the source of Abraham Lincoln's political genius. He was a great leader because he was an astute politician, knowing when to bend and when to stand firm in defending the Union. His essential genius lay in his capacity for empathy and his uncanny ability to understand the motives and desires of others. What propelled the Great Emancipator into politics? In a word, he sought esteem. Goodwin cites his declaration at age twenty-three, in his first run for elective office, that he had "no other [ambition] so great as being truly esteemed of my fellow men."[1]

What about the lesser Lincolns—the men and women who pursue elective office, wanting in varying degrees to effect change and win esteem? Where do they originate? Are they different from birth, as though born under a special star, preternatural politicians waiting to serve and to shine? Or do their life experiences tap them on the shoulder and beckon them forward, as they evolve from private citizens to community leaders to elected officials at successively higher levels? Once they enter elective office, do they become different people because of the seductions of power and status, or do they only *seem* different because of the constant media attention they receive? And realistically, can such people come and go from politics, as George Washington imagined they would, or does politics seep into the blood and make careerists of those who join society's politically active stratum?

These questions made me want to write a political biography. All the better that my subject, U.S. senator Mel Martinez, was a relative newcomer to politics, plucked from local office and pushed onto the national political stage by President George W. Bush, making Martinez seem like an "accidental politician," as some have called him.

Two thinkers stirred my interest in these topics. One is Niccolò Machiavelli, a progenitor of modern political science, whom I address in the following chapter. The other is Max Weber, the early-twentieth-century German scholar whose ideas laid the foundation for the field of sociology. His essay "Politics as a Vocation" dates back to the rise of modern democracies but remains relevant today. In it he assessed the essential qualities of this new historical actor: the elected official. Two qualities were uppermost, he said. One was "a passionate commitment to a realistic cause," which transformed citizens into politicians and connected them with their followers. The other was reason, understood as the capacity to determine a reasonable course of action. Too much passion led to demagoguery, making reason necessary to protect democracy from its bad cousin, mobocracy.

The challenge was finding politicians who combined "hot passion and cool judgment in the same personality," said Weber. I examine the Mel Martinez story through the prism of this challenge.

My interest in writing this book arose from watching Martinez's tough 2004 U.S. Senate race. The contest itself was disappointing. In Weber's terms, hot passion rather than cool judgment dominated the race. Personal attacks punctuated both the primary phase, in which five Republicans and three Democrats sought nomination, and the general election. In the November matchup, Martinez succeeded in making his opponent, Democrat Betty Castor, a former president of the University of South Florida, look soft on terrorism. His TV ads pummeled her for not firing a USF professor accused of supporting Palestinian "jihadists." In return she accused the former Bush cabinet member of running "the nastiest campaign in state history."[2]

Still, the campaign piqued my interest in Martinez. It was more than just his storybook American Dream saga, from his emigration from Cuba by himself at age fifteen through his rapid ascent from county chairman to secretary of Housing and Urban Development to U.S. senator in barely four years. His story was not just about him; it was emblematic of broader changes taking place in Florida and the nation—namely, the rise of Hispanic political power, pitched battles over religion, and heightened concern over terrorism in the post-9/11 environment.

Early in the general-election contest, before four hurricanes in forty-four days forced a temporary suspension of the campaign, I attended a political fund-raiser for Martinez in Winter Park, Florida, where I teach at Rollins College. As a political scientist who frequently comments on local and national politics in the news media, I normally avoid such events. Encouraged to attend by a Martinez supporter, I was intrigued by what had become of Mel, a person I had then known casually for a dozen years or so. How, I wondered, had he changed since becoming a cabinet member and a candidate for the U.S. Senate?

At the fund-raiser, Martinez greeted me warmly. I should say, he greeted me warmly but with a tinge of surprise. I think he said, "Rick, I'm surprised to see you here." We knew one another from participating in a local version of CNN's *Crossfire* talk show. The local show was called *Opinion Street* and was broadcast by PBS's Orlando affiliate, WMFE-TV, airing weekly in the mid-1990s. Mel and I were semiregulars on the program. Although we always got along personally—everyone gets along with Mel—we usually disagreed on the program. In our on-air exchanges I tried to be evenhanded, but most viewers probably saw me as liberal. For his part, Mel sounded consistently conservative and pro-Republican.

I particularly recall a 1994 program addressing U.S. policy toward Cuba. We discussed whether the American trade embargo with Cuba should be relaxed, and I said yes because "nothing sells capitalism like Nike," while Mel defended the embargo on political grounds, saying it weakened Castro's grip on the island nation. At the conclusion, he said that he would return to Cuba if the Castro government fell. I remember being struck by the remark. Sure, Cubans reflexively said those things—I knew that. But the remark surprised me coming from Mel. He was civically entrenched in the Orlando community. He had a lucrative law practice there, and he had a non-Cuban wife and three children born in the United States. I couldn't imagine his family preferring Cuba to their comfortable life in Orlando.

To me, an outsider to Orlando's civic and social elite, Mel looked like the consummate insider. For example, he chaired the Orlando Utilities Commission, a prize position in Orlando's old-boy network. He belonged to the Country Club of Orlando, the preferred club for Orlando's "old" families—the ones who made their money before Disney World came in 1971 and brought new sources of wealth. For these reasons and more, Mel seemed incidentally Cuban. That was how Orlando's Anglo establishment saw him, too, as my subsequent research confirmed.

Yet he couldn't resist repeating the mantra about returning to Cuba—

an apparent gesture of loyalty to fellow Cuban émigrés. Whatever roots he had established here, however entrenched he was socially and civically, no matter his family ties to his adoptive country, his Cuban identity remained strong, passionately so.

My surprise at his remark probably said something about me. In truth, I regard ethnic attachments as impediments to broader bonds of citizenship and community. My ancestors came from Germany but fought for the United States against their motherland in two world wars, and my great-great-grandfather was killed by the Germans in World War I, purging German identity from subsequent generations of Foglesongs. If anything, I regard myself as ethnically American.

Rather than fueling criticism, this difference in our identities stimulated my interest in Martinez. He was more of an insider than I, yet he retained the cultural identity of an outsider. It made him an enigma to me, even back then.

At the fund-raiser in 2004, Mel asked me: "Rick, what good book are you writing?" The question was flattering but said more about Mel than me. He possesses a knack for putting people at ease, a personality trait remarked upon in later chapters. His question referred to my book *Married to the Mouse*, which examines the economic-development marriage between Walt Disney World and Orlando. I had interviewed Mel for the book during his tenure as Orange County chairman. In that interview he had talked tough about dealing with Disney, and I commented favorably on him. "A former personal-injury attorney, he knows that corporations do not always do right," I wrote.

As county chairman—a referendum has since changed the title to county mayor—Mel always struck me as a pragmatic negotiator. I knew he felt passionately about Cuba and about abortion, issues that rarely arise in local government. On the issues that do, he seemed moderate to conservative, yet always reasonable. He cut government spending without imperiling social services, for example. He espoused a small-government philosophy but tied the permitting of residential development to school funding, so that classroom space kept pace with new home construction, something his moderate Democratic predecessor had failed to do. Within limits, his policy decisions seemed reason-driven, pragmatic, and nonideological.

In his Senate campaign, however, Mel was sounding like an absolutist, especially when he campaigned with President Bush. Had he, I wondered, found new passions? Some commentators said he had been "hijacked by the Bushies."

Mel said one more thing at the fund-raiser that caught my attention. "After the election, win or lose," he said, "I'd like to sit down with you over a cup of coffee and tell you about how this all came about." From a conversation with former U.S. senator Paula Hawkins, I assumed he was talking about Karl Rove, the president's chief political adviser, pressuring him to join the Senate race. There were also stories, from 2000, about Rove promoting him for HUD secretary, to help Bush secure Florida in an eventual reelection bid.

The Martinez story therefore seemed tied to the Bush-Rove story—to Rove's success in molding George W. into presidential timber and, after 2000, improving the GOP's standing among women, Catholics, and Hispanics, all important voter groups in the Martinez Senate campaign. I was definitely intrigued.

And my intrigue grew as the campaign unfolded, because Mel was sounding different. It was more than a matter of ideology; his demeanor seemed different. In his campaign mailings and TV ads, he was not the affable nice guy I thought I knew. He sounded mean. He accused his primary opponent, former congressman Bill McCollum, of supporting the "homosexual extremists," an act of gay-baiting that caused even Florida governor Jeb Bush to express disapproval, and he tried to associate his Democratic opponent with the "armed thugs" who took Elián González away from his mother's relatives. The reference was to U.S. agents acting on orders from Attorney General Janet Reno, in accordance with U.S. law, to return the twelve-year-old boy to his father in Cuba after his mother drowned trying to cross the Florida Strait on a raft.

In response to Martinez's attack on McCollum, the *St. Petersburg Times* withdrew its earlier endorsement of him, decrying his "unprincipled tactics." A candidate "associated with bigotry," their editorial declared, was "unworthy of support."[3]

In fairness, Martinez later apologized for his remarks about both McCollum and Reno. Still, political watchers in Orlando were speculating in the fall of 2004 about what had happened to Mel. Had he changed since going to Washington as President Bush's HUD secretary? Were his campaign aides to blame? Were White House operatives too involved? Or did his criticisms of McCollum simply reflect the triumph of "attack politics" over civil discourse in contemporary political campaigns?

After the election I decided to write about Martinez. Since completing my book on Walt Disney World and Orlando, I had searched for a suitable subject for a biography. As a recovering academic writer, alienated from most political-science scholarship, I wanted to put real people (not just data points gleaned from survey research) back in the study of politics, honoring that timeless homily that "people make history, though not always just as they choose."

Further, I wanted to write about a living person—to illuminate current forces and trends. And I wanted to write about a Floridian, not just for reasons of convenience and access, but because Florida has become a bellwether state. For all the strange happenings here, as told on tabloid TV and fictionalized in Carl Hiaasen novels, the United States is becoming more like Florida in its age structure, ethnic diversity, and political climate.

Recalling my earlier conversation with Martinez, I realized he was the ideal subject for a biography. He had not only replaced the venerable Democratic moderate Bob Graham, a self-described "cracker." Bridging the two worlds of Florida, in which one in five residents is Hispanic, he was the state's first Cuban U.S. senator—with an Anglo wife from Alabama. With luck on his side, he had enjoyed a rapid ascent from county chairman to cabinet member to U.S. senator in four years. Having metamorphosed so recently from private citizen to successful politician, he was a fit subject through which to explore the questions raised earlier about where politicians originate, whether they change once in office, how they combine "hot passion and cool judgment" in the same personality, and whether politics seeps irreversibly into their blood.

More, the qualities that made him an enigma to me made him interesting in human terms. How did his Cuban exile experience shape him, causing him to identify as an outsider even as he became an insider? Was he an absolutist or a pragmatic negotiator? Mean or a nice guy? A practitioner of Karl Rove's take-no-prisoners tactics or a conquering hero in national politics?

I wanted to know who he is, how he got where he is, and what his story means for Florida and the nation at the start of a new century. Does it mean, for example, that Hispanics (not just Cubans) are destined to vote Republican, with disastrous consequences for Democrats in Florida and the nation? That religious politics, which played such a prominent role in his Senate campaign, has decisively trumped class politics? That the soft-on-terrorism tag he stuck on Betty Castor signals a new era of Republican political hegemony, much as anticommunism bolstered Republican fortunes during the Cold War?

I therefore wrote Mel Martinez in December of 2004 and proposed writing a biography of him. Would he, I asked, grant me the necessary access? After a short phone conversation, he agreed to the project. His only reservation was that he wanted to write his autobiography, which he subsequently did. His book, *A Sense of Belonging*, appeared in 2008, after my own book had been accepted for publication and eight of its eleven chapters completed. As the senator and I agreed in 2004, our books would be complementary rather than competing. His autobiography focuses on his early life, before he entered politics, whereas my book traces his evolution from private citizen to elected official.

Senator Martinez agreed to give me personal access for this book, and I have interviewed him nine times. He also facilitated my interviews with his wife, Kitty, whom I interviewed twice, his mother and foster mothers, members of his staff, and assorted friends and advisers. He did not ask for any editorial guarantees in return, which I consider admirable given that his reputation could be at stake. I promised only that I would give him the opportunity to respond to any negative information that I turned up.

About names, I refer to Senator Martinez in various places as "Mel." In doing so I mean neither disrespect nor to imply a close friendship with him. People who knew Martinez before he was elected senator still call him Mel. In this regard he differs from most major political figures. For example, the previous occupant of his Senate seat, Bob Graham, is gracious and unassuming, but Democratic Party regulars call him Senator Graham or Graham, not Bob.

That Martinez remains addressable as Mel evidences his lack of vanity, bringing to mind Max Weber's aphorism that vanity is the "deadly enemy" of successful politicians.[4] Nonetheless, I use "Senator Martinez" or "Secretary Martinez" or "Chairman Martinez" when appropriate, to show respect for the person as well as his office. I thus seek to recognize both the private and public personae of this real person who—accidentally?—became a U.S. senator.

I also made the editorial decision to recognize the transition of Mel and his family from Cuba to the U.S. in the treatment of the family surname. In pre-immigration contexts, I use Martínez and Melquiades in recognition of the family's Hispanic heritage and Mel's unchanged legal first name (Melquiades); in post-immigration contexts, I use anglicized, unaccented Martinez and Mel instead of Melquiades.

In writing this book I have tried to be fair on both sides—fair to my subject and fair to my own political values. The reader is therefore doubly forewarned: I do not share Martinez's conservative political philosophy, yet I find him immensely likeable. To minimize both partiality and bias, I allow those whom I interviewed—particularly Senator Martinez—to speak in their own words as much as possible. In the convention of writing "creative nonfiction," which involves setting scenes and writing in narrative fashion, I try to "show rather than tell." That means that readers of varying political persuasions might come to different conclusions about Mel from what is written here. Only in the final chapter do I offer my own frank assessment.

My authorial hand nonetheless intrudes in constructing the stories to follow. None of the narrative is imagined; all quotation is substantiated by interviews with named sources. Still, another author might have constructed these stories differently, yielding different impressions of people and events. Hence, this is unavoidably my book; I alone am responsible for its errors and shortcomings.

LUCKY

"Mel is the luckiest son of a gun I know," said Ralph Martinez two months after his brother was sworn in as Florida's junior senator.[1] "First, he was there when Bush came to town to promote his education program, and Mel rode in the limousine with him." Ralph—who, like Mel, became an Orlando attorney after fleeing Cuba—was describing the occasion in 1999 when Mel escorted presidential candidate George W. Bush around Orlando on a campaign visit. At the time Mel was the chairman (now called mayor) of Orange County, the fast-growing county that surrounds Walt Disney World and Orlando. Martinez had won election to the Orange County job only one year earlier.

"Then Bush and [chief political strategist] Karl Rove pick him because they need a Hispanic in the cabinet," Ralph added. That choice followed Florida's 2000 presidential election controversy. Martinez had served as cochair of the George Bush campaign and advised Florida governor Jeb Bush as Republicans sought to halt the vote recount. After the U.S. Supreme Court decided the election, Florida's importance to the president's reelection chances in 2004, and in turn the importance of the Hispanic vote to winning the state, was clear. In joining the Bush cabinet, Martinez became more than the secretary of Housing and Urban Development: he became the Hispanic face of the new Republican administration, the bright shining example of the GOP's openness to Latinos, their troubadour for Spanish-language audiences.

"And then," Ralph Martinez continued, "Bush and Rove chose him to step into the Senate race." Former congressman Bill McCollum was the leading GOP candidate to replace retiring Democratic senator Bob Graham, but McCollum, who had lost a Senate race to the Democrats in 2000, was faltering. Congresswoman Katherine Harris, who had served as Florida secretary of state during the recount squabble, was poised to join the Senate contest. Bush and Rove wanted a stronger candidate than McCollum to help the president's candidacy in Florida, however, and they wanted to head off Harris, since she would galvanize the state's Democrats, who despised her. So they turned to their HUD secretary, whom the president loved for his personal qualities as well as his American Dream saga. (Not many cabinet couples got to weekend with President and Mrs. Bush at their ranch in Crawford, Texas, as Mel and his wife did.)

Before 2000, Martinez was little known outside Orange County. But that soon changed. His selection as HUD secretary, his many speeches before Hispanic audiences after joining the Bush cabinet, the rise of public affairs reporting on Telemundo and Univision and their demand for Latino politicians to cover, and the fact that the president always brought Mel along when he spoke to audiences in South Florida—all helped make him a folk hero among Hispanics.

During the primary campaign, the White House did not overtly endorse Martinez; after all, McCollum was a stalwart administration supporter. But the president communicated his preference in subtle ways. At an Orlando fund-raiser, for example, Bush mentioned his cabinet member numerous times, Katherine Harris once, and McCollum once.[2]

Rankled by the White House's involvement, McCollum lost to Martinez in the primary, and Martinez defeated a strong Democratic contender, Betty Castor, in the general election by slightly more than 1 percent of the vote. In the aftermath, a *St. Petersburg Times* article observed: "The strategy of recruiting Martinez to run for the seat was successful, but it leaves lingering questions about whether Martinez is his own man, or the creature of a Beltway crowd that correctly anticipated him as an irresistible bridge to victory in Florida."[3] Nonetheless, the value of the president's support for Martinez was clear.

"Now Mel sits on the Senate Foreign Relations Committee," said Ralph Martinez. "It's great that he's in a position to influence policy toward Cuba." To the loyal younger brother, it is a source of pride that Cuba's official Web site calls Mel the "number one enemy." It also accuses him of Mafia involvement, a typical Cuban government ploy. Believing this, an aunt in Cuba asked Ralph over the phone how Mel, who "was such a nice boy as a kid," could get mixed up with the mob.

Yet Ralph would be the first to say his brother's meteoric rise to power was unforeseen. In his words: "Mel had no plan. He just kept saying 'yes' whenever he was asked to serve." As Mel wrote in 2008, he did not set out to have a political career. Rather, it "sneaked up and tapped me softly on the shoulder."[4]

Indeed. Mel inherited a strong sense of obligation, a desire to give back, from all the public and private charity he received as a teenage refugee. In return, he compiled an impressive record of community service in the Orlando area, as we shall see in later chapters. Still the issue of luck arises. Not every community servant, not every hard-working refugee, not every politically connected local official becomes a cabinet secretary, U.S. senator, and "rock star" to his ethnic group.

Martinez's own words reveal his sense of good fortune. In a newspaper interview during his Senate campaign he said:

> How did I get here? I wasn't even a mayor of a major metropolitan area, and there I was, HUD secretary. I had a driver, a security detail. I was going off to Latin America. I have done some pretty cool stuff. It just feels incredible. Now I am on a private plane. I am flying to Miami—for dinner! In an hour, I'll be there. I can hardly believe it: I'm running for the Senate.[5]

Similarly, in an interview with the author, he acknowledged how his life changed after White House operatives pressed him to join the Senate race.

> I went through agony deciding whether to get into this race or frankly leave politics. I was inclined to leave the cabinet after four years. Had Graham not quit the Senate, my plan would have been to finish four years in the cabinet, come back to Orlando, keep a Washington presence, go to work and try to make some money and have a private life.[6]

The consequences have been little short of remarkable. Kitty, Mel's pretty and demure Anglo wife of thirty-five years, is willing to say what he is too modest to say. "He's an icon. There's not a restaurant that we go to in Orlando or Washington where the waiters and busboys, be they Mexican or Puerto Rican or Honduran or what have you, don't recognize him and express their appreciation. They regard him as a role model because he made it here in America." She credits part of his notoriety to Telemundo and Univision: "He's on Spanish television all the time."[7]

In a symbiotic relationship, like that between Michael Jordan and Nike in the 1980s, Martinez and the Hispanophone media use each other. When he gave his first speech on the Senate floor, in defense of President

Bush's nominee for attorney general, Alberto Gonzales, he spoke briefly in Spanish, a nearly unprecedented occurrence in Senate history. Telemundo, alerted in advance, interrupted its soap-opera programming to carry the speech live—a first for them.

Asked what the Senate GOP leadership thought of his Senate foray into Spanish, Martinez said: "They thought it was great."[8] Beginning with his HUD experience speaking to Latino groups across the country, he was surprised by the outpouring of support he received. His personal saga of coming to America and "making it" transcends party boundaries, earning him fervent support from Hispanic audiences across the country. "You'd be surprised how many Hispanics there are in places like Kansas City," he said, referring to his cross-country speaking schedule while at HUD.

One of his Republican House colleagues told him that she was speaking to a group of constituents in upstate New York, explaining that she was their representative in Washington, when a Hispanic woman raised her hand and proudly announced: "We already have a senator." As the congresswoman learned, "we" referred to Hispanics and the senator was Martinez.

Nor has Martinez been shy about claiming this cross-nation constituency. During the 2004 Senate contest, he campaigned in Puerto Rico, knowing that some residents move back and forth between the mainland and the island, and can vote in Florida. While there he told the islanders: "I will be your senator too," a promise repeated numerous times since his 2004 victory (though largely unreported in the mainstream media). The Commonwealth of Puerto Rico, a U.S. territory, has a nonvoting delegate or "commissioner" in the House of Representatives but no Senate representation.

In an interesting contrast, Democratic senator Ken Salazar of Colorado, the Senate's other Hispanic, also elected in 2004, did not claim to represent Hispanics outside his state. Perhaps Salazar found this a safer course, given his narrow victory over a well-financed opponent, Pete Coors. Looking back, Martinez's strategy of representing Hispanics *and* Florida would prove problematic during the Senate debate over immigration reform in 2007–8. Following his Senate election, though, this well-assimilated Hispanic became a Pied Piper for the GOP among Hispanics of all types, not just Cubans, who comprise but 2 percent of Hispanics nationally.

Unquestionably, Mel Martinez has been lucky. To repeat a cliché, he was in the right place at the right time. In more than one way, he also had the right stuff. Yet luck can be a fickle mistress, here today and gone tomorrow. Political theorist Niccolò Machiavelli addressed the role of luck in politics in his famous book *The Prince*, completed in 1513. (Ironically, I gave a copy of the book to Martinez after he attended a seminar for elected officials that I directed in 1992.) "Fortune is the arbiter of half of the things we do, leaving the other half or so to be controlled by ourselves," wrote Machiavelli, who sought a "prince" to unify a fragmented Italy.[9]

Machiavelli added this warning, however: "Those princes who are utterly dependent on fortune come to grief when their fortune changes." His remedy for such a prince was to "adapt his policy to the times." It would be good advice for Martinez as his Senate career unfolded. For Florida has a habit of electing one-term U.S. senators—Paula Hawkins in 1980, Richard Stone in 1974, Edward Gurney in 1968.

In his early Senate career, moreover, Martinez's luck seemed to change. During the Senate debate on the Terri Schiavo matter, when Martinez and his GOP colleagues wanted to extend federal legal protection to the brain-dead Florida woman, he inadvertently gave the Democrats a memo, written by one of his staffers for Republican eyes only, on how the GOP could exploit the Schiavo issue politically. Martinez earned a torrent of bad press, the anger of his Senate colleagues, and a charge against him before the Senate Rules Committee. The staff member who authored the memo was fired.

Overall, though, Martinez was very lucky—or so it appears on the surface. Peering deeper, *Immigrant Prince* explains why Mel Martinez's political career was no mere accident. For sometimes things that appear accidental yield to causal explanation on closer examination. The task of social science is to "peel the onion" so that surface impressions yield to deeper understandings, and this requires, among other things, distinguishing between the accidental and the organic, happenstance and force of will.

Thus, *Immigrant Prince* explains how Mel Martinez's political career arose from the confluence of good fortune, a remarkable personal biography, and a distinctive set of events and trends.

The role of good fortune was noted in the preceding pages. The power of Mel's personal biography is no less persuasive. It includes coming to

America at age fifteen on the Pedro Pan program—funded by the CIA, administered by the Catholic Church—that spirited unaccompanied children out of Cuba. Arriving in Orlando in 1962, young Mel blended into two successive foster families while helping his parents escape from Castro's grip four years later. After graduating from a Catholic high school, Bishop Moore, he put himself through college and law school at Florida State University in Tallahassee. He married an Anglo woman from Alabama, Kitty, and returned to Orlando to practice law as a personal-injury attorney. In a city that then had few Hispanics, he became both wealthy and a fixture in the power structure—without losing his Cuban identity.

A Democrat until the Reagan era, he not only was a trial attorney, a profession that Republicans have assailed in recent elections as pro-Democrat and antibusiness, but he was, in 1989, the president of the Florida Academy of Trial Lawyers, fighting against what Republicans call "tort reform"—their effort to cap medical malpractice awards and otherwise protecting physicians and insurance companies. Five years later Martinez ran for lieutenant governor with gubernatorial candidate Ken Connor, his college roommate, on the Right to Life ticket, competing in the GOP primary against Jeb Bush, who would lose the general election to former U.S. senator Lawton Chiles. That was the same Jeb Bush who, as governor in 2000, urged his older brother to name Mel to the cabinet.

This remarkable personal story has become a huge political asset for Martinez, attesting to the continuing power of the American Dream saga. For America loves conquering heroes who succeed despite the odds; they reassure us about the promise of America as a land of opportunity. That is why Mel's story was a godsend to Republicans seeking to unify Hispanic voters and mainstream Republicans in wresting Bob Graham's Senate seat from the Democrats. In their joint appearances, President Bush never failed to call Mel "living proof of the American Dream."

In fairness to Martinez, his difficult passage to America, coming to these shores alone at age fifteen, was a major obstacle to overcome, not a pathway to success. Not every immigrant kid becomes a U.S. senator, after all. But once these hurdles were overcome, the story of his immigrant experience became instrumental for him and for the GOP in their quest for Hispanic voters.

To the opposition party, however, the story was stale, tiresome, and platitudinous. As one Democratic elected official said to me: "He's been advancing himself on his personal story for the past twenty years." Hence the charge from Democrats that Martinez is an "empty suit."

But the Mel Martinez story is about more than luck and an inspirational personal biography. Understood more deeply, it is also about the events and trends that "conspired" to put him in office. For this Cuban American was not only in the right place with the right stuff; it was also the right time for someone like him. Notably, his path to power was paved by a series of historical circumstances—by Castro's takeover of Cuba; the Bay of Pigs fiasco and the Cuban exile community's anger toward President Kennedy and the Democratic Party; the successive waves of Cuban émigrés to the United States in response to decisions by Presidents Johnson, Carter, and Reagan; the Elián González affair, which probably altered the 2000 presidential election; the 2000 Florida vote-recount controversy; and, not least, the rise of public affairs reporting in the Spanish-language news media. Each of these will be explored.

Finally, *Immigrant Prince* relates Martinez's story to three broader trends—the growing importance of Hispanics in the racial and ethnic dynamics of the United States; the increasing role of religion in politics, especially on the part of Roman Catholics and evangelical Christians; and the heightened security concerns associated with 9/11 and the war in Iraq. On one hand, these trends provide context for better understanding Martinez's emergence as a major political figure; on the other, his story personifies the influence of these trends.

Regarding racial politics, brothers Earl and Merle Black offer a sophisticated analysis of black-white differences in their 2002 book *The Rise of Southern Republicans*. There they argue that the "partisan transformation of southern conservatism" from Democrat to Republican, and the Republican Party's incomplete conquest of national politics, is mostly about race—that is, about black-white racial differences.[10] Democrats began in the 1960s to moderate their staunch segregationist views, enabling the erstwhile "party of Lincoln" to gain inroads into, and eventually conquer, the once solidly Democratic South. With the South, the Democrats could dominate national politics; without it, wrote the authors, they can contest Republicans at the margins, but little more.

Numerous other books on southern politics have advanced the same argument: black-white differences have created a solidly Republican South, giving Republicans a huge head start in assembling a national majority, whether in the House, the Senate, or the presidential Electoral College.[11]

But this analysis underplays the growing importance of the Hispanic vote, in the South and beyond. In 2000, Hispanics became the nation's largest minority. They now represent 14 percent of the national population, compared with African Americans at 12 percent. In the South, the Hispanic population is growing faster than anywhere else in the nation. Virginia, North Carolina, Georgia, and Florida have all witnessed a tripling of the growth rates of their Hispanic populations since 1980, with population increases ranging upwards of 200,000.[12]

In the South as elsewhere, Latinos are still a political sleeping giant in many ways—because so many lack citizenship and cannot vote, and because only 58 percent of eligible Latino voters are registered, compared with 75 percent for whites and 69 percent for blacks. Latinos are nonetheless the fastest-growing segment of the electorate. Between the 2000 and 2004 elections, their number of eligible voters increased by about 20 percent to 16 million people, a growth rate six times that of the non-Hispanic population. In the Electoral College, moreover, they represent more than 10 percent of eligible voters in four key presidential battleground states— Florida, New Mexico, Nevada, and Arizona.[13]

Recognizing this, the two parties are locked in an epic war for the Hispanic vote. Nothing less is at stake than dominating American politics for the foreseeable future. Not only is the Hispanic electorate fast-growing; increasingly, Hispanics are swing voters. In 2004, President Bush improved his share of the Latino vote by 5 percent over his 2000 showing, winning 40 percent of the total. A key part of the Republican strategy is showcasing Republican elected officials who are Hispanic. As HUD secretary, Martinez's portfolio was to represent the administration to Hispanic audiences. And significantly, two Hispanic cabinet members replaced him in Bush II: Carlos Gutierrez, a fellow Cuban American, at Commerce, and Alberto Gonzales, a Mexican American and the child of farmworkers, as attorney general.

Not to be outdone, the Democrats scored a victory in 2005 with the election of Antonio Villaraigosa as mayor of Los Angeles, the city's first Hispanic mayor since 1872. Thereafter, both *Time* and *Newsweek* ran cover articles on rising "Latino power." In commenting on Martinez, *Newsweek* styled him a leader of the GOP's "Latin charge" in a story subtitled "How Hispanics Will Change American Politics."[14] *Time* called the Cuban American senator "perhaps the U.S.'s most important Hispanic lawmaker" in their own cover story, "The 25 Most Influential Hispanics in America."[15]

A related misconception is that Hispanics feel a natural affinity for the Democratic Party. On one hand, newer and poorer immigrants tend to vote Democratic for economic-class reasons. On the other, the Martinez and Bush campaigns in 2004 showed that Hispanic voters are culturally susceptible to the GOP mantra of faith, family, and country. Regarding faith and family, Martinez and Bush both attracted Hispanic support in 2004 by pushing social issues that resonated with Roman Catholics and evangelical Protestants—namely, gay marriage and abortion. President Bush did especially well with Hispanic Protestants, winning 56 percent of their vote.[16] Good for the GOP, Hispanic Protestants comprised a larger share of the Latino vote in 2004 (32 percent) than in 2000 (25 percent).

Regarding appeals to country, Hispanics have high rates of participation in the military, making them susceptible to patriotic appeals in the context of the war in Iraq and concerns over terrorism. In public opinion surveys conducted during the 2004 election campaign, 18 percent of Hispanic voters named terrorism as their highest priority. These voters also favored Bush by a 3–1 margin. Advantaging Democrats, however, younger Hispanic voters ages 18–19, the fastest-growing segment of the Latino electorate, were more skeptical of the president's conduct of the war in Iraq than Hispanic voters over 55. They were also the only age group of Hispanic voters in which a clear majority (56 percent) opposed a constitutional amendment banning same-sex marriage.[17]

Of concern to Democrats, Hispanics have lower rates of trade union participation and welfare dependency and higher rates of homeownership and self-employment—all Republican voter attributes. As John Micklethwait and Adrian Wooldridge write in their insightful book *The Right Nation*, "The flow of South American immigrants into low-paying jobs will always provide a flow of recruits into the Democratic Party. Nevertheless, the likelihood is that the Latino vote will split increasingly along class lines, as the more established Latinos follow the pattern of Italian Americans."[18]

Of course, ethnicity and country of origin greatly matter among Latinos. Most prefer to be identified by their country of origin rather than by pan-ethnic labels like Hispanic or Latino, although Hispanic is the preferred catchall nationwide. In terms of provenance, Hispanic America is overwhelmingly Mexican American (58.5 percent), followed by Puerto Ricans (9.6 percent), with Cubans a distant third (3.5 percent). Cubans famously vote Republican, though second-generation Cuban Americans are less conservative and also less Republican than their parents, no doubt because foreign policy matters less to them. Puerto Ricans and Mexican Americans, on the other hand, still vote overwhelmingly Democratic.

Led by direct-mail devotee Karl Rove, the Republicans tailored their messages to different segments of the Hispanic electorate in 2004, appreciating the importance of idiom and accent among distinct regional and ethnic clusters.[19] Looking at Hispanics as a whole, however, the political question is whether the cultural appeal of the GOP mantra, emphasizing issues like abortion and gay marriage, will trump Democrat appeals based on antidiscrimination measures, extending Medicaid, and raising the minimum wage.

A third misconception is that Florida Hispanics are primarily Cuban and Republican. Of the eligible electorate in Florida, Hispanics make up 14 percent, of whom 36 percent are Cuban, 32 percent Puerto Rican, and 21 percent Central or South American. Contributing to this dizzying diversity, more than 200,000 Puerto Ricans had migrated to the five-county Central Florida region by 2003, responding to Disney recruitment efforts and advertising in Puerto Rico by Florida homebuilders.

In Orange County surrounding Orlando, where Martinez got his political start, the Puerto Rican influx in the 1990s helped Democratic presidential aspirants win majority votes. Thus Bill Clinton won Orange County in 1996, Al Gore in 2000, and John Kerry in 2004. In the Senate race, Martinez ran ahead of George Bush but behind John Kerry in the county, meaning that some Kerry voters—probably Puerto Rican—voted for this Cuban American.

Demographics alone will not determine which party gets the Latino vote, however. Political leadership and creative politics will matter too, raising the importance of Martinez's political future. Though Puerto Ricans often dislike Cubans and typically vote Democratic, Martinez fared well among Puerto Rican voters. Marching in Puerto Rican Day parades in Orlando and Miami, he was greeted by signs saying "Martinez Sí, Bush No."[20] Consistent with this message, he won heavily Democratic Miami-Dade County while Bush lost there. In defeating Democrat Betty Castor by 2,500 votes in Dade, Martinez earned votes from many non-Cuban

Hispanics. As *Time* reports, Florida's Hispanic diversity gives Martinez "the opportunity to speak for all Hispanics"—benefiting him and his party.[21]

——→

Another backdrop to the Mel Martinez story is the rising importance of religion in American politics. Religion has always been woven into the fabric of American life, including its politics, but something new has occurred. As Andrew Kohut and his colleagues write, "It is the level and type of activism of the churches and their partisan mobilization that are new, not the reality that people of similar faiths have similar values and often vote alike."[22] The "diminishing divide" between religion and politics has brought new groups into politics, altered party coalitions, and influenced campaigns and election results, write Kohut and his fellow authors, drawing on Pew Research Center survey data.

Not so long ago, cohesion among religious groups grew indirectly from people of the same faith living in close proximity, often with a distinctive cultural identity. Now, parishioners' shared beliefs are often coalesced into a direct, blunt political force by the self-conscious actions of clergy, active laity, and specialized political groups. These trends are ominous for Democrats. In 2000 and again in 2004, more than 60 percent of those who attended church every week voted for George W. Bush.[23]

Since the 1970s, much of the energy fueling religious activism has come from evangelical Christians. The ascendancy of the right as the center of religious activism can be traced to evangelicals' response to the changing role of women in society and Supreme Court decisions regarding school prayer and abortion. In all faiths, people who show high levels of religious commitment tend to be more politically conservative, but the political impact of faith and religious commitment is most potent among white evangelical Protestants, who now represent 24 percent of registered voters and who have been overwhelmingly loyal to the Republican Party.[24]

In the 1960s, white evangelicals voted Democratic by a 2–1 margin, before moral issues like abortion, prayer in school, and homosexuality pushed them to the GOP. Roman Catholics have also shifted allegiances, though not quite as dramatically. In 1960, 71 percent of Catholics identified themselves as Democratic or leaning Democratic. By 2004, that number had dropped to 44 percent, with 41 percent favoring the GOP. Much of that change occurred in response to the presidency of Ronald

Reagan, as Catholics were drawn to his emphasis on traditional values and patriotism.[25]

In the new millennium, the Catholic Church has played a larger role in politics, following the lead of evangelical Protestants. This role was evident in the pronouncements of U.S. Catholic cardinals against Democratic presidential candidate John Kerry, a Catholic who supported abortion rights. During the 2004 campaign, a number of U.S. Catholic bishops announced they would deny Communion to Kerry and other politicians who supported abortion rights. It was apparent too in the encyclicals of Pope John Paul II on the importance of respecting a "culture of life," which entailed opposing abortion and euthanasia (but not war and executions), an emphasis that Pope Benedict XVI pledges to continue.

Applying this philosophy, the Church took a strong stand in the Terri Schiavo case. She was the Pinellas Park woman who persisted in a "permanent vegetative state," according to Florida courts, for fourteen years. Her husband, Michael, won approval from state courts to remove her feeding tubes in April 2005, and she died two weeks later—amid a firestorm of controversy. Consistent with his Roman Catholic faith, Mel Martinez helped involve the Senate in the Schiavo matter. He was one of four senators who, in an emergency session, pushed through a bill requiring a federal court review of Michael Schiavo's request.

As the next chapter underscores, Martinez's Catholic faith is central to his core identity. He is a devout Catholic, educated in Catholic schools in Cuba, a graduate of a Catholic high school in the United States. His parents removed him from Cuba when government agents harassed him at a high school basketball game with shouts of "Kill the Catholic." His Catholicism is entwined with his anticommunism, moreover. In Cuba his views were shaped by a beloved priest and headmaster who saw in Castro a remake of the Spanish Civil War—a message Mel brought home to his parents.

⬌

A third contextual factor is the power of antiterrorist rhetoric in the post-9/11 environment. Americans have long fretted about "the barbarians at the gate." For most of the post–World War II era, the barbarians were the Soviet and Chinese communists, and the Republican Party exploited this threat, assailing the Democrats as "soft on communism" and weak on defense. Absent a barbarian to guard the nation against, the Republican

Party faltered politically when Soviet communism fell in 1989, culminating in the election of Bill Clinton, the first Democratic president to win two terms since World War II.

In this regard, Mel Martinez might seem like a throwback to a bygone era. He is a refugee from communist Cuba, the only outpost in the Americas of Soviet-style communism. As an anticommunist warrior, his credentials are impeccable, his personal story vivid. But the communist menace has been defeated, raising the question of whether his life experience relates to the new threat of terrorism. The initial evidence from his Senate campaign suggests it does. In that campaign he vilified his Democratic opponent, former university president Betty Castor, for not firing a Palestinian professor with alleged ties to terrorists. It was his main attack on Castor, incessantly repeated in TV commercials.

Tactically, Castor played into his hands, taking credit as university president for decisively dealing with the professor in question. Her move enabled Martinez to link her, a nonincumbent newcomer to national politics, to the terrorist threat. In Florida the terrorist issue was especially potent: the state's economy had suffered when tourists were afraid to fly after 9/11; several of the 9/11 hijackers had received their flight training in Florida; and the state's infrastructure is acutely vulnerable to attack, with 14 deepwater ports, 21 military installations, 20 commercial airports— and Walt Disney World.

Accordingly, while the issues dominating the 2004 presidential and Senate campaigns were much the same with voters inside and outside the state, they ranked differently. National exit polls showed that concern about moral issues was the reason most often cited by voters who chose Bush over Kerry. But in Florida, terrorism was ahead of moral issues, 24 percent to 20 percent.[26] Castor understood that, in order to win the election, she would have to shift voters' attention to domestic issues. Unfortunately for her, national media coverage regarding missing explosives and the Osama bin Laden tape released in October refocused voters' attention on terrorism and homeland security issues.[27]

For Martinez, the link between his anticommunism and the new threat of terrorism is his commitment to freedom. Natan Sharansky, the former Soviet dissident who then became a far-right cabinet member in Israel, makes this link in The Case for Democracy, a popular book among Washington conservatives. (Martinez had a copy on his office coffee table and recommended the book to me when I first interviewed him.) Likening the fight against terrorism to the struggle against Nazism and communism, Sharansky describes a world "divided between those who are prepared to confront evil and those who are willing to appease it." Americans need "moral clarity," he says, to understand that "promoting peace and security is fundamentally connected to promoting freedom and democracy."[28]

On the other side are those like Michael Ignatieff who take a less connective view of this threat, who see the commitment to freedom as morally fraught. As Ignatieff argues in *The Lesser Evil*, force may be necessary to protect liberal democracy. But its use must be measured, not a program of torture and revenge. And we must not fool ourselves into thinking that whatever we do in the name of freedom and democracy is good; it is merely the lesser of evils. As he writes, "we cannot compel anyone to believe in the premises of a liberal democracy."[29] We are stuck with persuading others that we will respect their dignity and that, if they fail to respect ours, we will defend ourselves.

Once in office, Martinez fit his anticommunist credentials to the terrorist threat. Tellingly, his first act after winning election was a trip to Israel sponsored by the Israeli Public Affairs Committee (but paid for by the Senate)—in keeping with Sharansky's connective view of the threat of terrorism and the threat to democracy. Yet in June 2005 he called for shutting down the military prison at Guantánamo Bay in response to prisoner-abuse stories—consistent with Ignatieff's more restrictive view of the ethical challenge posed by terrorism.

Thus *Immigrant Prince* is not only about serendipity, a remarkable personal biography, and the power of the American Dream narrative. It is also about the political and social currents sweeping Florida and the nation. Altogether, the book addresses three overlapping questions—who Mel Martinez is, how he got where he is, and what his story means. In explaining who he is, coming chapters address the questions posed in the preface about his cultural identity (insider versus outsider), philosophical orientation (pragmatic negotiator versus absolutist) and disposition (mean versus nice). In explaining how he got where he is, this book also explores the influence of serendipity, personal biography, and social events and trends—notably, the rise of Hispanic politics, the contemporary influence of religion in politics, and antiterrorist politics in the post-9/11 environment. All of which contribute to our understanding of what his story means.

2

PETER PAN

Thomas Aglio didn't know what he was getting into.[1] His father was an accountant working for the Catholic parish in Orlando when he overheard a priest say the Church wanted to open a Catholic Charities office in Orlando. It was 1961 and Aglio was employed at a Boston hospital, having previously worked several "nine-to-five" social service jobs. He interviewed for the position and was hired, only to learn that a "huge rope" was attached. The Church was not yet ready to open the Orlando office; his first assignment was to administer Camp St. John, a converted summer camp in Switzerland, Florida, just south of Jacksonville, nestled along the wooded banks of the northbound St. Johns River.

The camp housed Cuban refugees, all teenage boys. They had been airlifted from the salamander-shaped nation as part of a church/government rescue program dubbed Operación Pedro Pan, or Operation Peter Pan. Soon to arrive at the camp was Melquiades Rafael Martínez Jr.—not yet using the nickname Mel—age fifteen. When Aglio came to Camp St. John in January 1962, Mel's parents were trying to get him out of Cuba after the execution of a hometown boy who, like Mel, opposed the Castro regime.

Aglio began his assignment by spending time with the Reverend Bryan O. Walsh, the American godfather of Peter Pan. Walsh was a Spanish-speaking, Irish-born priest serving as executive director of the Catholic Welfare Bureau in Miami. One of his early assignments after joining the priesthood in 1954 was aiding Hungarian freedom fighters who had sought refuge in the United States, an assignment that included placing unaccompanied teenage boys with foster families. Aglio, who was Boston Italian, spent a week shadowing Father Walsh, asking questions and getting advice. Among other things, he learned that the program was shrouded in secrecy. Walsh worked with a shadowy network that secretly distributed visa waivers and, in some cases, airline tickets—financed through contributions from companies whose property had been expropriated in Cuba—to parents wanting to send their children to the United States.

As María Cristina García reports in *Havana USA*, her valuable cultural history of the successive waves of Cuban émigrés, the program involved dozens of people.[2] The chief collaborators were Ramón Grau Alsina and Leopoldina "Polita" Grau de Agüero, the nephew and niece of former Cuban president Ramón Grau San Martín, and James Baker, the principal of the elite Ruston Academy in Havana. Employees of Pan Am and KLM airlines also aided the network. Walsh would secure blank visa waivers, up to six hundred at a time, and smuggle them to Ramón Grau, sometimes using staff from the British and Dutch embassies as couriers. The airlines assisted by setting aside seats under false names for unaccompanied children. Just before the flights departed, Ramón Grau would give the young passengers' actual names to the airlines, which then informed the Cuban Interior Ministry of the changes.

As punishment for their good works, Polita Grau served fourteen years and her brother Ramón twenty-one years in Cuban prisons for these and other counterrevolutionary activities. Ramón was brutally tortured at the infamous Villa Marista, the headquarters of G2, the Cuban secret police.

◁———▷

In the beginning, the program was small. Father Walsh and the Miami diocese expected no more than a hundred boys, because leaving Cuba was so difficult. Most countries do not restrict people from leaving; they require entry visas but not exit passes. Castro's Cuba was different, following the model of the Soviet garrison state: persons wishing to depart needed exit passes from the Cuban Interior Ministry. By the time Peter Pan arrivals ceased in September 1962, a total of 14,156 Cuban teenagers had escaped to the United States. It was the forward edge of a Cuban diaspora that would send 750,000 émigrés to the States, including 248,070 in 1959–62 alone.

As Victor Triay writes in *Fleeing Castro*, the Peter Pan program represented "the largest child refugee movement in the recorded history of the Western Hemisphere."[3] All social and economic groups were represented among the unaccompanied children, though the majority came from middle-class backgrounds, most wealthy Cubans having already fled the country in the initial stages of Castro's revolution. Poorer residents lacked the means to escape and, in most cases, supported the economic and social changes under way.

These middle-class parents sent their children into exile for various reasons. They feared communism partly because of Cuba's long association with the United States, which was engaged in a global struggle against communism, and also because of the influence of the Catholic Church. Many of the clergy were from Spain, where they had witnessed anticlericalism during the Spanish Civil War of 1936–39. Seeing leftist movements as threats to the Church, the priests were fervent in their anticommunism.

Influenced by the Catholic clergy, middle-class Cuban parents feared a civil war like the one in Spain, and they wanted to remove their children from the war zone. They also wanted to prevent Castro from drafting their teenage boys into the military, which explains why Peter Panners were mostly male.

In addition, these parents were worried by persistent rumors. One was that the regime was kidnapping children and sending them to Russia for indoctrination on state farms. Another concerned *patria potestad*, a Roman legal concept regarding the authority to make decisions for children. Aided by the CIA, the anti-Castro underground claimed that the Castro regime planned to strip parents of *patria potestad* and transfer it to the state when children turned three years old.[4] Throughout November 1960, Radio Swan, a CIA station beamed at Cuba, reported night after night that the Cuban government had plans to abolish parental authority and take children away from their mothers. Though false, these allegations were believable in the context of the regime's decision to close private schools and require attendance at state-run schools, where students were pressured to join communist youth organizations.

Though the program started small, Father Walsh was soon awash in Peter Panners. To secure funding, he turned to the federal government, meeting with State Department officials in late 1960. As the enigmatic priest recalled some years later, he entered the State Department by a side door, as if he were working for the FBI or a spy. In a three-hour conversation, he was asked to help take children out of Cuba, and was given assurance that visa waivers would be issued for children aged six to sixteen.[5] For the U.S. government, Peter Pan undermined the credibility of Castro's upstart communist government ninety miles away. Seeing the airlift, onlookers would ask: What kind of brave new society is this, if children are fleeing?

Secrecy was essential because they were spiriting children out of Cuba under the nose of Cuban authorities, which they had to do without endangering the children or their parents or, just as important, their Cuban contacts. As María de los Angeles Torres explains, the program had military origins: it arose from an effort to protect the children of persons fighting in the underground against Castro.[6] In her nuanced and impressively researched account, *The Lost Apple*, she shows that humanitarian concerns also drove the program, motivating Father Walsh and the Catholic Church, for example. So did propaganda interests of the CIA, which sought to destabilize the new regime and undermine its moral legitimacy. Torres concludes: "The interests of the [Cuban underground] activists, parents, U.S. bureaucrats, CIA agents, and Cuban officials [wishing to denationalize the disaffected] coincided."[7] It is this coincidence of a broad range of governmental and private interests that explains the massive nature of the exodus.

Evidencing this mixture of motives, James Baker had come to the United States in November 1960 to find help to take care of the more than two hundred children whose parents were fighting in the underground, and who would continue fighting only if they knew their children were safe. As most of the children were Catholic, Baker approached Father Walsh, knowing of his previous relief activities. Walsh was also approached by members of the American Chamber of Commerce of Havana, which likewise sought help for the children of parents fighting in the underground. In conversations with Walsh, a concern was found that transcended the physical safety of the children: a desire to save them from the dangers of communism.[8] It was this ideological concern that Walsh played upon in dealings with the CIA.

Walsh's first contact with one of these children occurred on November 15, 1960, when he met a fifteen-year-old boy named Pedro Menéndez who had been wandering the streets of Miami alone, going from home to home. Their contact spawned the program's name, though this Pedro had left Cuba before the program began.

Originally the children came to Camp Matacumbe, a converted summer camp run by the Miami diocese. As the inflow of kids reached tidal proportions, the Matacumbe camp was quickly overrun. It then became a receiving facility, processing the new arrivals and acculturating them to the area before sending them elsewhere. The Catholic Church would make other summer camps available, starting in Florida and spreading elsewhere as needed. It was unwelcome news at Camp Matacumbe, where many of the young refugees had Miami relatives whom they could call or visit. Most of all, the kids feared being sent where it snowed.

The Church then had two dioceses in Florida, one in Miami and the other in St. Augustine. The bishop of St. Augustine announced plans in mid-1961 to convert Camp St. John to receive Peter Panners as soon as summer camp concluded. When Aglio arrived in January 1962, the camp's census stood at 40 and would swell to 96 in six months. Married and the father of three, he found a house for his family in Jacksonville and commuted to the camp, where he frequently stayed overnight responding to one crisis or another. Assisting him were a Spanish chaplain whose corporal discipline made him unpopular with the boys, four elderly Cuban men serving as houseparents and bus drivers, an outside food service that was Anglo, and a part-time nurse.

"This was my baptism working for the Church," said Aglio. "I remember when I arrived and looked around at all those boys, and I thought, 'Oh my gosh, how am I going to handle this?'"

Besides relying on his wits, Aglio had the benefit of his graduate education at Boston College, where he earned a master's degree in social work, learning among other things the requirements of group care. He knew that teenage boys needed more than food, shelter, and clothing. Separated from their parents, anxious about their futures in a new country with a different language and culture, not to mention different food, they harbored powerful emotional needs. "I knew I had to make them feel wanted, appreciated, and important. I also knew their day of reckoning was coming, because the Church would not let them continue to live like this. It was not right for them, which the Church knew."

A drawback, Aglio did not speak Spanish. He remembered a few words and phrases from an early-life Spanish course but not enough to converse. Knowing the boys needed to master English—they were thrust into classes at Bishop Kenny High School in Jacksonville with English-speaking students, sans special treatment—he decided to bluff them. In his first camp appearance, he told the boys in English he would not speak Spanish to them. "You need to speak English to be successful here," he said. "If you speak to me in Spanish, I will not respond. I will only respond to English." The boys assumed he comprehended Spanish; he knew this because, when they occasionally spoke Spanish around him, they whispered.

Aglio was unaware of Peter Pan's funding back then. Only much later, after the program concluded in 1963, did he learn of the CIA's involvement. He was not surprised then, because much administrative red tape was involved. There was a strict funding formula of so many dollars per day for each boy once he was assigned to a foster home, which made it seem more like a government program than a church-run initiative, he reasoned. As well, the program was enveloped in the intrigue surrounding South Florida in the period before the Bay of Pigs invasion. Aglio knew from news accounts that "all sorts of special operations stuff was happening down there."

At the time, as we now know, the CIA was training a military force of 1,500 Cuban exiles, called Brigade 2506, preparing for an invasion. The agency had also organized a "government in exile" in South Florida, approved by President Eisenhower in March 1960.

Aglio grew more sensitive to these shadowy doings when Father Walsh called him in early 1962. "I shouldn't be telling you this over the phone, but I don't know when I'll see you down here next," the priest began. "You shouldn't tell this to your wife," he warned, "but you should watch your back. A price has been put on your head." Walsh then told him that the program had received considerable exposure, that he had been connected with it publicly, and that rumors had spread about "what kind of doctrines he adhered to." He added: "I'm not saying that you should do anything different."

Aglio listened as the good priest talked about the connection between his social work and his church role. After the call, he wondered whom he might have upset and "whether I should worry about starting my car." As best he could tell, the concern expressed by Father Walsh arose because he worked with children, possessed a social-worker background, and came from Massachusetts. Already stressed Cuban parents worried about their children and who was supervising them. Social workers were known as liberals if not socialists. And Massachusetts, seen from Florida or Cuba, was a suspicious place, despite or possibly because of President Kennedy's origins there. "I think they thought that I might be a double agent," Aglio speculated.

Such concern was not entirely unreasonable. Fidel Castro was aware of the clandestine program but had not consolidated his power enough to prevent it. He may have reasoned that it siphoned off discontent, as the Freedom Flights that brought Mel's parents to the United States in 1966 would later do. Nonetheless, the Castro government did spy on the Peter Panners, according to Yvonne Conde in *Operation Pedro Pan*.[9] Citing evidence from Cuban officials at the time, she says there were spies among the workers at the temporary shelters in Miami.

Overall, about one-sixth of the Peter Panners over twelve were female, though Camp St. John was all male.[10] Like Catholic schools, the camps were sex-segregated; in Florida, the girls went to camps in Tampa. They were typically younger than the boys, averaging ten to twelve years of age, the boys closer to fifteen. According to Aglio, the preponderance of boys was not only because parents worried about their sons getting drafted into Castro's military, possibly for training in the Soviet Union. It was also because Cuban mothers found it so difficult to part with their daughters, who were perceived to need more sheltering than boys. Some of the children were sent as far away as Portland, Oregon, while others went to Chicago and Baltimore, despite the children's fear of snow.

It was a massive relief effort organized under the auspices of the Kennedy administration, which would later earn the enmity of Cuban exiles for the Bay of Pigs fiasco. Beginning in 1961, the Kennedy government established the Cuban Refugee Program, which provided funds for resettlement as well as relief checks, health services, job training, adult education opportunities, and surplus food distribution. The amount of federal aid provided surpassed that available to U.S. citizens living in Florida.[11] In support of Peter Pan, the government provided foster families and institutions with per diems, paid for the children's transportation expenses and for winter clothes if they traveled to colder climates, and made special arrangements for children with mental or physical disabilities. It offered the most generous benefits in American immigration history, as Florida historian Gary Mormino writes, granting far more assistance than later immigrant groups—Haitians, for example—would receive.[12]

On the flip side, the Kennedy team failed to provide promised air cover to support the Brigade 2506 landing at the Bay of Pigs and Girón Beach on April 17–19, 1961, dashing hopes for an invasion that was probably doomed already. For this the Kennedy government earned the exiles' lasting enmity. So did the *Miami Herald*—though it has recovered somewhat by publishing a Spanish-language edition, *El Nuevo*—because it was one of several newspapers that reported on Brigade 2506 training exercises. The publicity spoiled the invasion plans, said exile critics.

When the CIA's strategy failed at the Bay of Pigs, it reportedly lost interest in the Peter Pan program and disengaged from it. Nonetheless, support continued from the anti-Castro underground operating in Cuba, even as it became involved in more substantial counterrevolutionary activities. According to Monsignor Bryan Walsh, the intelligence concerns that stimulated U.S. support for the program had created enough momentum after the Bay of Pigs failure to carry it through until the missile crisis of October 1962, after which the program ceased.[13]

Despite so much government assistance, the Jesuit-trained Aglio needed to "divide the loaves" to support his growing flock. It was a different time then, he explained, a time when a social services director could make a request of a store manager, rather than asking for a United Way grant, as would happen today. Thus he went to J. C. Penney in Jacksonville and said he needed bedspreads for his "teenage Cuban refugees." The store manager asked how many, and he said one hundred. Shocked, the manager said he didn't have that many, but after further conversation Aglio got the bedspreads. "You couldn't believe how much the boys appreciated them," he said. "It made it seem more like home."

For accommodations were rustic. The boys lived in barrack-style buildings with common showers, bunk beds, and footlockers for their belongings. A temperamental heater worked some days but not always. (They stayed at the camp through winter, when North Florida gets chilly if not freezing cold.) About the only amenity other than the natural scenery of oak forest and river was an Olympic-size swimming pool, where many of the boys learned to swim during the warm months. In all, the conditions were appropriate for one-week summer camp but difficult for anything longer.

Still, Aglio worried more about the boys' emotional needs. When chicken pox afflicted one-third of them, the part-time nurse addressed their medical needs—but they needed something more. "Sixteen-year-old boys still cry for their mommy when they have the chicken pox," the camp administrator learned. They also had pride and identity needs, he knew. When a forest fire threatened the camp, the boys succeeded in extinguishing it, a tremendous source of pride among them. Aglio assumed they also set the fire. One of the camp's biggest problems was loneliness. The boys would sometimes call home, often making them feel more miserable. Mainly, they had each other.

Cesar Calvet, now a bank vice president in Orlando, arrived with the first group of boys in 1961. He would become best amigo of Mel Martinez, whom he knew slightly in Cuba. His parents had moved to Havana from Mel's hometown of Sagua, but they went to the beach near Sagua, and Cesar would see Mel there. Like the other boys, Cesar thought their stay would be temporary. Arriving in Miami in June 1961, he expected to be home by Christmas; when that did not happen, he realized that "things were going to be different." For Christmas in the camp, he received a pair of socks and some candy. "I've never been so grateful for a pair of socks, but it was a far cry from what I would have received at home." In his middle-class family, he said, he would have received something like a bicycle.[14]

"They were mostly upper-class kids," said Aglio. Many of them brought expensive jewelry and fine clothes, such as French-cuff silk shirts and nice suits, reflecting their class background as well as their parents' misreading of the situation in Cuba and of how long their children would be away. Mel's mother packed him three wool suits and new leather-soled shoes, "as though I was going to boarding school in the North," he commented. Passionate about baseball, he packed his baseball mitt, a predictable but nonetheless symbolic choice. For baseball would become a cultural lifeline for him, linking Cuba and North America and facilitating his assimilation into American life. He felt guilty, though, about playing baseball at the camp in his new leather shoes.

By March 1962, Aglio and his fellow administrators knew this situation could not last. The Church had high standards for relief work, which could not be met with so many boys. As well, they knew from the worsening situation in Cuba that something different—more than an emergency stopgap measure—was required. They would find the answer in foster homes.

Mel arrived at the camp in March. Cesar Calvet knew that Mel was coming—an aunt of his in Jacksonville had heard from Cuba—and took him under his wing, protecting him from some of the pranks that older boys inflicted upon new arrivals. One initiation rite was depositing the new boy in a mud hole and spraying him with a hose. He remembers Mel then as levelheaded, less excitable than other boys, a good listener with a certain charisma—a "natural leader."

While the boys had previously gone to Bishop Kenny High School in Jacksonville, Mel and the last arrivals attended classes at Camp St. John. Aglio thought it too disruptive to place the boys at Bishop Kenny in mid-year, especially when they were not returning in the fall, so instead an adult-literacy teacher gave English classes at the camp. Looking back, Martinez called the classes "babysitting."

Initially, camp administrators kept mum on closing the camp. "They were all asking, 'When are we going home?'" said Aglio. "It took a long time for them to realize they were not returning." Looking back, the name Peter Pan was sadly ironic. In the 1953 Disney movie they all knew, Peter Pan had taken the Darling children to a place called Neverland. Yet for most of these real-world Peter Panners, the United States was a land from which they would never, never return.

Following the decision to decamp, Aglio assumed a new responsibility: finding foster homes for the boys. In response to appeals in the *Florida Catholic* and pleas from the pulpit, he began receiving applications from prospective foster parents. By day he interviewed the applicants, encouraging those he found suitable to take two boys rather than one, so the boys would have a companion. Applicants were offered $6.50 per diem, a clothing allowance, and reimbursement for medical and dental expenses, all administered through Aglio with tight controls, including a number assigned to each kid. It was these administrative procedures, not typical of the Catholic Church, that made him suspect federal government involvement, though he saw no direct evidence.

In the evening he returned to Camp St. John for administrative chores. He would sit at a cafeteria table, flow charts and lists spread in front of him, working into the night to match boys with foster families. The boys would often stand behind him, looking over his shoulder, sometimes shouting, "No, here, not there," pointing to a different city or parent, although to them the cities were much alike, all foreign places.

When the boys learned in May that they were going to foster homes, they had different reactions. Some welcomed it, others fought it; some never accepted they were going to a foster family rather than home to their parents until boarding the bus for the trip. Seeing how desperately the boys needed each other, Aglio let them propose a destination and a partner from the camp, but reserved a veto over unsuitable matches. Mel and Cesar partnered, having become fast friends. They chose Orlando because Cesar had originally gone to San Pedro Center, a retreat center owned by the Church outside Orlando. He had attended Bishop Moore High School for a semester before transferring to Camp St. John when San Pedro closed as a refugee camp.

Aglio placed about sixty boys in foster families and assigned close to forty more to relatives, mostly in Miami. From Camp St. John the boys went to foster homes in Jacksonville, Daytona, Melbourne, Cocoa, Orlando, St. Petersburg, Tampa, and Sarasota. Aglio took two boys himself, added to a growing family that eventually included eight natural children. The foster home had to be licensed and approved by Aglio, but the Church retained legal responsibility for the kids.

Before the boys dispersed from Camp St. John, the administrator made a final speech to them in the cafeteria. Figuring he should reveal his bluff, he spoke in fractured Spanish, having worked to learn the language over the previous six months. He began by telling them how much they meant to him, and how brave they were to leave their homeland and their parents behind. The "liberty bell" that called them to gatherings would ring no more, he said, but they would always remember what they had shared. As he spoke, he could see their astonishment at hearing him "murder the Spanish," in his words. He was amused that his bluff had worked.

"When I finally shut up—I spoke maybe five-six minutes—there was a long pause," he said. "Then one boy stood up, then another and another. Finally they all stood. They began clapping this rhythmic clap, clapping two times and then saying my name in Spanish. *Clap, clap—Aglee-o. Clap, clap—Aglee-o. Clap, clap—Aglee-o.* They all had tears streaming down their faces, and so did I. It was the most moving tribute I've ever experienced before or since. I finally felt the meaning behind what they called me: *padre segundo*, my second father." Forty years later, Aglio's voice cracked as he told the story.

———

In Cuba, Mel's natural mother and father suffered his absence, though he wrote to them weekly. For them, putting their elder son in Peter Pan was an act of passion—passion born of love for Mel and hatred for Castro. When a local boy was executed for opposing the government, after Fidel's 1960 death-penalty decree for anyone joining or helping the revolt against him, Mel's parents feared the consequences if he remained in Cuba. So, said Mel's mother, they "decided to make the big sacrifice and seek out Peter Pan."[15]

Describing the moment when Mel left, Mrs. Martinez said: "It was very sad. We never thought he would return. With another government, yes, but not with this one." She and her husband made it their goal to reunite with Mel in the United States, not knowing how or when.

Before Castro, their lives were good. Gladys and Melquiades Sr. lived in the midsized town of Sagua la Grande, population 35,000, located on the meridian directly below Miami in Villa Clara Province. It was a pretty town with a river running through it, its economy based on agriculture—primarily sugar and dairy farming—and manufacturing. There was a sugar mill in the town and a metal foundry that made parts for sugar mills. Ten miles away was a port, attracting import-export trade. As in similar American towns, a hundred or so families controlled the life of the town, said a contemporary of Mel's from Sagua.[16] These families were related through business as well as kinship ties. Their children played together and went to the same schools, the same resorts, and the same Christmas parties.

Gladys Ruiz came to Sagua from a nearby small town and met her future husband through relatives. He became a large-animal veterinarian who primarily served the dairy industry, inseminating cows. (Later, when the future senator tried to explain his father's occupation to his American foster parents in his limited English, he said: "He marries cows.") Smart and able, Dr. Martínez graduated number two in his class at the University of Havana. He was well respected in the town, as his father had been before him. "Back in those days in Cuba, being a veterinarian was a big deal," said his son Ralph.[17] There were only six veterinarians in Sagua, and a large-animal vet was valuable, because many people still rode horses for transportation.

Tall and distinguished-looking, Melquiades was gregarious and well liked, the kind of person who would stop people in the street and give them chickens. Said his son Ralph, four years younger than Mel, "He had a magnetism about him. People were attracted to him." And he enjoyed being the center of attention. Though not boastful, he did not display the humility that Mel would exhibit in later life. Dr. Martínez, as people called him, was the head of the family in keeping with Cuban patriarchal culture, presiding more by position than by decree. Most decisions in the family were his, extending to what they ate, where they shopped, and where they vacationed, said Ralph's wife, Becky.[18]

In this patriarchal culture, Gladys was largely dependent on her husband, seldom leaving the house without him. She neither cooked (they had a maid), nor grocery shopped, nor kept a checkbook, nor drove a car. Said Ralph, she was the "kind of mother you had in this country [the United States] thirty or forty years ago." Their household routine in Cuba was tied to their immediate family. Every night after dinner they visited Dr. Martínez's parents, who lived in Sagua; on Sundays after church, they drove to her parents' home fifteen miles away.

Reflecting birth-order traits, Mel was well behaved and studious as a child, Ralph more rambunctious. As Mel related, "My father used to say he could sit me down next to a well, tell me to stay there, and come back in an hour and find me still sitting there."[19] Though otherwise tranquil, according to his mother, Mel had a passion for sports, primarily baseball. Like their parents, both sons are big talkers, say family members. They also inherited their mother's joviality, according to Mel's wife, Kitty. A joke teller, she enjoyed making people laugh, while her husband was more serious and task oriented, focused on getting it done.[20]

As well, both sons are family-centric, a value fostered by the larger Cuban culture of their youth and reinforced by their small-town upbringing. At least among the leading families, everyone knew everyone else in Sagua. The town encouraged the traits that both parents modeled: warmth, friendliness, and grace.

⟵⟶

In most respects the Martínez family in Cuba was nonpolitical. Turned off by the graft and corruption of the Batista regime, Melquiades told young Mel: "Don't ever get involved in politics. It's dirty stuff."[21] When the Bay of Pigs invasion failed in April 1961, the government arrested most of the leading people in Sagua and put them in a theater. At center stage was a machine gun, trained on the nervous audience. The militiamen's instructions were to wipe them out if the invasion took hold, according to Ralph. But Dr. Martínez was not among those taken to the theater, as one of his colleagues who was a military veterinarian had vouched for him personally. He was placed under house arrest "under this guy's watch," said Ralph.

Yet the family belonged to the bourgeoisie that Castro opposed. They had a chauffeur and a maid. Their house was air-conditioned. And family ties linked them to the landowning class. An aunt and uncle owned a dairy farm, which Castro confiscated. The family also owned a small bottling company, founded by Mel's grandfather and a partner in 1919, which Castro also took. The plant produced a local cola that tasted like a cream soda with pineapple and lemon. Melquiades's veterinary practice was located in a corner of the bottling-plant building along with a small pharmacy that he also ran. At the time, a veterinarian could run a pharmacy. According to Cesar Calvet, whose family knew Mel's in Sagua, they were upper middle class.

Still, they welcomed the revolution at first. At least they felt that Fulgencio Batista should go, given his abuses in office. El Presidente had filled the prisons and ransacked the national treasury, making Cuba a haven for organized crime. As Mel recalls, his parents held out hope for the July 26 Movement that expelled Batista, thinking it would be liberal and humanitarian. Castro, the bearded Jesuit-trained lawyer from Oriente Province, had promised to hold elections in two years, and many Cubans expected him to reinstitute the nation's liberal constitution of 1940, which Batista had suspended, and restore civil liberties. But even as a young man, Mel was less sanguine.

At night, home from his Jesuit school, he would argue with his parents about Castro. This revealed a part of his makeup that would grow more pronounced over time. Though levelheaded and moderate in disposition, he also had passions—in this case, what evolved into a fierce anticommunism, an opposition to big-state solutions that restricted individual liberty as occurred under Castro. As would later be true on the abortion issue, the Catholic Church nurtured this passion.

In his secular life, Mel's passion was baseball. Family pictures show a serious-faced boy—because, his wife speculates, he objected to coming indoors from playing ball to have his picture taken. Through baseball he gained exposure to the culture of the United States, which many Cubans in the 1950s and 1960s regarded as the land of milk and honey. Young Mel's view of America could be summed up in three words: baseball, bubblegum, and movies. Before Castro blocked American TV and movies, Mel and Ralph could watch major league games broadcast from Miami. After Castro's intervention, the young baseball aficionado resorted to ingenuity. He would climb onto the roof and adjust the antenna, his brother, Ralph, shouting from in front of the TV, telling Mel when the reception was good.

In fact, American cultural influences in prerevolutionary Cuba ran deep. Second-run TV programs were available in Cuba with Spanish subtitles.

Felix the Cat, the Three Stooges, Woody Woodpecker, Laurel and Hardy, Mickey Mouse, Betty Boop, Buck Rogers, the Lone Ranger, Roy Rogers, Hopalong Cassidy, Donald Duck, Rin Tin Tin, Flash Gordon, Tarzan, and Zorro were known to Cuban children. Vacations to the United States were common among upper-middle-class Cubans, as was schooling in North America. Miami, the most frequent vacation site for Cubans, had a population of 30,000 *cubanos* before Castro's 1959 takeover; even then, *se habla español* signs were commonplace in the shops and restaurants of the Florida city.[22] Mel's father had wanted the family to take an American vacation but "waited too late," said Mel.

As Louis Pérez explains in his masterful book *On Becoming Cuban*, the intercourse between Cuba and North America nourished an ethos in Cuba supportive of individualism, personal responsibility, and capitalism. Pérez observes how North American styles became "standard in the definition of middle class," as Cuba became an extension of the market to the north: "In a complex process, North American market culture insinuated itself into virtually every aspect of public and private life, in tastes and preferences, as a means of self-representation and merchandise for self-esteem, prescribed behaviors for which appropriate attire was available, or perhaps it was the other way around." English, he states, was Havana's unofficial second language. And most "Cubans of means" had studied or worked in the United States.[23]

Before the nation's economic collapse in the 1950s, Cubans by the thousands journeyed to the United States to purchase TVs, washing machines, and other appliances, all much cheaper on the mainland. From their travels across the Florida Straits, as well as from American cultural fare, they gained exposure to the American Dream ideal. Visions of stardom, Hollywood, playing professional baseball, becoming a top doctor, lawyer, or other professional or entrepreneur, all blended seamlessly into Cuban culture, as Pérez chronicles, all part of the *yanqui* influence.

Nor did Cubans need to leave the island to experience American capitalism. As a diverse sample, Ford, Sears, Woolworth, Max Factor, Coca-Cola, Sherwin Williams, U.S. Rubber, and Portland Cement were active in pre-Castro Cuba. Economic doldrums that began in 1953, largely related to the inability of the sugar industry to sustain the nation's growth, put the American Dream of ever-growing consumption on hold for all but the richest Cubans. Island residents' average income was approximately $370, compared with an average of $2,000 in the United States, worsened by the fact that prices of consumer goods in Cuba were higher because of import costs.[24]

On one hand, the resulting economic dissatisfaction—accentuated by culturally available comparisons with life in America—played into the hands of revolutionaries. On the other, the infusion of liberal ideals of equality, participation, and democracy in the nascent anti-Batista movement raised hopes for a liberal outcome, rather than communism. That was before Castro routed the Liberals and consolidated power, as he did by 1961. On April 16, 1961—three days before the Bay of Pigs invasion—he proclaimed the revolution as socialist.

Certainly young Mel experienced these cultural influences, refracted through the medium of baseball, American television, consumer goods, and his parents' expectations for him. The stronger influence on him was probably the Church. Prior to college in the United States, his whole education was in Catholic schools, where he learned the catechism along with the three R's. His priests, as a fellow Cuban explained, would have taught or at least supported the idea of evolution and science, hallmarks of modernity. In other respects, they would oppose political-economic arrangements that suffocated the soul, with obvious implications for communism.

Said his friend and fellow exile Ernesto Gonzalez-Chavez, now an architect in Orlando:

> Mel is a person of deep belief. If he's guilty of anything, it would be that he is tied to his beliefs. It's hard for him to compromise his beliefs. We were raised as Catholics. In our hometown, the Catholic diocese was Jesuit and the Jesuits are strange people, because they are sometimes social liberals but also conservative. The priest told him as a boy that there was nothing wrong with Darwin's view of evolution. We were not raised as Bible thumpers. We did not believe that it was literally true that God created the world in eight days.[25]

What's more, Mel's priests were Spanish, providing a link to the Spanish Civil War conflagration. He felt so close to the Spanish rector of his Cuban school that, years later, he and Ralph traveled to Majorca to visit the then-elderly priest. From his Spanish priests he learned what the communists had done in Spain, how they had murdered priests and closed churches, knowledge that he brought home in conversations with his parents about Castro.

In the future senator's own words:

> I remember debating my parents hotly about the fact that it was a communist revolution. They were still buying the line that it was humanistic rather than communist, that Castro would hold elections in two years, and so forth. And because of the influence on me from my teachers, who were from Spain, and who had seen [the Civil War], they had a very different view of it. I remember Father Gayá, and how he was very clear about that and [how he] stressed that this is bad and people don't understand it, and this is going to be a problem. I carried this home and debated my parents.[26]

It made Mel's parents worry about their normally levelheaded, even-tempered son. Because on this issue he was rebellious, dangerously so for someone in Castro's Cuba.

Mel recalls several events that culminated in his departure. One was Castro's closing of Catholic schools and sending everyone to public school, the better to indoctrinate them. Another was him booting out priests, suppressing religious practices, and closing churches. A third was Mel's own "rebelliousness about the system." In his words, "I wasn't fitting in and adjusting. I wasn't willing to accept things and just live with it." Finally, friends of his began leaving. Kids would just disappear from school without explanation, though everyone knew they had gone to the United States.

Then came the basketball game. Tall and lanky, young Mel enjoyed basketball almost as much as baseball. To signify his devoutness, he wore a scapular—a large silver medallion imprinted with the Virgin Mary—on a ribbon around his neck that would bounce from his shirt as he played basketball. At one particular game, government people came and began to harass him for being Catholic, as evidenced by his scapular. Amid the crowd's shouting and cheering, they began to yell, "Get the Catholic." Then, "Grab him by the *escapulario*." And finally, "Kill him, kill him. Kill the Catholic." As Gladys Martinez said, "That's when my husband and I knew we had to do something."

Looking back, Mel commented: "My parents were horrified because I was wearing this scapular, which was kind of in-your-face. They saw these people were crazy, yelling at a fourteen-year-old kid playing basketball, saying to kill him just because he was Catholic. On top of that, they were thinking: 'It is our son out there wearing the damn thing.'" It was a conflict waiting to happen, and it frightened Mel's parents to the core.

Soon after the game Mel had a hush-hush conversation with his parents. They gathered in his parents' bedroom behind a closed door. Emblematic of the "fear state" created by Castro, his parents could not trust their maid. They also did not want Ralph to hear, knowing it would frighten him. Huddled at the foot of their bed, his parents asked him whether he wanted to leave. "They didn't counsel me one way or the other," he said. The decision was his, and he chose to go. As he related: "My mother said, if I had not wanted to leave, they would not have done it." Recalls his mother: "He wanted to leave and was very happy. He knew he had to and accepted it." She said he was totally against Cuba and wanted nothing more to do with it. "The revolution and its consequences had totally disillusioned him."

It was a pivotal decision for young Mel. Had he not chosen to leave, his family might have escaped later, but the consequences would have been different for him. He would not have been a Peter Panner. He might have wound up in South Florida rather than Orlando, delaying his assimilation into American culture. Or perhaps his family would have stayed in Cuba. As his mother explained, they could have stayed and remained safe. Her husband was a professional, not simply a bourgeois. He was a veterinarian, and vets were needed, making it difficult to depart once Castro sought to stem the brain drain. "If we had stayed, I probably would have become a physician, following in my father's footsteps," said Mel the devoted son. His decision to leave would culminate in a vastly different career path for him.

⊢——⊣

To get Mel out, his parents needed to connect with the Peter Pan network. Dr. Martínez traveled a lot in his veterinary practice and eventually met someone who gave him step-by-step advice on placing Mel in the program. The first step was to get a visa waiver to exit the country. The visa waivers were available from members of the underground Peter Pan network, but making contact with them was perilous. Castro had created an elaborate system of surveillance consisting of block committees backed by his dreaded G2 secret police. Parents wanting to connect with the network and those distributing the visas had to worry about both.

To secure a visa, Mel needed to go to Havana. It was a challenging trip, by train, for someone who had never traveled alone before, but a small step compared with what was to come. Fortunately, Mel had an aunt living in Havana who met him at the train station, making him feel more comfortable. She then took him to a house where he recalls a bunch of strange people asking him questions. In retrospect, he explained in an interview, he appreciates that they were trying to gauge his trustworthiness for the Peter Pan operation, but it all seemed frightening at the time.

"The secrecy was huge," he said. "They needed to be confident that we were not going to tell on this thing." He satisfied his interrogators, who agreed to provide a Peter Pan visa waiver and an airline ticket, which had to be purchased in dollars. His parents were to get an exit pass, which required applying to local authorities.

During this period Mel had acquired a baby sister, Margarita, born December 6, 1960. At the time, the plans for his departure were well advanced, and he knew that his time with her was precious. Her presence during these dark times provided "a beam of light and an inspiration to the whole extended family," Mel wrote in his memoirs.[27]

After a six-month wait, Mel's exit pass arrived, with a departure date two days later. His father did not go to the airport. According to Mrs. Martinez, her husband could not bear watching his elder son depart. So Mel's uncle drove Mel and his mother and brother to the airport in Havana. The family had also purchased bus tickets for five of his friends to see him off. At the airport he was almost prevented from leaving because authorities claimed that the family had an unpaid telephone bill. Before he could depart, his uncle paid an exorbitant bill at the airport office, which, said Ralph, "probably lined some local official's pocket."

For his mother, it was painful beyond belief. "His leaving was something from another world. You can't imagine how a mother feels letting her son go like that," she said, then became emotional and could talk of it no more.

Not knowing whether they would see their children again, the families watched through a plate glass window as the authorities processed the Peter Panners. As soon as they headed to the plane, the families went to an outdoor terrace where they watched the boys board. When the plane finally departed, the families began cheering, prompting the police to lock the door, imprisoning them on the terrace. Said Ralph: "We didn't know whether the firing squad was next," though the police eventually unlocked the door and let them go.

For Mel the experience was sad and frightening but also exhilarating. At least, it was exhilarating when they left Cuban airspace. The pilot of the Pan Am plane came on the intercom to announce they had reached U.S. airspace and "were free." Until then the plane was subject to recall as part of the harassment practiced by Cuban authorities.[28] While mesmerized by everything about his first plane ride, Mel remembers the boys cheering the pilot's announcement in jubilation.

◄══►

Mel's life was also shaped by the escape stories of others. Given his close-knit family and their connection to the larger Cuban diaspora, his political and philosophical views and his attitude toward communism in particular were also influenced by Ralph's escape story. And his parents'. And his aunts and uncles'. And others he knew in Sagua. All of them influenced the person he became.

When Mel left, Ralph was eleven and too young to go too. Besides, his parents could not afford it. He would leave within a year, however, driven by events at his public school. There, kids taunted him and called him bourgeois, some of them proudly saying, "I'm a communist," implying he was not. Then came the day when health officials were to administer an oral polio vaccine at school. Through the underground, Ralph and his parents had heard that the authorities were experimenting with kids and the pill might be poison. He went to school that morning determined to refuse the vaccine.

Health officials called students to the front of the room and gave them the pill, which they expected students to swallow in front of them. Ralph tried to foil the officials by holding the pill in his teeth and not swallowing it, but he accidentally dropped it when he returned to his seat. Seeing this, the girl sitting next to him—a girl whose mother was a prostitute, who might be especially attracted to a revolution that overturned the status hierarchy—began shouting: "He dropped the pill. He dropped the pill." The authorities came over to his seat and looked for the pill but could not find it.

Young Ralph thought he had won, but two weeks later a G2 secret policeman and four militiamen with machine guns came to the school. They called out his name and the name of a girl who had missed school the day the vaccine was administered. Then they marched them to secret police headquarters, a place where some people walked in and never walked out. There they sat them down in metal chairs, pointed the machine guns at them, and told them to take the pill. Ralph and the girl did as told, opening their mouths for inspection to prove they had complied, before being marched back to school.

Within two months of Mel's leaving, his parents wanted Ralph out too. The plan was for him to leave with an aunt and uncle living in Havana. To see whether he could handle being separated from his parents so young, he was sent to live with the aunt and uncle for a month. He passed the test and left, bound for Miami, with his aunt and uncle and their two daughters on May 12, 1962. In Cuba his uncle had been a prominent architect, living well enough to afford maids and butlers in their home, while in Miami he could not find work and became totally depressed. It was a typical experience for early refugees, 36 percent of whom were professionals or semiprofessionals who could not meet state licensing requirements, or speak the language, or find a job in their trades.[29]

Ralph's aunt put a dressmaker sign in their front yard and sewed dresses, while the two daughters worked as secretaries, providing the family's income. Ralph slept on the couch of their small rental house and attended junior high in Miami, waiting for his parents to follow them. (Born Rafael, he Anglicized his name without changing it officially after an Anglo teacher advised him that he would fare better in the United States as Ralph.)

Dr. Martínez and his wife endured four years in Cuba without their sons. In this early period of the Revolution, the Cuban government encouraged the departure of opponents, whom they called *gusanos* (worms or maggots). At the same time, they used exit permits to screen out individuals, like Dr. Martínez, who possessed needed technical skills.

A brief thaw occurred in 1965, however. President Johnson created the Freedom Flights, which began on December 1, 1965. The parents of Peter Pan children were given first priority, and about five thousand children were reunited with their parents in the first six months. These flights lasted until April 1973 and brought 260,561 Cubans to America.

Dr. Martínez and his wife and daughter could enter the United States on this program, but they still had to be screened in Cuba. Through a friend in the Interior Ministry, in what amounted to a cloak-and-dagger operation, they succeeded in securing passes, which arrived on Friday for a Monday flight. The people in Sagua did not know they were leaving. Saying goodbye to Gladys's mother, they departed on March 28, 1966.

In keeping with government policy, they could take only three changes of clothing, three pairs of underwear, a hat, and a one book apiece—nothing more. Not their bank account, nor other assets, nor anything from their house. Members of the Young Communist Pioneers, junior supporters of the Revolution similar to Hitler Youth, came and emptied the house, which the government then converted to a school for Pioneers.

———

Many Cubans did not seize the opportunity to leave. For every family story of harrowing escape there exists an equally compelling story of those left behind. A commonly heard version goes: "My grandparents didn't think Uncle Sam would allow a communist dictatorship to take root ninety miles from Florida." Mel's own father repeated this mantra, at least initially. In leaving, Dr. and Mrs. Martínez left behind not only her mother but also her younger brother, a sister, and a niece. In 1978 Gladys was able to visit her mother, then in her nineties, shortly before the mother died. Her siblings remain in Cuba.

Expecting "Uncle Sam" to intervene was plausible, given the historical record. At the time of Castro's takeover, Cuban independence and the struggle for democracy in the island nation were relatively young. Independence from Spain was secured only in 1902, following the Spanish-American War of 1898. Thereafter the United States continued to exercise a strong hand in Cuban affairs, intervening militarily multiple times, though more to support "stability" than democracy. So Cubans might reasonably think it would happen again. Of course, that was before Castro gained protection from the Soviet Union, raising the stakes for American involvement.

For Cuban Americans, stories of escape and emigration are the bonding material of the Cuban diaspora, which has scattered a million Cubans across the globe, three-quarters of them in the United States. (Some 11 million remain in Cuba.) Older exiles, especially those in Miami, the symbolic center of *el exilio,* speak reflexively of returning—emphasizing their status as exiles rather than refugees, the difference being that exiles intend to return. This distinction also marks the difference between *immigration* (entering a country to permanently settle there) and *emigration* (leaving a country in response to crisis, possibly to return).

In other respects, though, Cuban Americans are more passionately American than natural-born Americans, owing to their motivations in "emigrating" to the United States. As they often say: "We came for philosophical reasons—at personal sacrifice, sometimes at great danger—rather than for merely economic reasons, as other groups have."

In the choice words of Cuban American scholar and memoirist Carlos Eire, a Peter Panner who holds an endowed chair in history and religious studies at Yale University: "Cubans have a hard time letting go. We love much too deeply." Yet those Cubans who gave him "the Judas kiss," sending him away, "would also inch me towards paradise," the United States. For loss and gain, he writes, are "Siamese twins, joined at the heart."[30] Hence the dual identity that María Cristina García, in *Havana USA,* finds among many Cuban émigrés: as Cuban exiles and Cuban Americans, part of their identity in each country, one foot in each culture.[31]

In varying degrees, this characterization applies to all Cuban Americans, including Mel Martinez. According to García, it applies with special force to first-wave exiles living in the Cuban enclaves of Miami-Dade County, Florida, where more than half of America's Cuban émigrés reside. Martinez is a first-wave exile but not a Miamian. In coming to a foster home in Orlando, he had a different assimilation experience, one that facilitated his eventual election as Florida's first Hispanic U.S. senator. More than many Miami *cubanos,* he became culturally an *americano.*

3

⊶━━⊷

AMERICANO

The bus ride from Jacksonville to Orlando marked a transition for sixteen-year-old Melquiades Martínez—he was not yet Mel. Practically, it delivered him from the nondescript Jacksonville bus station, down the Atlantic coast past St. Augustine, Daytona Beach, and Cocoa to sleepy Orlando, 130 miles away. But symbolically, it marked the end of his Cuban exodus and the start of his American odyssey. Because until now, mid-June of 1962, he had not really entered America.

He had walked on U.S. soil for four months while at Camp Matacumbe and Camp St. John, where he mixed almost exclusively with his fellow Cuban exiles. Before that, in Cuba, he recalled only one encounter with an American. That was with his father, at a tender age, when an *americano* came to inspect some cattle he was buying. Otherwise Mel's image of America came from TV—from Rin Tin Tin, Roy Rogers, and Hopalong Cassidy—and baseball.

He rode on an ordinary Greyhound bus, of the kind that ferry those too old, too young, or too poor to drive themselves. With him amid the other passengers were eleven more Peter Panners assigned to foster homes in Orlando. They nicknamed themselves the Twelve Apostles.

Beneath their bravado, it was a nervous experience for all of the boys, said Mel's best amigo, Cesar Calvet. At the camp, they had each other. In Orlando they "knew someone was there to meet them, but they didn't know who." They were going to an unknown place with unknown people, in what was still for them an unknown country. "It felt funny," Calvet said.[1]

The bus station was Mel's first glimpse of life in America. Located on Amelia Street just west of Orlando's downtown, it looked like every other small-city bus station in the South, with buses angle-parked like the folds of an accordion next to a glass-front building where, inside, passengers and their families sat on wooden benches and listened as the loudspeaker squawked information about arrivals and departures. It was a southern bus station, because there were separate waiting areas for whites and "coloreds," something Mel found strange.

He recalls a confusing scene when they arrived, with lots of people milling about and somewhere in the distance a voice trying to say "Melquiades."[2] Like the other boys, he searched for the person calling his name. *Mel-kee-AD-es? Mel-kee-AD-es?* Finding the voice, he introduced himself in broken English to Eileen and Walter Young.

For reasons explained below, Mr. Aglio had assigned Mel to a home without another Peter Panner accompanying him. Culturally and emotionally, he was on his own, left to fend for himself. After introducing himself to the Youngs, he collected the suitcase that contained all his belongings and climbed into the Youngs' station wagon. They then headed "home"— home to the Youngs' family of two teenage boys and Mrs. Young's visiting mother; home to Pine Hills, a blue-collar suburb of Orlando; home to their modest three-bedroom house on that perfectly named street, Amigos Avenue. There, in a household in which no one spoke Spanish, Mel would enter America.

➞

Walter and Eileen Young typified the postwar migration to the Sunbelt. Attracted by the climate and defense-related employment, they had moved to Florida from the snowy cold of Chicopee, Massachusetts, a declining manufacturing town ninety miles west of Boston. High school graduates, Catholic, she of French Canadian origin, they sought opportunity down south, finding it in Orlando where the Glenn L. Martin Company had recently built a missile production facility.

Like a teething infant, Orlando was starting to grow suburbs, stimulated in part by Martin's arrival. The Baltimore-based aircraft company had headed south because the Pentagon wanted to disperse the nation's military arsenal away from Washington in case of nuclear war. Martin chose Orlando because it was near the U.S. Missile Test Center, recently established at Cape Canaveral on the Atlantic coast. The company's presence, with a workforce of 12,000, generated several new suburbs, including Dommerich Estates in Maitland, where Martin engineers located, and Pine Hills west of Orlando, where the Youngs and other production workers resided.

The family's modest concrete-block home typified postwar construction in Orlando and the Sunbelt. With a low-pitched roof and a carport on the side, the 1,200-square-foot house boasted three bedrooms, two baths, and a big picture window—the epitome of the American Dream. Two houses from the end of the street, it sat snug against a small wooded area, down the street and around the corner from Parkwood Plaza, Orlando's first shopping center.

It was not what Mel expected, for his image of America was basically drawn from TV westerns. But it was picture-perfect postwar Americana— culturally, an appropriate port of entry for this naïve young émigré.

⊷

Eileen Young had responded to a call from the pulpit in agreeing to take a foster child, said her son Dennis, two years younger than Mel.[3] His brother James was a year older than their Cuban foster brother. The Youngs first learned about Peter Pan at St. Andrews Church in Pine Hills. Intrigued, Mrs. Young called a family meeting, telling her sons they had an opportunity to help someone and asking what they thought. With their assent, she investigated further and reported back in three days, saying, "Here's the deal." It would be a short-term arrangement, maybe six months, just long enough for the boy's parents to come over, or for things to change in Cuba, she explained. The leader in household matters, she said: "Let's give it a try," and the family agreed.

Humanitarian efforts were common in the family. Walter Young was active in the Knights of Columbus and president of the Holy Name Society, which did good works in the parish. Walter and Eileen distributed food to the needy at Christmas and Thanksgiving, often bringing their children along. While Mel was with them, they took in a second foster son, Bill Hunt, a teenage friend of Dennis's who was "on his own," though the Hunt boy did not stay with their family continuously. The Youngs later helped parent a troubled niece too.

The Youngs were devout Catholics who prayed nightly and faithfully attended Mass. But taking in Mel "was not so much driven by religion" as it was a humanitarian gesture. "They just thought it was the right thing to do," said Dennis.

Because they had two teenage sons and a grandmother in the house for part of the time, they wanted only one Peter Panner. In placing the boys, Thomas Aglio had hoped to keep Mel and Cesar Calvet together. Another foster family, June and Jim Berkmeyer, had wanted them both, but Aglio demurred. The Berkmeyers had no children, and Mrs. Berkmeyer worked full-time as an executive with the Florida Bankers Association. In these circumstances, at a time when working mothers were the exception, Aglio feared that two boys would be too much for them.[4]

So Cesar and Mel were separated, living across town from one another, Cesar in a familiarly privileged setting, Mel with a blue-collar family. Through an odd set of circumstances, however, each would later stay with the other's foster family.

———

Eileen Young was the kind of natural mother who knew instinctively what to do. "She gave me just the kind of mothering I needed," said Mel. As soon as they arrived home from the bus station, she and Walter sat Mel down for a conversation.

"We have to know what you should call us," she said.[5]

Mel looked at her "with those big brown eyes," as she tells the story. "Mommy," he responded.

"No way, you still have a mommy. You have one mommy and that is all. How do you say 'aunt' and 'uncle' in Spanish?"

"Tía and Tío," he answered.

"Fine, then that's what you will call us," Mrs. Young said. "We will call you Mel." Tears streamed down both of their faces.

At the time Mel's English was limited. He had never spoken to someone whose first language was English. (In Cuba, he had learned academic English in his Jesuit school, while Cesar had attended an American school and learned colloquial English.) At the Youngs he would say, "Thank you, thank you, thank you." He was genuinely thankful and knew to say thanks, but "thank you" was also one of the few expressions he knew. In response, Mr. Young told him: "Mel, one thanks is enough."

Mrs. Young wisely perceived that Mel's limited English might get him in trouble. Soon after he arrived, she pulled aside Dennis and Jim and told them: "You need to tell Mel all the dirty words." Her sons were disbelieving. "You want us to do what?" She said it was to prevent someone from taking advantage of Mel by teaching him to say something inappropriate. So the two brothers gave him an "English 101 of dirty words," telling him: "These are the words you don't want to say publicly."

Mel's English was good enough to communicate his basic needs, and his skill improved rapidly. It did not help him with French, though. One Sunday afternoon the family was gathered in the living room after returning from church. Also present was Mrs. Young's mother, whom the children called Grand-mère, as she was French Canadian. Mel approached Grand-mère as she sat in a recliner, took her hand on bended knee, and began, "Ma grosse mémère—" She immediately started shrieking at Walter, who convulsed in laughter. Without realizing it, Mel had called her his "fat granny." As she instantly knew, her son-in-law was the culprit: he had told Mel she would like hearing this appellation from him. Walter, who played the harmonica for entertainment, was a frequent source of levity at home. That night he was laughing so hard he could not say his prayers.

Grandmother stayed with the family for several months, during which time the three boys crowded into a ten-by-eleven-foot bedroom. On weekends Bill, the second foster son, often spent the night on the couch. When Grand-mère moved back to Canada, son Jim had his own room, while Mel continued to bunk with Dennis.

Despite the mixing of two foster children with teenage sons in close quarters, Mel blended smoothly with the family. "We all got along very well with Mel," said Dennis. "He was very likable. We never had a disagreement." He added that Mel was obviously on his "best behavior."

This foster-child experience honed Mel's personal skills. For succeeding at the Youngs required a certain amount of personal diplomacy. Asked about this, he said:

> Absolutely, you had to walk lightly. They did everything they could to make me be one of them, but it was still a little artificial in the best of circumstances. There were all the normal family interactions— teenage sons not always doing what Mom says, husband and wife interactions, and money tensions, because they were not a well-off family. And you're trying to figure out your place in that little world. I've thought a lot about that: I had to be a real diplomat at a young age to make it work.

Other Peter Panners found such diplomacy difficult. "They felt entitled because of the spot they were in," said Thomas Aglio, who routinely visited the boys. "They didn't have it in their natures to be diplomatic," he reported. "Some of them struggled outwardly and became angry and aggressive." But Mel was different. He was "soft-spoken, mellow, accommodating, and easy to get along with," said the former camp administrator.

Here Mrs. Young no doubt helped. She possessed a big heart but would not have tolerated someone who felt entitled. By all accounts she was a stern taskmaster. She made it clear to her charges what was expected of them. For example, Dennis explained, they were expected to eat what was served—there was no special diet for the Cuban boy. They were also expected to practice good manners, say ma'am and sir, and stand when an adult entered the room.

Guided by these expectations, her children succeeded in later life. Neither parent was a college graduate. Walter Young was a purchasing expediter at the Martin Company who became a park ranger with the Florida Park Service after his children left home. Despite Walter and Eileen's modest education, all of their children, foster sons included, earned college and graduate degrees, working their way through school. They have also enjoyed good careers and stable marriages.

⟷

The Catholic Church was the Peter Panners' legal custodian, and Aglio, as the Church's representative, advised the foster parents not to Americanize the boys. Having observed at Camp St. John that the boys shunned American cooking, he recommended that foster parents take them shopping, let them pick out a few items, and allow them to "show you a few things in the kitchen." More broadly, he recommended that foster parents immerse the boys in American culture, showing them "our customs and traditions, but without trying to take away their Cubanness," in his words.

Even so, some foster parents forbade the boys to speak Spanish at home. Eileen Young did not: Mel taught Walter and her some Spanish during his stay—which stretched, from the anticipated six months, into two years. But she did tell him to speak only English at school, advice he took. "She told me not to speak Spanish. If you do," said Mel, "people will think you're talking about them."

It was very different from exile life in Miami, as Mel appreciated because Ralph was living there with his aunt and uncle. "In Miami, they had a Cuban Refugee Center where Cuban refugees could go and get food," said Mel. "In Orlando, we had El Refugio," the city's lone Spanish restaurant in the mid-1960s. "The difference was, at the Cuban Refugee Center the food was free. At El Refugio it was capitalism—you had to pay."[6]

⟵⟶

Yes, Mel's life experiences—his acculturation to America—would have been different in Miami. As Cubans in South Florida say: "We like Miami. It's so close to the U.S."

The city became the center of *el exilio* because it was so familiar. Before 1959, it had a Cuban population of 30,000. Its subtropical weather was like the island's. Its palm trees and pseudo-Spanish architecture were like Cuba's. And *español* was widely spoken. By March 1961, just two years after Castro's takeover, an estimated three-fourths of the faculty from the University of Havana resided in South Florida.[7]

As Mel recognized, Miami provided assistance to Cuban refugees. When first-wave exiles arrived in the 1959–62 period, the city was experiencing a recession, and most exiles found menial jobs, if that. As resident aliens, they could not receive conventional government assistance. But social services, medical examinations, and surplus food were available from the federally funded Cuban Refugee Center. As well, they received assistance from faith-based organizations—the Catholic Hispanic Center in downtown Miami, the Protestant Latin American Emergency Committee, and the New York–based Hebrew Immigrant Aid Society. (Some 12,000 Jews left Cuba after Castro's takeover.)

The initial refugees primarily settled in a four-square-mile area southwest of Miami's central business district, an area soon dubbed Little Havana. Largely white and affluent, these early refugees used their business acumen to renovate and start businesses in the old buildings along Flagler Street and SW 8th Street (Calle Ocho), important thoroughfares running through the heart of Little Havana.

This became a distinctive cultural zone, one where street vendors sold *guarapo* (a sugarcane drink) and *granizados* (snow cones), and the smells of *puros* (cigars), *pasteles* (pastries), and *café cubano* filled the air. The exiles could shop in stores owned and operated by Cubans, read and listen to the Spanish-language media, and live and work alongside fellow exiles.

In Miami, Spanish never became a private language among Hispanics, a language spoken only at home or in hushed tones among Anglos.[8] It was used in public and private places, in the myriad interactions with fellow Cubans and other Latin Americans. In recognition of this, the Dade

County public school system experimented with bilingual education as early as 1963, encouraging the retention of Spanish-language skills, as well as the learning of Spanish by native English-speakers.

How different it was for Mel in Orlando, where no alternative culture existed. No "foreign smells" of Cuban cigars or *café cubano* wafted through the air. No Cuban or Latin American brands lined the grocery shelves. There were no *quinceañeras*, the Hispanic celebration of a girl's fifteenth birthday. Nor *periodiquitos*, political tabloids, to keep *la causa* in the public consciousness. Nor simply many Hispanics. As Cesar Calvet recalls from this era in Orlando, "If you were riding a bus and you heard someone speaking Spanish, you definitely turned to see who they were. It was that unusual."

In Miami, Cubans were successful in this early period because they had a strong sense of who they were. They had a support system for maintaining a sense of *cubanidad*, an appreciation of the customs, values, and traditions associated with being Cuban. As María Cristina García explains, for early exiles *cubanidad* entailed preserving an identity that was both political and cultural. For despite their refugee status "they were still—and always would be—Cubans; complete assimilation would be a rejection of their past and of their heritage, as well as a negation of the forces that propelled them to the United States."[9]

All of this irritated many non-Cubans in Miami. It seemed that these new immigrants refused to blend in, to become culturally American, to dissolve into the proverbial melting pot. As the refugees moved west and south of Little Havana into other residential areas, "white flight" occurred to cities north of Dade County. (Blacks, having less mobility, remained largely in Dade.)

Carving out a distinct cultural zone also afforded protection from discrimination. Cuban American writer and activist Miguel De La Torre writes in *La Lucha for Cuba*, his analysis of religion and politics on the streets of Miami, that his life changed when his family moved from Miami to Louisville, Kentucky. There his family encountered institutionalized racism for the first time in their adult lives, both in the workplace and in church. He writes: "The day we moved, I woke up 'white' in Miami, but that night in Louisville I went to sleep as a man of color."[10]

In Orlando, which Miami Cubans call "the country," Mel Martinez lacked this cultural support system. His only semblance of support for maintaining *cubanidad* was the company of his fellow Peter Panners, the

Twelve Apostles. But they were separated among different foster families in different parts of the city. They saw one another only at school, where they took pains to "fit in" and avoid speaking Spanish.

As we shall see, this separation from Cuban culture was both a challenge and an opportunity for young Mel. It was a challenge because he was pushed into the proverbial melting pot, which privileged Anglo ways. It was an opportunity, though, because once he overcame that challenge, he was able to advance in the cultural mainstream without seeming "alien."

In that sense, his coming to Orlando—to monocultural, Anglo Orlando—was a lucky break. Had he been relocated to Miami like so many other Peter Panners, he might have been trapped in a Cuban American enclave, delaying his assimilation into American life. Had he pursued a political career in that context, winning statewide office would have been virtually impossible.

<hr>

The bishops of Florida, in sending the Peter Panners to foster homes, ordered the dioceses' schools to accommodate them tuition free. Orlando had only one Catholic high school, Bishop Moore, so the boys of high school age went there.

Bishop Moore was a conservative place, socially and culturally, according to Mel's classmates. For equality's sake (God loves all children the same) the students wore uniforms: blue blazers, white shirts, and gray pants for boys; for girls blue blazers, white blouses, and gray pleated skirts that covered the knees—with regular hemline checks by the nuns. Consistent with Catholic thinking of the day, the boys and girls were segregated; the only mixing occurred in advanced math and science courses and at athletic events, where the girls cheered the boys' teams.

Paying private tuition, though only $35 a month, the students hailed mostly from economically privileged families, and saw themselves that way. At a time "B.D." (before Disney) when "citrus was king," the school boasted children from leading citrus-growing families, among them the Battaglias and Carusos.

When Mel attended, in 1963–64, the school had no black students. Nor were there Hispanic students before the Apostles arrived. In the yearbooks from these years, one mostly sees the names and faces of Ireland and Italy.

Nonetheless, Mel's integration at Bishop Moore was fairly seamless. Likewise for the other Apostles. Said one of his two best friends, Rick Steinke: "I don't remember a time when Mel wasn't one of us. He just seemed to fit right in."[11] He was part of a "three musketeers" group that included Steinke and Gary Preisser. Speaking of the Apostles, Preisser said: "I didn't think of them as being Cuban. I don't think we really looked at them as being different from the rest of us back then."[12] The same message was heard in a half dozen interviews with former classmates.

Some males worried the Cuban boys would "steal the girls," said Steinke, a concern possibly related to the "Latin lover" stereotype. But that concern soon faded. The guys discovered that the Cuban boys were actually shy around the girls. "They were less aggressive than the rest of us," Steinke reported. In fact, the Apostles dated the Anglo girls—there were no Hispanic girls—without apparent incident.

This acceptance of the refugee boys occurred without special preparation by school administrators. Instead, the Cuban boys just showed up the first day of school, said former students. "We were all aware that they were refugees from communism and how difficult it was for them," said William Dunn, who would become a newspaper executive.[13] Yet this appreciation of their plight remained largely unspoken.

Even with his close friends, Rick and Gary, Mel didn't talk about his situation. "We probably should have talked to him about it," Steinke said. "We might have learned something, but we didn't." Added Preisser: "He never complained. He was just getting on with his life."

For Mel, Cuban life and politics were compartmentalized—something to discuss with Cesar and other Cubans, in private and probably in Spanish, but not with his Anglo friends. He would follow this path until the Elián González affair, in 1999, which marked the beginning of his career as a *Hispanic* politician.

By all accounts, Mel and Cesar were more successful at integrating than the other Cuban boys. Classmates cited Mel's charm and desire to fit in as reasons for his success. Ron Edwards, who played basketball with Mel, recalled that he always had a smile on his face and a positive attitude.[14] Cesar Prado, a Peter Panner who would became an auto sales executive, described Mel back then as hard working and "pretty humble." He was "more levelheaded than I was," said Prado, who admitted having a hard time adjusting.[15]

His language skill was another reason for Mel's success. In his words, "I learned that you had to get rid of the accent if you wanted to communicate effectively." Cesar agreed that Mel had only a slight accent, less than most of the Cuban boys. "You could hardly tell that English was not his first language," said Rick Steinke.

Plus, girls liked him. Though a bit "gawkish," reported one female class-mate, he had a "baby face that was attractive on a tall sports-minded boy," which made him popular with girls in a school culture that valued athlet-ics.[16] Mel had a steady girlfriend his senior year and escorted her to the Homecoming Court, a status marker in the school's culture.

Rick Steinke recalls how he and Mel became fast friends. In October 1962, soon after Mel's arrival at Bishop Moore, the Cuban missile crisis un-folded. It was a more frightening affair in Florida than elsewhere, because of the state's proximity to Soviet missiles in Cuba, and because of the signs of military preparation as convoys rumbled down the roads, headed to South Florida. At the height of the crisis, Bishop Moore canceled classes so that students could go to the chapel and pray that nuclear war would be averted.

Of course, for Mel and the other Apostles, the missile crisis was a dou-ble-edged threat—to them and to their parents in Cuba.

In a World History class the students were talking about the crisis as Soviet warships steamed toward Cuba. Steinke turned to Mel and asked what he thought would happen. Mel responded confidently and without hesitation: "They'll turn back." Fortunately, events proved him right. "I was impressed with the guy," said Steinke. "It was the start of our friendship."

Neither Steinke nor Preisser came from Bishop Moore's privileged set. Preisser's father was retired from the Air Force and Steinke's father was a masonry contractor. (Both boys would become coaches and high school principals.) As Aglio observed, "None of Mel's friends were rich." In this regard he followed a different path than the other Apostles. They tended to find friends from wealthy families like their own families back home. Though Mel came from an upper-middle-class family in Cuba, his forma-tive experiences in the United States—in the Young family and among his friends at Bishop Moore—were grounded in the lower middle class. Those experiences would make him a more open and accessible person in his later political career.

More than anything else, playing sports integrated Mel into the social life of Bishop Moore. Virtually all of his friends were athletes. Preisser was a standout football, baseball, and basketball player, the best athlete in the school. Steinke was a top basketball and baseball player. Other good friends were Tim Durkin, who played basketball and baseball, and Ron Edwards, a football and basketball player. As sociologists appreciate, sports teams enforce an ethos of equality: players are valued for their contributions to the team regardless of their race or ethnicity.

It was thus with Mel. He was an above-average athlete, an intense competitor, a dedicated team player, and above all a good sport.

In basketball, he was the sixth man on the squad his senior year, playing forward and center behind Steinke. At 6'2" he was the third tallest member of the team. As teammate Ron Edwards recalls: "He was not the most skilled player, but he made up for it with hustle." On a good team with an 11–10 record, playing mostly public schools two or three times their size, he scored 64 points for the season his senior year and averaged 3.2 points per game.

Baseball was of course Mel's real love. Taller than other Cuban boys, he was a good choice for first base but also played catcher. Preisser, the team's best player, called him a "real good player." Mel batted behind Preisser, who said: "I'd get on base luckily and he'd hit a line drive." Lacking a suitable practice field, and playing much larger schools, the team was not competitive. In most of their games, the opposing team "run-ruled" them, meaning the game was called because Bishop Moore was so far behind. They were lucky if the game went five innings.

Compared with the other boys, Mel played at a disadvantage: He recalls looking into the bleachers and seeing that all the other players had their parents there. He didn't.

Still, playing sports was a bonding experience for Mel at Bishop Moore. It also helped keep him out of trouble. Steinke acknowledged some mischief-making among the "three musketeers" but says nothing serious occurred. "We didn't go to jail or anything." Moreover, as athletes they neither drank nor smoked, though their sobriety ended in college. The musketeers were decent if not great students: according to Steinke, in a class of 127, Preisser graduated about thirtieth, Steinke about sixtieth, and Mel somewhere in between. In fairness, though, Mel's academic performance should probably be "curved" to account for English being his second language.

Reflecting his character and demeanor, Mel was a good sport who kept his temper. Said Preisser of their baseball days: "He was pretty classy.

When he fouled out, he might get angry with himself, but he kept it in check. He didn't swear or throw the bat or kick his helmet." As a basketball player, Steinke reported, "He was a fierce competitor who gave it all he could. He wasn't timid, but he wasn't dirty either. He was not one to swing his elbows or hit people in the nose, which the coach wouldn't have permitted." Nor did he talk trash to opposing players. He engaged in good-natured razzing of the other side, with the likes of "We'll show you guys" or "We'll kick your butts," but he observed a limit and was never insulting or mean.

Interestingly, several of his teammates thought Mel seemed mean in his Senate campaign, especially in calling former congressman Bill McCollum, a staunch conservative, a representative of the "radical homosexual lobby." Emphatically, no one remembered Mel ever acting mean himself. Preisser, who lives close to Mel today, asked him during the campaign why the race descended into personal attacks. "Maybe I shouldn't have asked him, because he just looked at me and didn't say anything. I guess that's how politics is these days," he said, adding, "I don't know why anyone wants to be a part of it."

Assisting Mel's seamless integration at Bishop Moore was Orlando's uncomplicated racial caste system at the time. Essentially, there were two racial groups: blacks and whites. With a negligible Hispanic population, there was not yet a "brown" category, nor were Hispanics a perceived threat to Anglos.[17] Orlando in 1963–64 was a racially segregated, black-white city not far removed from the Old South. Accordingly, the Cuban boys—all Spanish-European in origin rather than black Cuban—were socially defined as "white" rather than "colored."

Ostensibly affirming this, one Peter Panner became indignant when asked about "integrating" at Bishop Moore. "It wasn't like we were black. We were white, for God's sake," he responded.[18] In the same vein, Tim Durkin, who played basketball with Mel, said: "Before these kids came over, we didn't have any Hispanics. It just wasn't an issue that they were Cuban."

⇌

Mel and the Apostles arrived in Orlando at a time of economic and social transition. By Mel's senior year, what the media described as a "mystery land buyer" was assembling a large parcel of land southwest of the city. That land buyer was Walt Disney. In November 1965 he announced plans for a giant theme park in Orlando, one ten times bigger than Disneyland in California. Opening in 1971, it would transform Central Florida into the world's most popular tourist mecca—the biggest economic boon to Florida since the air conditioner.

The other transition was social, as African Americans struggled to overthrow Orlando's racial status quo. In 1962, activists in the black community began conducting sit-ins at lunch counters and other public places that were designated whites-only. The following year, a committee appointed by Orlando mayor Bob Carr recommended that all public park and recreation facilities be integrated, while reserving the integration of public swimming pools until the following year. Their recommendation was accepted by the city council on a divided vote.[19] Orlando thus chose a path of racial moderation characteristic of much of the state.

Though part of the Confederacy, Florida (except the northern region) differed from other southern states. Its geography and small population at the turn of the twentieth century encouraged land schemes that continually attracted newcomers, diversifying the population and giving the state a frontier mentality while also encouraging urbanization. As well, the state's economic diversity enabled it to escape from the curse of relying on one crop, cotton, and the oppression of tenant farming. "Florida thus never had the same commitment to a 'southern way of life' that so influenced its southern neighbors," writes David Colburn.[20]

The Great Coming of Disney also steered Florida down the path of racial moderation. Disney, and the theme park operators who followed, wanted above all a secure environment in which to operate. Their economic importance to the state proved a deterrent to the racial extremism and social instability observed in other states of the Old South.[21]

When Mel arrived there, Orlando's population was almost one-third black, yet the city had no black elected official.[22] The first black commissioner would not be elected until 1972, after a switch from citywide voting for commissioners to election by district. Though the city's public schools were legally integrated since 1963, de facto segregation prevailed until a federal court order in 1969. Residential areas were segregated as well, protected by racial zoning codes. Blacks were confined to scattered residential districts on the city's west side and the black town of Eatonville, the nation's first black-founded community, lying just north of Orlando.

In Pine Hills where Mel lived with the Youngs, there were no blacks then, though it is predominantly black now. Mel probably encountered very few African Americans in his day-to-day life, so extensive was the pattern of segregation at the time.

Gary Preisser recalls going to Minnesota Twins games with Mel and other Bishop Moore baseball players. The Twins had spring training in Orlando, but Preisser and his friends knew that the black players could not stay with their white teammates, rooming instead at the Sadler Hotel on Church Street in the city's black quarter. For Mel's school chums "that's just the way it was." In Orlando in the mid-1960s, these arrangements were accepted practice, at least among whites.

Mel found all this surprising. The Cuba that he knew was 27 percent black or mulatto.[23] Though it had a racial caste system as well, there was more interaction among the races. "In Cuba I went to school with blacks, I played ball with blacks," he said. "Here they had colored water fountains and restrooms, which seemed very odd. The interactions or lack of them with people of other races seemed very odd." He remembered the first time blacks were allowed to go to theaters in Orlando. "That was a big deal in Orlando and created a big controversy."

Similarly, Orlandoans might be surprised by the racial composition of Cuba. Though Cuba was 27 percent black, only 3 percent of the Cubans migrating to the United States before 1970 were black, a percentage that changed with the Mariel boatlift in 1980, when a substantial number of black Cubans crossed the Florida Straits.

Mel kept quiet about his observations, though. He was not particularly outraged by what he saw; it was just not what he expected—not in the land of the free. "It seemed out of place," he said. Sounding like an anthropologist observing a strange tribe, he explained: "I'm here learning how to eat this food I don't much like, and I'm trying to get along with these people I don't understand, and this is how they do this. I didn't feel like I was any position to challenge the status quo but just to figure it out."

As he finished high school, Congress removed the civil rights issue from state control by adopting the Civil Rights Act of 1964 and the Voting Rights Act of 1965. The following year, the GOP captured the governorship with the election of Claude Kirk, aided by the growing number of retirees and Cuban Americans who had come to the state. That election and Republican Ed Gurney's victory over former Democratic governor LeRoy Collins for the U.S. Senate two years later "reflected the expansion of an electorate that was not committed by racial and historical ties to the

Democratic Party and . . . public dissatisfaction with President Johnson's Great Society programs."[24]

In retrospect, Martinez appreciates how the civil rights movement of the 1960s aided Hispanics. As he told a predominantly Hispanic audience in 2005, "We did not participate in [those] struggles, but we benefited from them." But this recognition arose after he formed an American political consciousness, which occurred slowly for this young émigré. In the 1960s his focus lay elsewhere—with his parents in Cuba.

⊷

In the national news media the Peter Panners and other first-wave exiles were celebrated heroes of the Cold War. *Life, Fortune,* and *Newsweek* mythologized what they called the "Cuban success story," proclaiming the Cubans "golden immigrants" and the newest Horatio Algers.[25] In 1962, when the exodus was new, *Business Week* found good chiefly in the relief money pouring into Miami.[26] By 1969, however, it was praising the exiles for "their determination and capacity for hard work."[27] They were part of the continuing American Dream saga, examples of people who came for political reasons—to find freedom—rather than for economic opportunity alone. Such stories are always poignant in America.

Mel's own story included several poignant moments, the kind that help a young man grow up fast. One such moment was when he realized that his parents might not get out. It happened for him during the Cuban missile crisis. "I'm at the Youngs'," he recounted, "glued to the TV. My parents were down there, after all. That's when I began thinking, this thing is really serious." Before then, his parents were on track to get out; after the crisis, there was no communication, no travel. "That's when my obsession began to get my parents out."

Another poignant moment was telling Ralph their parents might be trapped in Cuba. Ralph was visiting Mel in Orlando as he sometimes did, spending the night at the Youngs' house, sleeping in the same bed with his brother. Mel is still not sure he did the right thing. At the time, he felt Ralph was banking too much on their parents escaping. "He had put his life on hold, thinking they were going to get out in a few months," said Mel. "Maybe it was too harsh, but I told him: 'Ralph, you're not being realistic.'"

As Ralph recalls, "I didn't believe it. I said: 'You're being too pessimistic, they will get out.' It was the lowest of the low moments for me." He added that he was always an optimist like his mother, while Mel and his dad were more pessimistic.

For their parents to escape, the sons needed to help. Basically, there were two avenues. One was coming through Mexico, which required purchasing a $1,000 visa. The other was coming through Spain and staying there six months before they could enter the United States, which would require supporting their parents in Spain. Mel told Ralph that they might have to work after high school, postponing college, to fund their parents' escape. "It was a lot of money at a time when the minimum wage was something like a dollar," said Ralph.

Mel's main outlet for discussing such issues was Cesar, whose parents were in the same dilemma. At Bishop Moore, the Cuban boys did not self-segregate. As Mel said: "We wanted to integrate, not segregate." He and Cesar were frequently together at the Berkmeyer house, which was larger and less crowded than the Youngs', and when they were together they would converse—in Spanish—about what Castro was doing, and so forth.

These colloquies with Cesar were not like bathing in Cuban culture as Miami émigrés could do, however. That may explain why, today, Mel's sense of *cubanidad* is more political than cultural. In Ralph's words, "Mel's 'Cubanism' is more of a love for something he left behind. It makes you feel guilty doing well [here]. We hear about things happening to people over there, and it almost makes us cry." At the start of Mel's Senate campaign, some South Florida Cubans wondered whether he was sufficiently Cuban.

At the Berkmeyer house, Cesar's foster parent situation was far different from Mel's. Jim and June Berkmeyer lived in the expensive Rio Pinar country club district. As they had no other children, Cesar only displaced their dog, Floppy, from his bedroom. In addition, he had access to a car.

Thin and energetic, Mrs. Berkmeyer was an accomplished woman who was "ahead of her time" in the early 1960s as a female executive in Orlando. Without children to dote upon, she committed to helping the Peter Panners. When one had a foster parent situation that proved unworkable, she persuaded a Rio Pinar neighbor to take in the boy and, afterwards, checked on him regularly. She also took a shine to Mel, who was frequently in her home.

For Cesar and Mel, socialization to America entailed shedding some old-country ideas about work. In Cuba, menial work was performed by "someone else," often someone black. Thus Cesar tells of trying to mow the lawn at the Berkmeyer house as Mel watched. When Cesar "finished," there were unmowed strips all over. Though he was seventeen, he had never mowed before. Likewise, one day Mrs. Berkmeyer asked Mel to clean up some grease left on the patio by their barbecue grill. His solution was to pour gasoline on the grease and light it, sending flames over the roof of the house (fortunately, nothing caught fire). As Cesar explained, Mel didn't know better. Middle-class boys in Cuba did not do such work.

Within the larger Peter Pan program, doing chores was frequently a problem, especially for teenage boys. As Victor Triay writes, some of these boys sensed exploitation when asked to take out the trash or help with housecleaning. "Because of their exalted position in the home, Cuban males were shocked when asked to help around the house." Others found it a "welcome shock," one that proved useful to them later.[28] Mel and Cesar fell in the latter category.

Cesar had stayed with the Youngs for a short time when the Berkmeyers were building a new house and were temporarily "between houses." Now, in August 1964 after graduating from high school, it was Mel's turn to move into the Berkmeyer home. Cesar had gone to New York to care for his parents and sister, who had recently got out of Cuba. (He would soon join the Marines and be assigned to Guantánamo, of all places.) Eileen Young's mother was in ill health and was moving in with them, so Eileen asked June Berkmeyer to take in Mel. Mrs. Berkmeyer agreed on one condition: "If I take him," she said, "you can't have him back."

Mrs. Berkmeyer provided Mel with a different kind of guidance. As an executive who had attended Columbia University in New York before graduating from Rollins College, where she also earned a master's degree in business, she inhabited a different world than the Youngs. Accordingly, she gave Mel helpful counsel on attending college, making connections, and pursuing a professional career. Following her advice, he enrolled at Orlando Junior College, an officially whites-only Christian college. Other than Rollins College, which was far more expensive, it was Mel's only higher-education option in Orlando. He had hoped to win a baseball scholarship to Rollins but was unsuccessful.

Mel resisted one bit of advice from Mrs. Berkmeyer, however. While at OJC he heard a presentation from YMCA officials about working at their Orlando-area summer camp, Camp Wewa. He wanted to take the job, attracted by the opportunity to work with kids in a setting like Camp St. John, though it paid less than his job as a grocery bagger at the Publix on Colonial Drive. Mrs. Berkmeyer told him he couldn't afford it, but he persisted.

In the end the job was financially feasible, because through it he earned a $1,000 college scholarship from the Optimist Club. Mrs. Berkmeyer could see that Mel was lucky, telling him: "Mel, you could land in a pile of poop and come out smelling like a rose." She later remarried, becoming June Brewer. At her funeral in June 2005, Mel choked up in trying to deliver a eulogy and couldn't speak. He turned to the priest and asked, "What should I do?" He had spoken in the Senate and at the United Nations without difficulty, but found this far harder.

Camp Wewa opened up a whole new world to Mel. Living in the camp as a resident counselor, he had his "own place" for the first time since leaving Cuba. The counselor-in-training job also gave him entrée—more so than Bishop Moore—to Orlando's upper echelons. The city then had few summer camps, and the Wewa campers and their parents were a who's who of Orlando's elite, past and future. In Mel's words, "It was an all-star cast of old Orlando—the Country Club of Orlando folks, the lawyers, bankers, and car dealers. It was a huge opener for me to the community."

Attesting to Mel's newfound social connections, Cesar recalls coming home from the Marines the following year and going to a party with Mel at the Country Club of Orlando, the city's oldest, wealthiest, and most "southern" country club. Seen on a map, it was only a few miles from the Youngs' house as the crow flies. Socially, however, it was worlds away. Much later Mel would join the club, only to resign as his political career began, on discovering it was moving too slowly to admit blacks and Jews.

⊷⟶

It was while working at Camp Wewa that Mel learned that his parents and his sister, Margarita, were getting out of Cuba. On September 28, 1965, Castro declared that persons with relatives in the United States who wanted to leave could depart from the small fishing port of Camarioca, in the northern province of Matanzas. That had led to a chaotic "boatlift," prompting the Johnson administration to negotiate the airlift agreement that spawned the Freedom Flights of 1965–73. As Mel's parents were given only two days' notice that they were leaving, Mel had little time to prepare.

Their arrival on March 28, 1966, was a minor media event. Under the headline "Cuban Family Arrives in Orlando," the *Orlando Evening Star* related that Dr. and Mrs. Martínez stepped off a National Airlines plane "into freedom and a new life." With them was daughter Margarita clutching three dolls, "all they were allowed to bring when they fled Castro's tyranny." They were met by "their son, Mel, handsome 19-year-old sophomore at Orlando Junior College." Quotable then as now, he told the reporter: "We've been waiting a long time. It's a big day for us all."[29]

TV news covered the arrival as well. Film footage shows Mrs. Martínez descending from the plane holding Margarita and rushing into the arms of Mel at the foot of the plane's steps. Looking like Mel but heavier, Dr. Martínez is directly behind his wife, smiling broadly and waving. As Gladys would say: "It was sweet to see the tall man my little boy had become."

In a well-burnished story, liberally used in Mel's Senate campaign, he famously gave his father $450, his entire savings, which Dr. Martinez used to buy a $300 car and make a rental deposit. Mel's savings came from working at Publix, Camp Wewa, and the Orlando Public Library, where he moved and shelved books when the library relocated to a new building. A key requirement of the American Dream saga—"hard works pays off"—was thus fulfilled.

(As media critics observed, Mel acquired his savings from working minimum-wage jobs. Yet in the 2004 Senate race he followed Governor Jeb Bush in opposing a referendum to hike the state's minimum wage by one dollar. According to the measure's supporters, the real value of the minimum wage in 1966 was a dollar more than in 2005. The referendum passed overwhelmingly.)

With the help of Mrs. Berkmeyer, Mel had also found a job for his father. Despite his limited English, he went to work for T. G. Lee Dairy as a quasi-veterinarian, the same work he did in Cuba. Without a license, he could not write prescriptions, but he could examine the dairy herd, calling a licensed vet as needed. Mrs. Berkmeyer knew T. G. Lee, who made the job available. Two years later Dr. Martinez passed a foreign-language veterinary exam and went to work for the State of Florida in a different kind of veterinary work: as an inspector at a poultry slaughter plant in Gainesville.

For two weeks the newly assembled Martinez family (now Martinez rather than Martínez) stayed in the Berkmeyer home. They then moved into a three-bedroom, one-bath rental house at 2822 E. Pine Street, just four blocks from the T. G. Lee dairy farm, which was surrounded by commercial and residential development.

It was a difficult time for Ralph, who was finishing junior high in Miami and had to wait until June to join his family. "Those last three months of the [school] year were the roughest of my life," he said. For the family, it was also a difficult time financially. Dr. Martinez made $60 a week at the dairy farm, and the rent was $150 a month. That left precious little for necessities in a situation where, leaving Cuba with only three changes of clothing, they were starting from scratch.

Ralph recalls the day when his father needed a dime to buy a cola to drink with lunch at work. It was two days before payday, and he had dropped a dime in the yard. With the whole family involved, they could not find it there. Nor was there ten cents in the house; they were stretched that thin.

Orlandoans proved compassionate, however. T. G. Lee had moved into a new house and left behind a house full of furniture, pots and pans, and so forth. He told the Martinez family to go and take what they needed. He also gave them ground meat whenever a cow was slaughtered at the dairy farm. In response to news coverage of their plight, others offered help. One man drove up to their house and gave them a used washing machine.

In words that Mel would echo, Ralph expressed thanks for this help: "The American people were wonderful. We were huge beneficiaries of American generosity, which helped us to get acclimated to America."

It was a large debt of gratitude that Mel inherited. He became an American Dream success, yes. But he did not do it alone. From Peter Pan to June Berkmeyer, T. G. Lee to the Optimist Club, the Kennedy administration's assistance policy for Cuban refugees to LBJ's Freedom Flights, he received generous help. That was the other side of his success story, not to diminish his personal accomplishment. It shows how assistance and individual initiative are inextricably linked.

Living in Orlando rather than Miami, Melquiades urged his sons to learn the culture of America. Where other Cubans were focused on the past, hoping to return, he was more reconciled to remaining in America. There was still a split identity: if they could return, he told his sons, they would. They should continue to appreciate their Cuban heritage. But for now they were Americans, and they should do right by America, he advised. The message was important for the sons to hear from their patriarch. Culturally they already had inferiority complexes. Their father's words, said Ralph, helped give them courage to overcome the roadblocks ahead.

In the lessons he absorbed from his experience, Mel typified the Peter Panners. Yvonne Conde reports from surveys of former Peter Panners that 70 percent found their experience positive.[30] Only 7 percent reported a negative experience. This group said their ordeal made them grow up too fast and left them with separation anxiety. But most said it made them stronger, tougher, more hard-working, more independent, and more disciplined. It also made them become adults overnight and drew them closer to their parents.

Not long after Mel's parents arrived, a bright, pretty Spanish major and daughter of the South at FSU would complete his Americanization.

4

KITTY

They met in a pre-Columbian anthropology class at Florida State University in 1968. Mel was majoring in international affairs, and his adviser encouraged him to take the course. Seated next to Mel that first day of class was his close friend Ken Connor, also an international affairs major. Professor George Milton had just started lecturing when a pretty blonde breezed into the room, her long hair bouncing from her shoulders as she walked. Mel and Ken nodded at one another with a look that said, "This is going to be better than we thought."[1]

Her name was Kathryn Tindal, she was from Mobile, Alabama, and unlike Mel and Ken that first day of class, she was genuinely interested in pre-Columbian artifacts. She stayed after class and asked the professor question after question, while Mel and Ken lurked in the background, feigning interest in the conversation. But their real interest lay in the young woman known as Kitty. A sophomore while they were seniors, she belonged to a sorority and had a fraternity boyfriend. As Mel would later say: "She seemed way beyond my world."

At Bishop Moore he felt safe, having integrated into a tight-knit group of fellow athletes. There he could pursue his interest in girls, and did so. But FSU was a whole new world, far larger than Bishop Moore, and populated by a broader social mix, from antiwar activists to Greek-letter types. Though he would eventually oppose the war himself, he found left-wing opposition to the war frighteningly reminiscent of Cuban communism, and he could not comprehend "the whole fraternity and sorority thing."

Before FSU, he meandered through two years at Orlando Junior College during what he calls his "dark period." He almost flunked out his first year and needed a fifth semester to complete the school's two-year program. Looking back, he understands his difficulties. He felt dislocated by the move from the Youngs to the Berkmeyers. More important, he had lost his peer group of friends and fellow jocks. Gary Preisser had gone off to the University of Dayton to play football. Rick Steinke, the remaining musketeer, was at OJC, but they saw one another infrequently because of their different class schedules. And Cesar Calvet, with whom he shared his Cuban side, had left for the Marines.

Plus, in his second year at OJC, Mel acquired family responsibilities. His parents' arrival, while a tremendous source of joy and relief, also brought new demands. As elder son, he assumed a parental role with his own parents, who had never been off the island and who looked to him for guidance in this new land. On the joyous side, he adored his little sister, Margarita, and he delighted in the company of Ralph, who joined the family after finishing the 1966 school year. At last the family was reunited in America, realizing his parents' dream.

Contributing to his academic difficulties, Mel worked long hours at the YMCA to help pay his tuition. He could not get government-subsidized student loans because OJC was a whites-only school and ineligible for federal funding. Like Mel, Steinke could not afford going straight to FSU from high school. Nor, as the son of a masonry contractor, was the fraternity world accessible to him. But his grades were better than Mel's, and he was able to start at FSU in his junior year. One semester later, in January 1967, Mel joined him in Tallahassee, where the two shared an apartment.

Foretelling Mel's future, they lived in the Senator Apartments, only two blocks from the football stadium, a paradisiacal location for campus merrymaking. There they ended the sobriety practiced in high school and joined in the bacchic ritual surrounding Saturday football games.[2] Steinke took a job with the student newspaper, the *Flambeau*, and helped Mel land a job there selling advertising. Together with student loans, the job enabled Mel to finance his junior and senior years at the university.

He selected an international affairs major because it matched his interest in politics beyond the United States. At the time, his political views were ill defined, and U.S. domestic politics held little interest for him. International affairs was an interdisciplinary major, enabling Mel to take courses in the politics, history, and geography of Latin America. The head of the program, Professor Richard Gray, was an expert on Latin American politics who had written his dissertation on the Cuban leader José Martí.

As Gray explained, the program was small, with only thirty to forty majors when Mel was there. The professor hoped to expand the major by creating a graduate program, which proved controversial. The state Board of Regents was alarmed because Young Socialists were active on campus, and "international affairs" sounded suspicious to board members. So Gray was called to a Regents meeting, where he allayed their concern that the program was communist inspired.[3]

The Regents' attitude was not unusual for the time. Between 1956 and 1965 a special committee of the Florida Legislature, formed in response to the U.S. Supreme Court's school desegregation decision in 1954, conducted an extensive investigation that targeted a range of allegedly subversive elements in the education establishment. Officially called the Florida Legislative Investigation Committee, it was headed by Florida senator Charley Johns and became known as the Johns Committee. As historian Karen Graves writes, the committee first targeted civil rights activists, then suspected communists teaching in the university system, and finally gay and lesbian instructors in public schools and universities.[4] Because the state legislature held their purse strings, the Regents stood watchful against these perceived threats, obliging Professor Gray to appear before them and acquit himself of being a communist.

Having taught Mel in four courses, Gray remembered him fondly. He was a good student, interested in Cuban and Latin American affairs, who "didn't wear his Cubanism on his sleeve," said the professor. It was Mel's personal qualities that impressed him most. "He was the kind of person who would do well in his personal relationships." In an interview, Gray admitted being disappointed in the 2004 Senate race, however, saying it "got meaner than I would have liked." Mel had never impressed him as someone who could be mean, he said.

As Mel's adviser, he remembers encouraging him to take the pre-Columbian anthropology class with Professor Milton. George Milton was a friend, and Gray knew the course would be valuable for both Mel and his friend Ken Connor. He had no way of knowing just how valuable it would be for the Cuban émigré.

⟷

In Professor Milton's class, Mel and Ken worked to get seats close to Kitty. With her long blonde locks, she represented for them the epitome of southern womanhood and Anglo good looks. "I was pretty focused that she was the one," Mel said, adding, "To her, I think that Ken and I were like a couple of puppies seeking attention." Her lack of interest in them, he now appreciates, wasn't personal: she was more interested in the course.

Accepted in the university's honors program, which meant her out-of-state tuition was deferred, she came to FSU on the advice of her high school guidance counselor to study marine biology. Fortunately for Mel, she would change her major to Spanish education in her second year. She was building upon her self-taught Spanish, acquired while in grade school from listening to records in the Learning Language series. She would practice her pronunciations in front of the Motorola each day during summer vacation, for her mother expected her to be productive when out of school.

Mel observed her at church in Tallahassee, so he knew she was Catholic. For a southern girl that was unusual—a stroke of luck for him. But there was another obstacle: she had a boyfriend. Undeterred, he worked to overcome his shyness and find ways to get close to her. Professor Milton's teaching method worked to his advantage, as the course had no textbook. Instead, Milton sent the students on field trips to the campus museum, giving Mel an opportunity to talk with her outside of class.

Eventually Connor pushed Mel to ask her out, saying he would if Mel didn't.[5] Mel figured Connor was bluffing, but credits his friend for goading him to act.

As Kitty recalls the story, she was aware of Mel's romantic interest. At some point he asked her to "go out for a Coke."

"I don't drink Coke," she told him.

"Then how about a 7-Up?" he responded.

"I just had one, but thank you."

"Then how about ice cream?"

"Ice cream I eat," she said.[6]

So the little date occurred, and soon afterward she dismissed her boyfriend.

Ken Connor met Mel in one of Richard Gray's classes. A dual major in international affairs and economics, he began his college career like Mel at a junior college, graduating from Chipola Junior College in his hometown of Marianna, Florida. He described Mel back then as "very interested in sports and athletics and crazy about girls." With another friend, John Harris, who also became an attorney, they bought a beagle as bait for attracting girls. However, they could not agree on a name. Mel wanted to call it Ben, and the other two wanted Lance, so they called it Ben, or Lance, or sometimes Bengal Lancer. As Ken said, "The crazy dog never knew its name." But it worked as bait: as they walked the dog across campus, girls would stop and ask to pet it.

Though from a small country town, Connor fit into FSU culture more easily than Mel. He belonged to a fraternity, ΣAE, and through it gained membership on the student Supreme Court. As he said, "Mel really didn't have a place to plug in politically, because he was not a Greek." Mel was not interested in student politics, which seemed frivolous after his refugee experience. And antiwar politics—the campus had an active chapter of Students for a Democratic Society that conducted demonstrations, marches, and vigils against the Vietnam War, even taking over Westcott Hall on campus—repulsed him.

As Mel's roommate Rick Steinke explained, they felt a patriotic duty to serve in Vietnam going back to high school days. But like many others at the time, they were conflicted. "We wanted to stay in school so we would not have to go," said Steinke. In Orlando the three musketeers had registered for the draft as the law required after they turned eighteen. As full-time students, they had 2-S deferments, but Mel lost his during his "dark period" at OJC, and he was summoned for his draft physical, the first step toward military induction. To his surprise, he learned he had high blood pressure—something for which he still takes medication. Essentially, that kept him from military service.

As Steinke and Mel confirmed in separate interviews, the future senator's views on the war changed after his cousin was killed in Vietnam. The cousin had joined the U.S. military soon after coming from Cuba. "After that," said Steinke, "Mel thought we should get out [of Vietnam] as soon as we could." In Mel's own words, "My parents were worried sick about me having to go after my cousin died. I guess the good Lord had another plan for me."

At FSU Connor gradually replaced Steinke as Mel's wingman and protector. Steinke was majoring in physical education, and Connor and Mel had more in common as fellow international affairs majors. In the evening, while Connor and Mel were studying in the apartment Mel shared with Steinke, the phys ed major would come home after a few beers and announce that he was turning in early—"because I had an archery test or something like that the next morning," Steinke said with a chuckle. (Though possibly exaggerated, Connor and Steinke both tell this story.)

Connor took Mel home to his small town of Marianna, located west of Tallahassee in the Florida Panhandle, where he remembers getting an uncomfortable response from townspeople. "It was as if they were saying, 'What's Kenny doing bringing a wetback home with him?'" Immigration was just becoming an issue in Florida, and people in Marianna did not know "international people," in Connor's terminology. But that was before they met Mel. "My family embraced him right away, and so did other people once they met him," said Connor.

This experience captured Connor's sense of Mel. "There wasn't anyone who Mel didn't get along with. He just has a magnetism about him. He draws people in and builds relationships quickly, gaining people's trust and confidence." Part of the attraction was Mel's "maturity" and "sense of the world," born of his refugee experience, said Connor. These qualities would continue to pay social and professional dividends for him.

Together, Mel and Ken decided to apply for law school. As Mel remembers, law school seemed beyond his reach, culturally and intellectually. His grades were average to good, handicapped by his language ability, though Connor called him "plenty smart." Still, he lacked confidence. Mel credits Ross Oglesby, a popular and gregarious professor who taught international law and who now has a building named for him at FSU, with instilling that confidence. "You ought to go to law school," Oglesby told him one day.

Thus encouraged, Mel took the LSAT along with Connor, and the two of them formulated grandiose plans for attending Harvard Law School. That was before they received their test scores. From working for the university's Department of Government, Connor knew they needed scores above 500 to get accepted. When their scores arrived on the same day, Mel opened his letter first and learned he scored in the low 400s. Next Connor discovered he scored under 500 as well. They were devastated, though they would earn admission to FSU's start-up law school.

⊨⇒

As Mel and Kitty's relationship progressed, the time came for him to meet her parents. Earlier, when she had told them about the guy from Cuba she was dating, their response was, "Cuba?" Said Kitty: "I don't think my father knew where Cuba was at the time." She imagines that her parents thought Mel would be short with a big mustache, the stereotype of a Mexican. But Mel's charm triumphed and her parents fell in love with him right away.

Kitty's father always had trouble saying Martinez. He would Anglicize the name, making it MAR-ti-nez. Though Ken Connor teasingly accused Kitty of being a "southern belle" and "putting on airs," her widowed grandmother had supported Kitty's father and uncle by laboring in an Alabama cotton mill. "They were really, really poor," said Kitty. However, her father won a full scholarship to Auburn University, where he breezed through, earning a degree in mechanical engineering.

While he was working in Pennsylvania for Westinghouse, he went on a blind date with his future wife, Pauline Otto, who also worked there. Interestingly, Mr. Tindal's first name, Lorenzo, sounded Cuban. (Following a southern custom, he was named for the doctor who delivered him.) Accordingly, Kitty imagines her mother thought *she* was meeting a short Mexican with a mustache. A woman ahead of her time, Pauline learned to fly a plane and became an accomplished person, writing an "All About Bridge" column for the Mobile newspaper and organizing bridge tournaments throughout the area—"professional" work for a southern woman of her generation.

Knowing Mel and Kitty had dated for a long while, her mother finally said to her: "Kitty, if you don't marry him, I will." They had met in January of her sophomore year, Mel's senior year. They dated until the June following her junior year, marrying in Mobile on June 5, 1971.

As the new bride prepared for her senior year, Mel was entering law school. The year before, Mel had got his first taste of Florida politics from working for Secretary of State Tom Adams, who became a huge fan of Mel and Kitty. Loading up his twin-prop Beechcraft airplane, Adams took his whole staff to Mobile for the wedding.

⊶

Tom Adams won the Democratic primary for secretary of state in 1960, when Doyle Carlton and Ferris Bryant ran against each other in the Democratic gubernatorial primary. The big issue in the governor's contest was racial integration—whether to scuttle Jim Crow in Florida. Bryant, who opposed integration, won the primary, which was tantamount to election in the solidly Democratic state. But Bryant was reluctant to sit down with John Kennedy, the Democratic presidential nominee, whom he regarded as pro-integration. So the task of managing the Kennedy campaign in Florida fell to Adams.[7] From his association with Jack and Bobby Kennedy during the campaign, Adams became involved in the new administration's opening toward Latin America. Through work with the Organization of American States, the Florida officeholder was invited to tour Colombia and meet its president, Carlos Lleras. While Adams was there, Lleras got the idea for creating a "Florida-Colombia alliance." The alliance, which would send Adams to Colombia twice a year, involved twelve sister cities in Florida and more than 2,000 Colombian students studying at community colleges and living with families in Florida. An equal number of Florida students studied in Colombia and lived with families there.

As Adams explained: "I was in bad need of an interpreter since I did not speak Spanish. That's how I met Mel." Following his graduation from FSU, Mel put his specialization to practical use, something few international affairs majors were able to do, said Ken Connor. Though he went to work for Adams as an interpreter, unsurprisingly his duties grew over time. Once again Mel's language ability proved decisive, particularly his ability to suppress his accent, this time in Spanish.

"Mel did a wonderful job for us," said Adams. "Though he was Cuban, he could speak impeccable Spanish without a Cuban accent." As the former Florida official related, that was important because Latin American leaders feared Castro and would be suspicious of a Cuban accent. "They might think he was a wolf in sheep's clothing."

Everywhere Adams went in South America, Mel went with him, whether he was talking to a president, a provincial governor, or a mayor. As Adams explained, an interpreter needs an intimate knowledge of the policies being discussed, so he can fill in details with the proper words. "Mel never missed a beat," said Adams, "and he always presented himself well. Whether he was talking to the president of Colombia or someone on the side of the road, Mel knew how to handle himself."

In 1970, as Mel finished his first year with Adams, the secretary of state was preparing to run for lieutenant governor with Reubin Askew, a pro-integration state senator who would become one of Florida's most admired governors. Mel thus faced an important choice. He could follow Adams and potentially win a place in the Askew administration, as many of his young counterparts in Adams's office would do, or go to law school as planned.

The choice was made difficult, in part, by the excitement of working in the governor's office, but also by the opportunity to make money rather than enduring poverty as a married law student. Plus, the politicking beckoned him. Adams had ties to local and county officials throughout the state, and Mel, who was starting to perform some campaign-related duties, found the political machinations fascinating. Back then, before TV became so important in statewide campaigns, winning office depended upon lining up the sheriffs and Democratic Party chieftains in each county, and "Adams had all those connections."

In the end Mel chose law school as the wiser course. He was committed to becoming an attorney, and working for Askew-Adams might derail that plan. The whole point of working for a year was to save money for law school—that was what he had told his parents and Kitty. So, taking the long view, he pressed ahead with law school.

Looking back, Mel's choice was well advised. Though another young Adams staffer, Jim Smith, would work for the Askew administration and eventually become Florida secretary of state and run for governor, the "Adams connection" would prove perilous. In 1973 Adams narrowly survived an impeachment vote in the state legislature, after allegations that he improperly used state employees on his farm. He avoided impeachment by two votes, but Askew replaced him as his running mate for his second term.

FSU law school had opened in 1966, five years before Mel entered. The state legislature had authorized it in response to demand for a second state law school at a time when the University of Florida law school in Gainesville was over capacity and baby boomers were seeking entrance in growing numbers. But the legislature, thick with UF law graduates, did not fully fund the FSU school, leaving its president to cobble together start-up money from his discretionary budget. In these early years the emphasis was on "getting bodies into the classroom," as one initial faculty member remarked. By 1970, the year Mel entered, the school achieved full accreditation, and applications zoomed from 1,000 to 1,500 for the roughly 200 seats in Mel's class.

Bill VanDercreek, who taught on the law faculty from 1968 until 1987, remembered Mel well.[8] He called upon him frequently in his federal civil procedure class in Mel's first year, and recalls him as a personable young man who could speak and write well. VanDercreek, who supervised the school's moot court team, remembers Mel best in that context.

Ken Connor, who entered the law school a year ahead of Mel, participated on the school's nationally recognized moot court team. Helping his friend once again, he urged Mel to try out for the team. At the time, FSU had no oral advocacy or trial court clinic. Moot court was students' only opportunity to practice trial work, though it resembled appellate work more than trial practice. In the competitions, students argued different sides of a hypothetical appellate case.

The key to moot court work, said Professor VanDercreek, was being "persuasive without being argumentative," an important skill for lawyers, since "if you argue with the court, the court always wins." Foreshadowing his future political career, Mel's real forte in this competition was his pleasant delivery and listening skill, said the adviser, explaining that good listening helped attorneys handle questions effectively. He added that people sometimes underestimate Mel because his affability masks his intelligence and analytical skill.

Mel's moot court partner was James Corrigan, who now practices in Pensacola. They had bumped into each other as new law students and clicked right away. Following a pattern for Mel's early friends, Corrigan was of humble origin—born in New York City, the grandchild of Irish immigrants, his father a mailman. Reflecting back, he extolled Mel's teamwork skills. "Mel had a gift for going into a group and working hard at making everyone feel comfortable," he said. In their teamwork, Corrigan was the litigator while Mel "took care of the big picture."[9]

(Extrapolating from their moot court experience, Corrigan imagined how Mel might rely too much on staff. Referring to the mailer associating Bill McCollum with the "homosexual extremists" and the memo from a Martinez staffer on exploiting the Terri Schiavo affair, he explained that Mel "doesn't feel the need to control everything." He would defer to someone he thought was capable without needing to know everything that was done. "I can't see him sitting down and thinking up something mean," said Corrigan. "There would be plenty of others to do that.")

Their partnership extended from moot court to the playing field. Both married, they lived in the university's Alumni Village housing complex for married students. There they played flag football on the law school team, competing against fraternities and other independent teams. They indulged the fantasy of being big-time athletes, said Corrigan. Mel was the team's main receiver and loved the competition. "He could get hot. He was very competitive and wanted to win, just like in moot court. But he always played clean and fair," said his friend.

Another law school friend and coathlete was John Thrasher, who would become Florida Speaker of the House, capping a twenty-year legislative career. Fitting the pattern for Mel's early friends, he was the son of a gravedigger who worked his way through law school following military service. Married with children and living in the Alumni Village like Mel and Kitty, he remembers Mel from their intramural softball team, calling him "a great athlete and enthusiastic team player."[10] With Mel at first base, their slow-pitch softball team won second place overall.

Apart from sports, Corrigan's favorite experience with Mel was at the state finals of moot court competition, held at a convention of the Florida Bar in Miami. Professor VanDercreek, who was given to flamboyance, rented a pink Cadillac convertible to transport the team to Miami, and insisted on taking Corrigan and Mel to the city's Playboy Club while there. In VanDercreek's description, "Mel didn't drink very much. He was our designated driver." Driving the Cadillac was a new experience for him, though. He had trouble working the automatic windows when they stopped at turnpike tollbooths, explaining to the others that he'd driven Chevrolets and Fords, never a car with power windows.

In the Miami competition, Mel and Jim competed along with Ken Connor and another barrister-to-be, Bill Jennings, losing in the final round to the team of Schwartz and Levine from the University of Miami. The highlight of the competition was the convention itself, however. Wearing his first suit, Corrigan was thrilled to mix with the state's legal elite, as was Mel. They walked into a reception, dazzled by the impressive crowd, and vowed to meet as many important people as possible. Said Corrigan, "Mel was very good at mixing." From this experience, the two branded themselves "professional mixers," a term memorialized years later by Mel on a photo he gave to Corrigan, inscribed "To Jim, two professional mixers," and signed Mel Martinez, Secretary of Housing and Urban Development.

Connor remembers Mel's prowess as a "professional mixer" as well. Commenting on the Miami gathering, he said: "We were the lowest of the low on the food chain, because we were students." He recalled riding an elevator with Mel in the high-rise resort hotel where the convention was held. When the president of the Florida Bar and his wife stepped onto the elevator, Ken and another law school friend shrank back while Mel glided into easy conversation with them. By the time the elevator reached the couple's floor, the future senator had secured invitations for himself and his buddies to an elegant reception in the president's capacious suite.

Professor VanDercreek pinpointed Mel's effectiveness as a professional mixer, saying he was pleasant and interesting to talk with on a variety of subjects, whether sports or current events. "He was a very solid person as far as his psychological makeup and got along and worked well with other students, who liked and respected him. He had a lot of peer leadership ability," said the professor, adding that he was always relaxed and comfortable around other people.

Connor described much the same traits, attributing them, first, to Mel's innate temperament and, second, to his refugee experience and consequent desire to "fit in." Here Mel's professor and friends are delineating the characteristics of someone with "emotional intelligence," as described by Daniel Goleman in his popular book of the same name. Goleman defines emotional intelligence as a set of skills including control of one's impulses, self-motivation, empathy, and social competence in interpersonal relationships. Those who have it, says Goleman, succeed in work as well as play, building flourishing careers and lasting, meaningful relationships.

Though Goleman distinguishes emotional intelligence from the academic intelligence associated with good grades, Mel succeeded in the classroom too. He graduated in the top quarter of his law school class— a noteworthy accomplishment, said VanDercreek, for someone taking timed exams in a second language.

━━◆━━

Kitty described Mel's law school years as a "very, very happy time" for them. They managed the Stadium Apartments next to the FSU football stadium, and could see the iconic stadium out their apartment window. As she said: "I collected the rent and Mel fixed the toilets and cleaned the pool." The job gave them free rent and utilities, though their finances were nonetheless tight. By this time Mel's father had passed the foreign-language veterinarian exam and begun work as a poultry inspector at a chicken slaughter plant in Gainesville, 130 miles away, and he would give Mel and Kitty chickens from the poultry plant. In her words, "We ate chicken one whole year."

She had a VW bug and dropped Mel at law school on her way to her state job. Making more than she could with her teaching degree, she worked as a paralegal taking unemployment claims. They got by, scraping, she said. They never went to the mall, and she had two pairs of corduroy jeans, her perpetual outfit. For their first Christmas, Mel gave her a plastic piggy bank with $10 toward the contact lenses she wanted, and she gave him a pair of desert boots.

While in law school Mel made a dramatic decision, even if it seems predictable now: he decided to become a U.S. citizen. Both culturally and legally, he was affirming his desire to be an American. Am I here or am I there, am I going back or what? he had pondered. Kitty was a key factor—after all, he was married to an Anglo woman, a U.S. citizen. So was his career goal—he needed U.S. citizenship to join the bar. Affirming these choices, he went to the federal courthouse in Tallahassee on February 25, 1972, and took the citizenship oath, becoming the first member of his family to do so. To celebrate, Kitty fixed an all-American meal of fried chicken and apple pie.

⬩——⬩

Mel made another life-shaping choice in deciding where to practice law. He first considered Miami, which had only a half dozen bilingual attorneys. But he decided that Miami with its burgeoning Hispanic population would be too overwhelming for his wife from Mobile. Initially they saw Palm Beach, halfway between Miami and Orlando, as a compromise, and he applied for jobs there. However, a trip to Orlando during which he and Kitty stayed with the Berkmeyers made him realize it was the place for them. Orlando then had fewer than 500 Cuban residents, compared with almost 110,000 in Miami.[11]

Cementing the attraction, his friend Ken Connor told Mel about an opportunity with the Orlando law firm of Billings, Frederick, Wooten, and Honeywell. The young lawyer from Marianna had interviewed there himself. At a time when Orlando was growing by leaps and bounds, stimulated by the opening of Walt Disney World in 1971, Connor decided the city was too big for him and took a job in the small town of Lake Wales, southwest of Orlando. Mel also interviewed at the large corporate firm of Akerman, Senterfit in Orlando, knowing the managing partner, Don Senterfit, through June Berkmeyer. The Billings-Frederick firm proved a better fit, however.

Specializing in personal injury work, Billings-Frederick was founded in 1965 by Bill Frederick, who would become a three-term mayor of Orlando, and Jerry Billings, who came to Orlando from a Miami law firm headed by Perry Nichols, the godfather of plaintiff attorneys in Florida. The firm expanded slowly, hiring Council "Butch" Wooten and Dan Honeywell by 1970. One year before hiring Mel, Billings and Frederick sold the practice to Wooten and Honeywell, agreeing to stay for seven years to ensure the firm's continuity and reputation.

Thus it was Honeywell and Wooten rather than Billings and Frederick who made the key decisions in hiring Mel. Honeywell recalls interviewing him in his downstairs office and saying, "Stay here," while he went upstairs to consult Wooten, telling him, "I think we really need this guy."[12] Winning agreement, they hired Mel because he "pulled it all together," said Honeywell. He met people well, had confidence about him, "and if we didn't hire him for those reasons, we might have because of Kitty," the attorney said.

Jerry Billings, who continued as the firm's rainmaker, was especially impressed by Mel's refugee background. "You could see that wonder in his countenance at the enormity of the potential and opportunity that America gave to him. It was something unlike what you see in a native-born American, a humility and gratitude for being here."[13]

Candidly, Mel recalls hearing that one of his colleagues had misgivings about hiring a Hispanic attorney. In interviews, none of the senior partners would say so. To the contrary, Dan Honeywell recalls thinking that with "Miami starting to turn" and Orlando's Hispanic community enlarging, having a Hispanic attorney might be good.

Still, their comments about Kitty suggest a slight unease with hiring her Hispanic husband. She was important because of the "juxtaposition," said Honeywell. They were hiring a Hispanic attorney and assumed he would have a Hispanic wife, and instead he shows up with a "southern belle from Alabama." To the partners, the contrast was startling: "We figured she would cover for any weakness that he had." For her age, she was poised and self-assured, a classy young woman, the partners all agreed.

Jerry Billings used similar language, saying he never saw Mel as Hispanic. "Kitty dispels that," he said. In his view, Mel was "as American as apple pie."

At the time, personal injury work was the stepchild of the legal profession, disliked by doctors and insurance companies and disdained by the lawyers representing them. The Billings-Frederick firm basically represented four types of cases: auto accidents, trip and fall cases, medical negligence, and product liability disputes. Mel was drawn to such work by the opportunity to litigate. To him it was more "high wire" and more interesting than "sitting behind a desk and writing contracts."

"It was not an inbred desire to right the wrongs of corporate America" that attracted him to personal injury work, though practicing in this field stimulates "a little bit of that feeling," he admitted. Developing a legal specialty is like jumping from a cliff, attorneys will tell you. Once you begin a specialty, it becomes difficult to change after a few years of practicing. Mel's choice to become a plaintiff counsel, driven by his attraction to litigation, would shape the person he was when he entered politics.

He was drawn to Billings-Frederick because he wanted to practice right away, rather than "carry someone's bag" for a couple of years. As Bill Frederick explained, their new hires learned through trial by fire. "We pretty much rehearsed the cases with them and let them go." Though one of their attorneys might have an inventory of fifty to sixty cases, he would try only three or four a year. "We did that to maintain credibility with the insurance industry," said Frederick. "It was usually worth the time."[14]

In his legal work, Mel honed two skills that would aid his political career. One was negotiating. Honeywell said that Mel enjoyed negotiation more than litigation. He called Mel an "inclusionist"—someone who takes other people's thoughts into account in making up his own mind. A good negotiator needs to understand the other person's position, which Mel did well, said Honeywell.

In his legal career as in politics, Mel would excel as a negotiator. Opposing counsel liked negotiating with him because with Mel you could "avoid having a fight," said one of his law partners. "Mel didn't try to get the last piece of meat."[15]

Building upon his experience with moot court, he also honed his skill of persuasion, which required being honest and fair-minded as much as being articulate. He communicated well because he mastered the emotional aspect of communication, contributing to his future political career. As Billings put it, "The lawyer that comes across to the jury as the fairest wins every time." If an attorney presents the truth honestly and fairly, the jury will figure it out. "Mel did that very well," said the firm's rainmaker. Dan Honeywell made a similar comment, saying, "He's the kind of guy whom you can disagree with and not walk away angry."

Plaintiff attorneys—Mel included—tend to have a distinctive worldview. Taking cases on contingency, they hold the proverbial keys to the courthouse. Corporations have attorneys on retainer to represent them, while ordinary people depend upon the contingency-fee attorney. Since this attorney's work is free if he loses, in a small firm like Billings-Frederick he needs to scrutinize potential cases. To prevail, he needs a combination of hot passion and cool judgment, as in politics.

Specifically, the plaintiff counsel develops a worldview supportive of the underdog. As Honeywell said, "You can't do this kind of work for twenty years [as Mel did] and not feel a kindred spirit with the little guy." People who send their children to college may not appreciate the experience of those who do not, but personal injury attorneys do, he stated. "They see the other side, issues that affect little people."

Looking ahead, Honeywell thought Mel's refugee experience, of knowing what it means to lose everything, prepared him to be a statesman rather than a partisan. He doubted this would happen in the short term, however. "Mel is a very loyal person," he said. In the short term, he expected him to support the Bush administration steadfastly. With another White House occupant, Mel would revert to the worldview of his refugee and plaintiff-counsel roots, Honeywell opined.

⚬⟶

Mel and Kitty experienced two important bonding events early in their marriage. First, during their honeymoon, her father suffered an aneurysm. When he was five, his own father had died, felled by a tree he was cutting down. Lorenzo Tindal would die early as well, two weeks after the stroke. Looking back, Kitty describes her father, who spent most of his life working as a turbine-engine expert for International Paper, as a character from Tom Brokaw's popular book *The Greatest Generation*. Not an extraordinary person, just a good man who worked hard and took care of his family, she says.

Mel's support for Kitty during this period of loss, so early in their marriage, tightened their marital bond. The bond was further strengthened when Kitty's mother followed them to Orlando ten years later.

The other bonding experience came when Mel's sister was struck with neurofibromatosis, a rare illness that causes tumors on the skin, like those of the Elephant Man, or on the brain, as happened to Margarita. She was thirteen, living in Gainesville with her parents, when she began having painful headaches. Her parents were preparing to take her to Disney World one day when she developed sudden-onset pain, prompting them to take her to the hospital instead. At Shands Hospital, the University of Florida teaching hospital, doctors delivered the bad news: she had two brain tumors, one on each side of her head. She would lose her hearing to the cancerlike illness and later incur facial paralysis following surgery.

That year, 1974, Mel and Kitty had just moved to Orlando. Kitty worked as an insurance adjuster, using skills from her state job in Tallahassee and serving as the office's contact person for Spanish speakers. She was always very fond of her young sister-in-law, and when Margarita fell ill, Kitty quit her job in Orlando and moved into the hospital in Gainesville with her.

Kitty lived in Shands Hospital with Margarita for forty days. At first Mel's mother had stayed with her, but that proved unsatisfactory because she could not communicate with the hospital personnel in English. As Mel said, the experience "was very searing for our relationship." It deepened the bond, not only between the two of them, but also between Kitty and his family. "Kitty's love for my sister and caring for her during a difficult time endeared her to all of my family in a way that transcended whether," he said with a smile, "she cooked Cuban food for me or not."

Margarita lived another eight years. During that time Mel's parents moved back to Orlando, where they struggled to take care of her at home. Said Ralph: "It was a horrible situation. She couldn't move her arms or legs, but she always had a good sense of humor." In his mind, it was part of the family's American Dream ordeal, of their struggle to triumph over adversity. Near the end, she attended Ralph's wedding in a bridesmaid's dress, her wheelchair pushed down the aisle by her father. At age twenty-two, in 1983, she choked and died. In 2005, Mel and Kitty would liken her situation to that of another Florida woman: Terri Schiavo.

Though he acquired a veterinarian's license in Florida, Dr. Martinez suffered in the way other exiles of his age and background did. He seemed fallen, said Mel's friends. From all descriptions, Mel performed a delicate balancing act with his father. As eldest son, the first-come to America, he became the parent to his parents, yet he never belittled his father, always according him the respect of a patriarch. He used his dad as a sounding board for all of his thoughts and plans, even as he taught his father how to manage a checking account and drive in traffic. Though difficult for Dr. Martinez—he used the title socially as well as professionally—he adapted reasonably well, gaining limited English proficiency and modest driving skill.

The family joked about Sagua having only two stoplights, indicative of how much faster, more complicated, and more dangerous life was here, even in slow-paced Orlando.

In marrying Kitty, Mel introduced his parents to American daughters-in-law. Ralph, who followed Mel to FSU law school after graduating from the University of Florida in Gainesville, married an Anglo woman too. He and Becky, also an attorney, were married in 1983. In Mel's view, his parents respected that he and Kitty wanted to create a hybrid Cuban-American family. Still, Gladys Martinez regards her daughters-in-law as radically independent. From her traditional perspective, they seem on-the-go a lot; she has trouble understanding why they are out of the house when she calls.[16]

The life that Mel and Kitty constructed was very different from Gladys's. Today it would be described as a traditional family life, but traditional American rather than traditional Cuban. Unlike in Cuban culture, Kitty enjoys independence and gives career advice to her husband. Said their priest, Father John McCormick, the rector of St. James Cathedral in downtown Orlando, "Kitty is well spoken in her own right. She doesn't just live in Mel's shadow."[17]

As well, their nuclear family spends time together, rather than always being with parents and in-laws as Gladys was in Cuba. In keeping with an older American tradition, however, Kitty ceased working outside the home after children arrived, and Mel protects his family time from work demands. In a further contrast with his parents' practice, Kitty and Mel speak English at home.

Agreeing that they do not have a Cuban marriage, Mel said: "We made accommodations out of respect for each other's cultural background. I'm not a domineering husband, telling my wife what to do, and she has more choices than a traditional Cuban wife." Kitty had worked outside the home, except when she took care of Margarita, until daughter Lauren came along in the seventh year of their marriage. Afterwards she became a full-time mom, but not necessarily a stay-at-home mom. Like her sister-in-law Becky, she is active in civic and church affairs, explaining why her mother-in-law finds her away from home.

As their friend Ken Connor says of Kitty, "She is not some pudding-head, emotional person, and she always tells Mel what she thinks. They are a unit." He describes Kitty as a strong woman, more willing than Mel to stick her neck out. Before they married, Connor wondered how she would fit into Mel's family, especially when her in-laws spoke no or little English. "Here she is this elegant southern belle," he says laughingly, "it's the most unlikely transformation you have ever seen. Then she masters the language and becomes the hub of the family." In his observation, Hispanics are often bowled over when they see Mel's attractive blonde wife with him and then discover that she is just as fluent in Spanish as they are.

Protecting their America-style nuclear family, Kitty has always enshrined their family meals as occasions when they sit down together to eat and talk, with the television off. As part of the appeal, she sets an attractive table and cooks a varied menu, including Cuban food once a week or so, says her sister-in-law. Supporting this endeavor, Mel professes to compartmentalize work and family, cutting off work when he gets home. "I always tried to get home for dinner and was not much for going out for a drink with other lawyers," he says. The exception was Tuesday night, known in their family as "firm night," when members of the Billings-Frederick firm met for dinner at a local restaurant, comparing and rehearsing cases over dinner and wine.

Still, as part of their hybrid marriage, they gather with their extended family more than most American families probably do. When their family was young and they went to the beach, for example, Mel's parents came along. For Mel, this comes from his heritage; on Sundays in Cuba they traveled to his mother's parents' house, fifteen miles away, for Sunday dinner. (As he grew to bicycle age, he chafed at this practice, not wanting to miss afternoon baseball games.) For Kitty, this was part of "her adoptive culture," said Father McCormick.

Mel has been a different kind of parent than his father. Reflecting his generation, the elder Melquiades stayed focused on his career. He looked after his children and provided for them, but he did not become a Little League coach or Boy Scout leader, as Mel Jr. has been. Living in a close-knit neighborhood, Lancaster Park, an area of large old homes on Orlando's near south side, Mel served as Indian guide leader, was president of Little League, and helped coach YMCA basketball. Beyond that, he enjoys family outings on their sailboat, and taking his sons hunting and fishing. About hunting, he said, "I was never a huge hunter, but I love the outdoors. When we hunt, we mess around as much as we hunt." He never took up golf because "it takes too long" and would mean too much time away from his family.

———

Starting a family proved a struggle for Mel and Kitty. Confronting fertility issues, Mel turned to his old protector Thomas Aglio, head of Catholic

Social Services in Orlando, for help in adopting. Foreshadowing their later collaboration on pro-life issues, Mel's friend Ken Connor and his wife were adopting at the same time. Mel recommended Connor as a prospective parent to an adoption agency; Connor recommended Kitty and him to Catholic Social Services. They were blessed with their daughter Lauren in 1977. Connor named his daughter Kathryn after Kitty.

As frequently happens, they had natural children after adopting. Given their earlier fertility problem, they were surprised when Kitty became pregnant with John four years after Lauren. Twelve years later, they were surprised again when she became pregnant with Andrew.

As a measure of Mel's and Ralph's assimilation, neither of them named their children after their parents, the traditional practice among Cubans. (Ralph and Becky have two daughters and a son.) This was a very independent act on their part, and was shocking to Mel's parents. When Mel and Kitty named their first son John rather than Melquiades, Gladys had trouble explaining it to a Cuban friend. Her solution was to say he was named after the pope, which her friend found acceptable. Besides, John's middle name is Melquiades, so he can use the name if he wants.

If naming John signified Mel and Kitty's embrace of American culture, Lauren proved more important to their core political values. In Mel's words, "It was the experience of wanting children and not having them while waiting [for an adoptive child] that made it clear to us that life is precious and should be preserved. Beyond what the Church teaches, it taught us in a personal way that this is important. It solidified our pro-life position."

As Ken Connor says and Mel and Kitty affirm, she is the more passionate on this. It is more of a core issue for her. She always opposed abortion as a Catholic but lacked a strong opinion on it. Then Lauren came into their lives, and she came to see abortion as "a selfish way to solve a problem." In her words, "Thank God, a woman was thoughtful enough to give life and share that life with someone else."

These sentiments, combined with Mel's bond of friendship with Ken Connor, culminated in Mel's first bid for elective office. With Kitty's strong backing, he would run for lieutenant governor on the Right to Life ticket with Ken as his governor-candidate partner. It was one of several experiences that transformed Mel from private citizen to civic leader to politician and elected official.

5

CITIZEN

It was 1980, the dawn of the Reagan Revolution. The septuagenarian former movie actor swept into the White House with a crushing majority, defeating the hapless Jimmy Carter and ending the 444-day Iranian hostage crisis. To national politics Ronald Reagan brought a renewed assault on "big government," a fervor for tax cuts and defense spending, and fierce anticommunism. White southerners loved it, easing their transition to the GOP, as did Cuban Americans. Many of the latter found in President Reagan their first American hero.

In Florida, the political tide was turning. Reagan won the state by 17 points, amassing large majorities across the South, save in Carter's home state of Georgia. In Reagan's wake, Paula Hawkins earned election to the U.S. Senate, the first female member without a family tie to a previous senator. Though she opposed the Equal Rights Amendment, saying women already had more rights than men, she had reformer credentials as the lone Republican on Florida's elected Public Service Commission, attacking the commission's old-boy Democrats for being too cozy with the power companies they were supposed to regulate. After her, other Republicans would win state office as reformers.

Also in 1980, Orlando voters elected Bill Frederick as mayor. A moderate Democrat in a city with a Democratic majority, he defeated Shelton Adams in a close contest for the nonpartisan post. Duke-educated, handsome, and urbane, with a powerful baritone voice and a leader's bearing, Frederick would win two more terms, compiling an impressive record that included political reform as well as downtown redevelopment. He fancied running for governor and might have gone further had the political opportunity arisen.

Mel, whose political opportunities would be greater, assisted his law partner in the mayoral race. Having bypassed the Askew campaign for law school, he now embarked on his first election campaign. Within their law firm, Frederick was political, having managed the Edmund Muskie campaign in Florida and served as general counsel to the state Democratic Party, whereas his partner Jerry Billings was not. "It was okay if that's what you wanted to do," Frederick said of the firm's attitude toward politics. And he knew Mel shared his interest: "He always had a glimmer of interest in politics," said Frederick.[1]

To politics the young attorney brought the attitudes forged by his refugee experience and the skills honed in his law practice. He would become involved as a reformer, change advocate, and proponent of inclusion. He would be a Democrat at a time when most Cubans were Republican, cemented by his affiliation with Frederick, who would switch parties after leaving the mayor's office in 1992. And though Mel proved adroit at politics, drawing upon his interpersonal and negotiating skills, he would make mistakes and learn from them. His political game would improve.

◂═══▸

During the 1980 Frederick campaign, Mel reached out to local Cubans. From interviews with both Frederick and Mel, it is clear this outreach was driven by politics, pure and simple, though it brought about greater inclusiveness of Hispanics—mostly Cuban Americans. Frederick needed votes; Mel wanted to help and knew people in the Cuban community, so he solicited their support for Frederick, involving many of them in the political process for the first time.

As Frederick recounted, they knew the Cuban community was growing. In those days there was no real "Hispanic" community in Orlando. There were Mexican Americans, mostly farmworkers, and there were Cubans, with little in common save for language. There were not yet many Puerto Ricans in Orlando, though that would soon change. Census statistics reveal 5,000 persons of Spanish origin in a city of 87,282 residents in 1980.[2] But over the next twenty years, the Puerto Rican population of metro Orlando would balloon to 200,000.

One of the persons Mel engaged was Marcos Marchena, who came to the United States in 1971 at the age of twelve. Marchena, a college senior in 1980, would become a prosperous, politically connected local attorney. He respected Mel then as now because "he had penetrated the Anglo power structure more than anyone else" in the Cuban community. As Marchena recalls, Mel introduced Frederick to local Cubans and said, "He is my law partner. I know and trust him, and he will listen to us on issues that are important to us."[3]

Another campaign ally was Ernesto Gonzalez-Chavez, an architect and the son of a physician from Mel's hometown of Sagua. He likewise regarded Mel as a pioneer who brought others along. "He could not have succeeded in Orlando as a Cuban," said the architect. "The only way for him to succeed was to be absorbed into the [Anglo] community." As both Marchena and Gonzalez-Chavez attest, the Frederick campaign was a huge political opening for Orlando Cubans. In political science language, it "incorporated" them into the political process, giving them a sense of belonging and political efficacy, not least because their candidate won.[4]

"Thanks to Mel, the Frederick campaign brought us to the party," said Marchena. Pointedly, he was not talking about the Democratic Party. The same day he became a citizen he also registered to vote as a Republican. At the time of the Frederick campaign, "all of us Cubans were working for Ronald Reagan," Marchena explained. Yet he happily joined Mel in working for a local Democrat.

A smart politician, Frederick did not let their involvement with him end. He would need their votes again, so after the election he organized a Hispanic Advisory Committee, naming Mel chairman. Other members recruited by Mel in addition to Marchena and Gonzalez-Chavez were Bertica Cabrera, who became the first high-ranking Hispanic administrator at the Orange County School Board; Dr. Hermino Orizundo, a surgeon who operated on Mel's father; Dr. Alberto Bustamante, an obstetrician-gynecologist; Dr. Armando Payas, an attorney and university professor of Spanish; and Dr. Manuel Coto, a urologist.

Dr. Coto's story is interesting. He met Mel when the teenage refugee brought his father to the emergency room of Orange Memorial Hospital (now Orlando Regional Healthcare System). Melquiades Sr. was suffering from hypertension, and Dr. Coto, the only Spanish-speaking physician on duty, attended him. Well established in his profession, active in the Orange County Medical Society, but not yet politically involved, he credits Mel with introducing him to politics by involving him on the committee.[5]

Coto, like most Cubans, was a committed Republican. He "hated John Kennedy," not so much for the Bay of Pigs fiasco as because "Kennedy sold Cuba to the Soviets following the Cuban missile crisis." Asked about supporting Frederick, a Democrat, Dr. Coto said that he liked Frederick personally and regarded service on the advisory committee as an honor for him as well as his fellow Cubans. Pressed further about supporting a Democrat, he explained the *caudillo* principle, or how Cubans follow people more than parties. "We followed Batista, Machado, and some have followed Fidel."

When the Hispanic Advisory Committee met with Frederick and advised him on matters affecting their community, their primary recommendation was for Spanish-speaking staff in city agencies and on city boards and commissions. While partly a patronage request, it was also an attempt to extend government access. With relatively few Hispanics in Orlando, finding Spanish speakers in public offices was difficult.

About their patronage request, Bertica Cabrera explained the ethos of the Cubans on the advisory committee. "The point was to open the door," she said. "That's what Mel did. He did it for the others and me by appointing us to the advisory committee. It was as though he said, 'I'm already on the inside,' referring to the Anglo social and political establishment. 'You make your own way, but the door is open.'"[6]

Here Cabrera represented the views of Orlando's figurative Cuban Mafia, as she called it. The group included Cesar Calvet, now a banker; Tony Rey, a builder; and the above-named members of the Hispanic Advisory Committee, with Mel as the honorary chair or "godfather." As Gonzalez-Chavez explained in an interview, "Cubans"—first- and second-wave Cuban Americans—"were programmed for success," meaning they came to America with the drive, talent, and ambition to succeed in the capitalist marketplace.

In sharper terms, Cabrera proudly called Cuban Americans the "Jews of the Caribbean," saying she dislikes being called a "minority" because it connotes dependency. In her words, "I have never been discriminated against." Cubans have moved ahead professionally and economically, in part because "they never thought of being separated or asking for favors." After her mother died, two uncles—one a veterinarian, the other a physician—raised Bertica. In her Orlando neighborhood, there were eighteen Cuban doctors, evidencing the work ethic and professional achievement common among first-wave émigrés from the island nation.

Mel's big contribution to the Hispanic Advisory Committee lay in assembling it, said Cabrera. As chairman he presided with a light hand; Dr. Coto did most of the talking at their meetings. Because the physician was a decade older than Mel and had treated Mel's father, the young attorney deferred to him.

The other loquacious member was James Auffant, a Legal Aid attorney and the lone Puerto Rican on the committee, who took a more activist stance than the others. Where the Cuban members favored a conciliatory approach, not wanting to be cast as minorities, preferring quiet diplomacy and insider connections as the way to solve problems, Auffant was willing to talk about discrimination by name, and he favored bolder steps, if not lawsuits.[7] Concerned that Orlando had no Hispanic police officers above the lieutenant grade, he encouraged the promotion of a Hispanic sergeant—who was Cuban—to lieutenant, and participated in police job interviews to ensure that Hispanic applicants got a fair shake.

Describing the difference in perspective of the Cuban members, Cabrera said: "Our approach was to get involved and become part of the community. Show them [referring to Anglo leaders] what we can do, and they will come to us." Even back then, she added, "the Cuban and Puerto Rican approach for achieving the same end was different." But Auffant questioned whether the Cuban members wanted benefits for persons outside their group. In his view, they were unwilling to share their connections to the Anglo elite with other Hispanics. And Mel, he said, was their unquestioned leader: "He had the ability to take a group of Cubans, unite them, and they would follow him blindly."

As Mel explained, the Hispanic Advisory Committee was the "first time I looked up from my law books."[8] To that point his community activity was linked to his faith. He was active in his church, St. James Catholic Cathedral in downtown Orlando, "where I participated in giving the catechism to teenage boys" and served on the board of Catholic Charities, repaying the debt from his Peter Pan experience. According to Thomas Aglio, he was the only Peter Panner in the Orlando diocese to serve on his board. Otherwise, Mel focused on his family and his law practice in the 1970s and 1980s, participating in bar association activities, advancing himself professionally, making money—and doing all of it well. Still, he wanted something more.

⟸⟹

The advisory committee wanted Hispanics appointed to city committees, and Mel became a product of their success. "I was sort of in the Cheney mode," Mel said with a chuckle, referring to Dick Cheney's service as chair of the committee that recommended a running mate to George W. Bush. Mayor Frederick appointed Mel to the Orlando Housing Authority, which oversaw Orlando's fourteen public housing complexes, whose residents were mostly African American with a sprinkling of Hispanics.

Before his mayoral administration, "it was not part of the political sensitivity of the time to appoint someone Hispanic to a board," said Frederick.[9] He appointed Mel in part because he was Hispanic, responding to the Hispanic Advisory Committee. But the main reason was that he knew Mel. Even though the Cuban American was politically untested, the mayor had faith in his abilities and needed someone he trusted for a difficult assignment.

At the time, Frederick was troubled by news stories about the Housing Authority. "We had an ex-colonel running the Authority, and according to rumor he was running it like a plantation," said the mayor. Relayed through his chief of staff, Jacob Stuart, he gave Mel an assignment. "I had enough to worry about in trying to revitalize downtown. I didn't want any more bad-news stories about the Housing Authority," said Frederick.

Once on the Authority, Mel quickly made common cause with board member Bill Warden, a longtime social services executive whom Mel called a "dyed-in-the-wool Democrat." Together, but with Mel taking the lead after becoming board chairman in his second year on the Authority, they succeeded in making the meetings more accessible to their clientele: the tenants.

The practice had been to conduct lunchtime board meetings in the Authority's executive office building, which made it difficult for tenants to attend. Over the objection of the executive director, Ray McDaniell, they began holding their meetings in the recreation room of a different housing complex each month. "That way, we could sit down and see them and they could see us, and they could tell us their problems," said the future HUD secretary.

Mel and his allies also got the Authority's informational pamphlets printed in Spanish and English. Again, this was done over the opposition of McDaniell, "who thought people who live here should speak English," said the Cuban American refugee. Little by little, he and Warden along with Dr. John Washington, an African American university professor serving on the board, began raising the issue of McDaniell's leadership. In changing the Authority's practices over the executive director's opposition, they won plaudits from the *Orlando Sentinel*, which continued to write stories critical of the Authority.

Then Frederick applied the brakes. "I had to rein him in a little bit," recalls Frederick. The mayor had hired a city manager from Jacksonville, Lex Hester, who advised Frederick that Orlando's public housing problems were minuscule compared with the fraud and red ink in the Jacksonville Housing Authority. The advice relayed to Mel was "make waves but don't rock the boat so much that it capsizes."

Looking back, Martinez admits he "got a little carried away by youthful enthusiasm." Yet he found his time on the Authority an invaluable political learning experience. "You might be full of great ideas, but you can't carry them out all in one day. You learn a little restraint, you learn a little pacing, you learn how to coalesce with others to get something done . . . to bring others along who may not be as enlightened as you think you are at the moment."

Still, he showed his integrity as board chair, proving he had not forgotten where he came from. By now he was a wealthy attorney, a member of the Country Club of Orlando, someone who moved in elite circles. Yet he had assaulted the status quo at the Housing Authority, instinctively siding with their minority tenants and earning praise from board member Bill Warden, a self-described political liberal.

Said Warden, "I have a great deal of respect for him as a person, even though I disagree with his later political views." During their joint service on the board, he found Mel a breath of fresh air. "He was courteous and polite but had a goal in mind for the Authority. He proved he could work well with people from all kinds of backgrounds, the conservatives, yes, but also liberals like me. He knew how to mold a group of people together."[10]

The experience steeled Mel for his next big assignment from Mayor Frederick: appointment to the Orlando Utilities Commission, where he was again a reformer, and where he again learned from his experience, continuing his path to elective office. But meanwhile, he was engaged in other civic work—in his profession and in the Cuban community.

⇐⇒

Mel was not someone who believed he belonged only to himself. He belonged to his family, his faith, his Cuban American friends, his profession, his community, and the nation. Affable and at ease in groups, he was a joiner by nature. And because he kept his ego in check—ironically because of that—he gravitated to leadership roles. It seemed to always happen, as though by design, though he denies having a plan to prepare for public office prior to the mid-1990s.

In Orlando's Cuban community, Mel became a *padrón*: someone who grants favors, dispenses advice, and looks out for others. His work as a personal injury attorney, helping people right wrongs, supported this role. And he got "help" from his father, who was always meeting someone from Cuba who had a legal problem and directing him to Mel or, after Ralph started his practice, to his younger son. Clients would reward the two attorneys with baskets of fruit and other comestibles, if not with money.

But not all of his legal work for Hispanic clients was pro bono. As Orlando's Hispanic community grew, especially with the rising tide of Puerto Rican in-migration, his Hispanic identity became more beneficial to his law partners. In his words, "I had a pretty good following in the growing Hispanic community, so what was a potential liability turned out to be a big plus."

Yet as law partner Dan Honeywell observed, Hispanic clients sometimes shied away from Mel, especially Puerto Ricans.[11] From having a Spanish wife, Honeywell knew that Hispanics do not always feel a bond just because of their common tongue. But Mel usually won over Puerto Rican clients, succeeding with them as with Anglos on the basis of his grace and charm.

By the mid-1980s, Orlando had developed a small infrastructure of Hispanic institutions, consisting of Cuban sandwich shops and bodegas, or grocery stores. There was also a newspaper, *La Prensa*, founded in 1981, and a Cuban-American Club, which dated from the late 1970s. Probably the most important such institution was Medina's Marketplace, located east of downtown in a lower-middle-class neighborhood within walking distance of the neighborhood where Mel's parents first lived in Orlando. Starting as a proverbial hole in the wall, Medina's expanded to include a bodega and restaurant covering half a block. Its proprietor, Rafael Medina, a bookkeeper in pre-Castro Cuba, is sometimes called the Cuban mayor of Orlando. He hosts a yearly festival for Hispanics, the Medina Festival, and the walls of his restaurant are lined with autographed photos of local politicians, who court his approval to win Hispanic voters.

For years Medina would take a U-Haul trailer each week to Tampa, which has a much larger Hispanic population. He would return with coffee, crackers, and fresh bread, all Cuban style. For his clientele, Medina's was more than a place to buy Goya products, pick up Spanish magazines, and sip *café cubano*. It was a place to see fellow *cubanos*, exchange gossip from Miami, speak *español,* and express solidarity with *la causa cubana.*

For the aforenamed leadership group—the figurative Cuban Mafia—Medina's was a frequent gathering place, along with José's Sandwich Shop on Michigan Avenue on the near south side and Habana Joe's, a sandwich shop in Orlando's College Park neighborhood. The members of this group were heavily invested in the mainstream culture and commerce of Orlando. At Medina's, José's, and Habana Joe's they could share their Cuban side—their *cubanidad*.

Armando Payas described the scene when they gathered.[12] People talked at the same time, unable to finish a thought without someone interrupting. Making liberal use of Cuban expressions, they spoke excitedly and emphatically, each seeking to impress his opinion on the others. During the conversation, one of them might get up from the table to get something to eat without giving offense. To an outsider such behavior might appear rude, but not to this group; they were among friends.

Upon occasion their conversation was guarded. Then they would retreat to one of their homes, protected from outside ears. One topic discussed in private was the decline of first-wave Cubans within Orlando's Hispanic community. Once a majority among Orlando Hispanics, people like themselves were increasingly a minority as later-wave Cubans from lower social strata arrived, joined by Puerto Ricans migrating from the Commonwealth and New York. With them these newcomers brought drugs and criminality, as recounted in lurid newspaper stories, posing a challenge for the first-wave Cubans who had sought to project a positive image to the Anglo community.

As Payas delicately put it, "We were sympathetic to these new arrivals, but we didn't understand them entirely. They were different from us. Yet the average Anglo doesn't see a difference between them and us." It was now easier to find Spanish speakers, whether on the street, in government offices, or in stores. But the image of "Hispanic," to the Anglo community, was changing. The progress of first-wave Cubans, their efforts to blend into mainstream Anglo culture as upstanding citizens and accomplished business people and professionals, was threatened by the newcomers.

One byproduct of these meetings of the *padrones* was their involvement in the Cuban American National Foundation, or CANF, organized by Jorge Mas Canosa, a Miami multimillionaire and Bay of Pigs veteran. Mas, who earned his riches in the cable telephone business, was encouraged to form the group by Richard Allen, President Reagan's first National Security Adviser. It was modeled on the American Israeli Public Affairs Committee, or AIPAC, the nation's richest and most influential foreign-policy lobby group. For the Reagan administration, CANF offered support in the escalating global war against communism. For Mas and his compatriots, it was a way to influence U.S.-Cuba policy.

CANF had no Orlando chapter—Mas, who guarded his power closely, would not have permitted that. But he did come to Orlando in 1984 to recruit members. Mel, who had maintained a membership in the Cuban American Bar Association, took the lead. Paying $5,000 a year, he became a CANF "trustee," as did Drs. Coto and Orizundo, thereafter traveling to the group's meetings in Miami and Washington.

Among other activities, CANF successfully lobbied to create the U.S. Information Agency's Radio Martí in 1985 and TV Martí in 1990, while vigorously defending a complete embargo on Cuba. Weaving their hatred for Fidel with the administration's global anticommunism, they opposed any U.S. contact or negotiation with Castro's Cuba. In return for Mas's support, the Reagan-Bush administration made him the virtual president of the Cuban exile community, the designated liberator who would "return democracy" to Cuba.

As quoted in the *Orlando Sentinel* at his death in 1997, Mas famously declared: "I have never assimilated. I never intended to. I am a Cuban first. I live here only as an extension of Cuba. My friends, my social activities are all Cuban."[13] By the early 1990s, several high-profile members had departed from the organization, put off by Mas's dictatorial leadership. Dr. Coto resigned, feeling that Mas had abused Cubans' penchant for a *caudillo*, a strong leader. But Mel remained in the organization until 1994. This was the period in which he declared on local TV that he would return to Cuba if Castro fell.

◆━━━▶

Throughout the 1980s Mel was also involved in his profession. His participation started with the Young Lawyers' board of governors, part of the American Bar Association, then shifted to the Florida Academy of Trial Lawyers, essentially an organization of plaintiff-counsel attorneys, which he found more relevant to his day-to-day work. For the Wooten-Honeywell firm, which did not believe in advertising, participation in FATA was a way to gain referrals. They committed $10,000 to advance Mel in the Academy, running him for treasurer and secretary as a prelude to vice president and finally president. Their money went for mailers to law firms and to send Mel glad handing around the state.

In 1989 Mel became president of the Academy, an experience he called "kind of a hot potato" because no-fault insurance had been adopted, and the insurance industry was pressing for "tort reform" to combat lawyers and lawsuits. John Thrasher, Mel's old friend from law school, was on the "other side" as general counsel for the Florida Medical Society. As the lobbyist for physicians, he was accustomed to frosty relations with Trial Academy presidents. But Mel was different. "We had a cordial relationship, never a harsh word," said Thrasher.[14] Honeywell concurred, saying that Mel was different from other Academy presidents, "not as confrontational as others had been," adding, "A lot of personal injury attorneys have to break eggs, but not Mel."

Though Wooten-Honeywell financed Mel's initial run for office in the Trial Academy, he left the firm before becoming the group's president. "That created a little bit of hard feeling," said Honeywell, mentioning the $10,000 spent to promote Mel for office. When he announced he was leaving, in 1986, to practice with old friend Ken Connor, they could see that "Mel wanted to do something else." It was apparent from his involvement in the Frederick campaign, CANF, and the Housing Authority that Mel had a taste for public life. Soon after he departed, he was the low bidder to provide legal service for an Orange County charter review commission. It was an unexciting area of the law but a valuable stepping-stone for someone with political ambitions, since the work entailed interacting with local officials and political insiders. (It was also here that the author first met Mel.) As a personal injury attorney, Mel lacked the background for the job, but he hired an assistant to do the actual legal work.

Leaving their firm in order to dabble in the public sector took a lot of backbone, said Honeywell. Mel could hardly imagine making more money with another firm, his colleagues thought. At the time, he was earning more than $300,000 a year, in some years up to half a million, besides having a free car and liberal benefits.

Before long he would run for lieutenant governor with Connor. But first, Mayor Frederick beckoned him for another assignment.

⟵

The Orlando Utilities Commission or OUC fits oddly in conservative Orlando. At the turn of the nineteenth century, American socialists were dubbed the "light and water socialists," as their local agenda mostly consisted of municipal ownership of light and water utilities, which they maintained would offer low rates, reduce taxes by turning their profits to local government, and demonstrate the virtue of broader public ownership. Except for the latter, OUC does all of these things, providing water and electricity to more than 150,000 customers spread over 400 square miles in Orlando and part of Orange and Osceola Counties.

This "nominally socialist" institution arose in Orlando, whose conservative leaders have historically favored small government, almost by accident. John M. Cheney, a local judge whose family owned the water and light utility, decided in 1922 that the utility business was too risky and offered it to the city. Under Mayor Eugene Duckworth, the city bought the utility for $975,000. Yet conservatism reigned in the state's enabling legislation for OUC. Rather than allowing direct municipal control, putting the mayor and city commission in charge, the utility was founded as a hybrid public-private company with a self-perpetuating board.

In 1990, Mayor Frederick wanted to change the OUC culture. The utility was successful in business terms: it offered good service at low rates and earned a high bond rating from Wall Street. But the utility's "old-boys club" had lately become embarrassing. The *Orlando Sentinel*, in a series of investigative reports, had exposed their practice of giving lifetime utility discounts to managers and directors, granting liberal bonuses to employees, and using company employees to perform personal work for top executives.

Many of the newspaper's accusations came from a vengeful former executive who was fired for repeatedly violating OUC policy. Utility executives denied many of the charges about getting special perks and defended granting bonuses as acceptable business practice, overlooking the public character of OUC. Still, the charges raised credibility issues for the nominally public agency.

Concerning to Frederick, these issues might obstruct plans for building a second coal-fired power plant to accommodate Orlando's mushrooming growth. Knowing the power of appearances, he also worried about the message of an old-boy network running the city's pinnacle institution, as Orlando struggled to shed its small-town image at a time when Disney was transforming the face of Central Florida. He had already named a Jewish member to the commission, raising eyebrows in some quarters; now he wanted to appoint the first Hispanic.

For a recommendation on whom to appoint, he asked Mel, who turned to his brother, Ralph. The two brothers distinctly recall their conversation, which occurred in Mel's front yard. "I remember telling Ralph that Frederick had asked me to find someone Hispanic to be on the OUC board," said Mel.

"This is a heck of an appointment. It needs someone really good. Who do you think we should put there?" he asked Ralph as they chatted in the yard. They considered various possibilities but none seemed appropriate.

"You ought to do it," said Mel.

"No, I could never give it the time. You should do it. That's the kind of thing you should do," Ralph responded. He followed Mel to his door, telling him all the reasons he was the right person.

Half convinced, Mel called Mayor Frederick to report.

"I don't know if we found anyone any good," said Mel. "Frankly, I suggested to Ralph that he do it."

"And what did Ralph say?" asked Frederick.

"Well, he said that I should."

"Well, I think you should," said the mayor. He asked Mel what reasons Ralph had given for him taking the job, and offered support for each one of them.

Mel accepted the nomination, though it needed City Council approval. At the Council meeting, Clive Thomas, a local talk-radio host and Frederick foe, lowered his sights on Mel, calling him a Frederick crony and not a real Hispanic, erroneously saying he "didn't even speak Spanish." In defense of the Cuban nominee, the City Council's lone black member, Nap Ford, said "Mel Martinez isn't a Hispanic leader in Orlando. He is an Orlando leader who happens to be Hispanic."[15]

Mel, unanimously approved over two female nominees, paid a small price. Kitty attended the meeting—he did not—and was so unsettled by Thomas's maligning remarks that she had a fender bender exiting the city-hall parking lot. But the experience also baptized Kitty in the rough and tumble of politics, steeling her for future battles, said Mel.

Responding to newspaper reports on OUC, Mayor Frederick asked Mel to look into their charges "so we can take action." Soon after his appointment, the board named him to lead an investigation and hired an attorney, Teresa Gallion, and an accountant, Jim Hunt, to assist. As reported in near-daily *Sentinel* articles, the investigation quickly became adversarial, and Mel's comments in the media reflected this. He complained that "people don't need to rehearse . . . to tell the truth" after disclosure that OUC staff spent two hours rehearsing their public hearing testimony.[16] He stopped the utility from sending a labor attorney to accompany staff as they gave testimony to Ms. Gallion. And he repeatedly said the utility needed "a deep cultural change"—all reported in the *Sentinel*.[17]

For Mel, fresh from his experience on the Housing Authority and still in a political learning mode, the politics of the situation were daunting. In Max Weber's term, the circumstances required hot passion and cool judgment. As Mel said of his lessons from the Housing Authority experience, the problems at OUC required "restraint . . . and pacing . . . to bring others along who may not be as enlightened as you think you are at the moment."

On one side stood the *Orlando Sentinel* with the power to confer hero stature on board members who followed the paper's lead. The *Sentinel* had started the OUC investigation, and it was publishing continual front-page articles reporting new facts and restating old ones, supported by editorials denouncing utility management and imploring the board to clean things up. On the other side was Orlando's old-boy network with the power to confer access and social status. It supported the status quo at OUC and the embattled general manager, Ted Pope, a former Chamber of Commerce president. Pope, a Horatio Alger character like Mel, was entrenched in the community and well liked at the utility by employees at all levels.

In between was Mayor Frederick, Mel's political patron, who wanted to calm the waters so OUC could build a second power plant, ideally without ruffling too many feathers in Orlando's civic establishment. He would prove a tempering force in the affair.

At a June 9, 1992, board meeting, the chickens came home to roost. Ms. Gallion presented her list of findings, which included utility company workers being asked to fix homes and cars for OUC executives, excessive spending for parties and travel, and hiding expenditures from the board. At the end of her report, a hush fell over the meeting before board president Jerry Chicone announced: "The results are not what we wanted to find."[18]

Before the meeting, Mel had called Ted Pope into his office and said, "Ted, you have a real problem." Telling the GM in advance about Ms. Gallion's findings, he said: "You can do one of two things. You can stonewall it or change some things." Two weeks after the report, Pope announced his immediate resignation and another top executive took early retirement, resolving the crisis.

In Mel's own postmortem, Pope's arrogance defeated him. "I did not start with the preconceived notion that we needed to fire Ted Pope," he said. "I'm not that mean." Instead he played the lawyer, getting the facts, trying to create public understanding of what was happening, working in tacit partnership with the news media to sway opinion in the community and on the utility board. "By the time he was asked to leave, most people were saying, 'This needs to happen.'"

For his good efforts Mel earned a halo from the *Sentinel*. They had defined the problem and framed the issue: Pope needed to go and OUC's management practices had to change. Mel entered the scene and, *voilà*, the problem was solved. In return, as reporter Jim Leusner said to the author, he became the *Sentinel*'s "golden boy," a partiality that continued as his political career unfolded. In his later Senate race, for example, the *Sentinel* was one of two newspapers among the state's sixteen dailies that endorsed him.

Nonetheless he experienced social fallout from his efforts. Though he does not name names, the pressure was fairly intense. "There was an atmosphere" at OUC, said Mel, that "if you dare peep about what's going on, we'll get after you." As his brother, Ralph, recalls, Mel received numerous calls from local notables who objected to the treatment of Pope. Likewise his friend Bertica Cabrera says, "Mel lost a lot of friends on that one." In resisting this pressure Mel was making a career-defining choice about what he wanted to become.

In his own assessment, Frederick parses his words about Mel's performance, saying his attorney friend was new to full-tilt media coverage. Mel may have liked the coverage a little too much. He may have done some "grandstanding." Still a political novice, he may have let the media control him too much, rather than using them to achieve his policy goals. The *Sentinel* did submit its investigative series on OUC for a Pulitzer Prize nomination, which was arguably the goal. However, many of the charges proved spurious—the result of relying too much on a single questionable source, a disgruntled former employee.

Still, Mel succeeded politically on this issue. Regardless of the factual basis of the *Sentinel*'s charges, he got the board to go along with him. Fellow board member Rick Fletcher, who still defends many of the practices that got OUC and Ted Pope into trouble with the media, credits Mel with acting from principle. "I am convinced that he felt he was doing the right thing," said Fletcher.[19] Mel went on to become OUC president as the utility approved and built its second coal-fired plant at a cost of $550 million—with virtually no opposition. In the view of utility executives, this huge investment in coal-fired power generation, not small-dollar perks and privileges, should have drawn the news media's critical eye.[20]

The Ted Pope affair proved a major turning point for Mel. Ralph Martinez, who was active in student government in college, had imagined a political career for himself. But he turned down the OUC appointment at a critical time. It was Mel's tenure at OUC that "catapulted him into politics," says his brother.

———

Influencing the next step in Mel's political career, Kitty became "convicted"—a code term in the pro-life movement—about abortion. Her Catholic faith, and, more important, her experience as an adoptive parent after Lauren came into their life in 1977, provided the backdrop. But the trigger event was a speech course that she took at a local community college to maintain her teaching certificate. Asked to give a "persuasive speech," she decided to talk about abortion and learned from her research "how right the antiabortion position was." Fundamentally, she said, "It's a human. You are stopping the life of someone human."[21]

After numerous conversations, she and her sister-in-law Becky decided to put their principles into action, forming a pro-life discussion group, Moms for Life, in 1991. Believing that the abortion issue had become too much of a battleground, they wanted to form an educational group, as Becky said, "to educate mothers about the sanctity of life."[22] With Becky as president and Kitty vice president, they met at Kitty's house, initially just fifteen to twenty of them, all "Christian pro-life women" and stay-at-home moms.

As their membership reached forty, they moved to the Winter Park Baptist Church, where they met once a month to discuss issues ranging from the history of the abortion issue to partial birth, fetal experimentation, and volunteer opportunities. As mothers, they were more interested in providing alternatives for pregnant teenagers than in proselytizing against abortion.

Earlier, Mel and Kitty's friend Ken Connor became "convicted" on this issue too. Also an adoptive parent, he joined Florida Right to Life and served as its president. During that time, in 1989, Florida governor Bob Martinez called a special legislative session on abortion, prompted by the

Supreme Court's decision in *Webster v. Reproductive Health Services* upholding state restrictions on the use of public medical facilities for abortion.[23] More broadly, the Court decision gave states permission to adopt restrictions on abortion, hence the special legislative session.

In support of his pro-life efforts, Connor turned to Mel and Ralph and their wives, though "in terms of engagement it was more Kitty and Becky," Connor explained.[24] Describing Kitty as "one of the most principled persons I know," he said, "I tell people, don't worry about Mel as long as Kitty feels strongly about an issue." Reaching out to Moms for Life, he asked them to organize a conference for Florida Right to Life in Orlando. Kitty and Becky and their fellow moms handled logistics.

In 1994 Connor decided to push the pro-life issue by running for governor on the Right to Life ticket. He knew he would need a strong running mate, and he knew he wanted Mel. As Connor recounted in an interview, he talked with Mel about it on the Orlando attorney's front porch. Mel, he saw, was in obvious discomfort. Connor had encouraged him to run for office before, "knowing he would be fantastic," but Mel always demurred. This time there was an additional problem: his mentor Bill Frederick was weighing a run for governor. But Connor knew that if he asked his old college friend, "he couldn't do much except say yes." And he knew that Kitty would affirm her husband's decision, because she always recognized his potential as a political candidate.

"I said, look, there's only six weeks to go in the race. It's not going to hurt your reputation, which will only be enhanced by your getting into the race." Mel finally agreed and was "instantly terrific," said his running mate. As a first-time political candidate jumping into a statewide race, the former refugee seemed to come into his own, said Connor. Unlike him, Mel was not closely identified with the abortion issue; he was viewed instead as a civic activist, based on his OUC and Orlando Housing Authority experience.

It was not the first time Kitty's passion influenced Mel's political involvements. In 1990 Orange County was electing its first county chairman, after a change in the county's charter approved by voters in 1988. This was the same position that Mel would win eight years later. Most of his Cuban Republican friends were supporting the front-runner, Linda Chapin, a moderate Democrat whom they liked and trusted. Mel offered his support as well.

Bertica Cabrera explained the dénouement. Linda Chapin called her early in the campaign, saying, "What's happened to Mel?" She had just read a campaign finance report showing that Mel had given $1,000 to her opponent, Republican Tom Drage. Bertica called Mel, who told her that Kitty had put her foot down. Though Bertica and other Cuban friends of Mel's stayed with Chapin, she understood Kitty's problem: several weeks earlier Chapin had spoken openly of her support for abortion rights.

⟵⟶

The 1994 campaign marked a transition for Mel, from *homo civicus*, for whom political activity is remote from the main focus of his life, to *homo politicus*, for whom politics is everything.

In the governor's race, he and Connor won 83,504 votes, or 9.3 percent of the total. Connor would not run for elective office again, though he would earn national stature as an abortion foe, becoming head of the influential Family Research Council in 1999. Jeb Bush, who won the Republican primary, lost to the self-described "old he-coon," incumbent governor Lawton Chiles, in the general election. But he would try again in 1998 and win, and afterwards win reelection.

Likewise, Mel was just getting started. After the 1994 race, he had the political bug. Enamored of campaigning, of meeting and greeting and appearing before crowds, he looked forward to running again, the next time in his own campaign. Perhaps he would run for governor, he thought.

James Auffant recalls talking to Mel during the gubernatorial race. Puerto Rican, arriving in Orlando from New York in 1977, the former Legal Aid attorney had served with Mel on the Hispanic Advisory Committee in the early 1980s. The occasion was a Hispanic Bar Association meeting at the Citrus Club in downtown Orlando. Just back from the campaign, Mel was standing with Auffant and several others at the meeting when James asked: "How's the campaign going?" Mel was almost giddy, Auffant recalls. "It's going great," he responded. "I could see myself running for governor."

At the time, Skip Dalton was Mel's law partner. Handsome, the son of a staff navy pilot killed in a plane crash, and a Democrat, he was a fraternity brother of Ralph's at the University of Florida, where he also earned his law degree. In 1987 he ran into Mel at a trial lawyers' conference, where they exchanged pleasantries and talked about their legal careers. Dalton had recently left a major firm to practice solo, and Mel had started his practice with Ken Connor, though they worked in different cities, Ken in Tallahassee and Mel in Orlando. Mel told Dalton that he liked working with his college friend but doubted whether their two-city practice was viable long term. Almost on a whim, Skip said, "Why don't you come practice with me?"[25]

Following this encounter, the two joined forces—forming a partnership, adding attorneys, and building their own office building. "Our practice thrived," said Dalton. In the division of labor, Dalton took the complex, time-consuming cases that, while risky, generated big payoffs. Reflecting his risk-averse nature, Mel took the shorter-term cases, negotiating most of them and generating a steady income for the firm. As well, Mel cultivated the Hispanic community statewide, yielding considerable business for the firm.

Graciously, Skip gave Mel leave to pursue his quixotic campaign with his former law partner, Ken Connor. He described Mel's decision to join the campaign as a good indicator of who Mel was. In Dalton's words, "Ken was his friend, and Ken believed very passionately in the cause." Mel's decision to participate "shoved him into a realm he'd never been before and put him where he is today."

The grind of the campaign was an epiphany for Mel, said Dalton. From stump-speaking around the state, he realized he could be more than a trial lawyer. He liked interacting with people, the hallmark of his legal career, but he also enjoyed dealing with big ideas, as opposed to the minutiae of legal work. And as he campaigned in South Florida, he realized his incredible rapport with Hispanics. "I don't think before then that he appreciated the power he had," said Dalton. His presence and charisma worked for him as a trial lawyer; now he saw they were transferable to politics.

"Mel came back invigorated, despite their dismal performance in winning votes," said his law partner. "It was then that I began to see him interested in doing something else, though maybe not to the exclusion of law."

Rick Fletcher said the same. A friend and confidant of Bill Frederick, he served with Mel on the OUC board and knew him from the Billings-Frederick law firm. He and his wife were social friends of Mel and Kitty and admired Kitty as much as Mel. Rick described Kitty as "intelligent, authentic, and soft-spoken . . . the kind of woman who, if Mel ever got too caught up in himself, would be quick to bring him back to earth."

Following the governor's race, Fletcher knew that Mel aspired to public office. The buzz was, Mel would run for mayor and then governor. But when Bill Frederick stepped down after three terms in 1992, he left an heir apparent, City Commissioner Glenda Hood. She had been anointed in a crushing victory and gave every appearance of being a long-term mayor like Frederick. That left the position of county chair, which under Linda Chapin had become a powerful and high-profile position, potentially a good launching pad for higher office.

Chapin, having won without Mel's support, served two modestly successful terms. She was now term limited, and Orlando's political establishment was searching for a consensus candidate, someone they could all get behind. Charlie Gray, a local power broker and attorney with a long history of government involvement, wanted to "get a good candidate and get the ball rolling," as he said.[26]

Gray and his allies—Fred Leonhardt, Rick Fletcher, and Pat Christensen, all attorneys, and banker Jimmy Hewitt—were worried about a potential candidate, former county commissioner Fran Pignone. She frequently opposed Chapin on development issues and was not considered "business friendly" by the group. They were also worried by reports that Republican state senator John Ostalkiewicz was mulling a run. A multimillionaire diamond merchant, he would be business friendly, but he was also a conservative ideologue considered difficult to work with. Leonhardt, a state Chamber of Commerce president who frequently lobbied the legislature, said the word among Tallahassee lobbyists was that when you went to see Ostalkiewicz you "got a good listen" because he did all the talking.[27]

Charlie Gray had canvassed other potential candidates including Rick Fletcher, who was unwilling to make the commitment, so attention turned to Mel. Gray said, "I saw Mel as a person of integrity and ability" but also as a "big-picture person" who would need help with the details of government policy. To run and to govern, Mel would need a kitchen cabinet of informal advisers, the group thought.

A decisive meeting with Mel occurred at the University Club, Orlando's last all-male bastion, in late 1996. Present were the above-named individuals, plus Ralph and Mel. Then president of OUC, Mel was warm to the idea of running, said Leonhardt. "He said that his community and country had been good to him, and that he felt an obligation to repay this debt." But he was wrestling with the economic and family issues involved.

In 1997 the chairman's job paid $112,500. A personal injury attorney at Mel's level could make $1 million a year, said Fletcher. Mel had achieved that pinnacle, but only for a half dozen years, he suspected. From experience, Mel's mentor Bill Frederick knew the problem and wondered whether Mel had earned enough money, over a long enough period, to embark on a political career.

As both Fletcher and Frederick appreciated, it was more than a question of lifestyle, more than whether he could afford to support his wife and family, send his children to school, and assist his parents financially on a public officeholder's salary. It was also about taking time away from his family, about new and different stresses that would make compartmentalizing work and family more difficult. And it was about Kitty and him living in a fishbowl, losing their private lives, their every move subject to public scrutiny. Mel's attraction to public life and his commitment to family were at odds.

He needed to talk to Kitty and his brother, Ralph.

He could no longer talk to his other important counselor, his father. Except when they were separated during his Peter Pan years, Mel had sought his father's advice on every major decision in his life, down to and including every car he bought. But Melquiades had died from the effects of a stroke, on August 12, 1995, the day of his fifty-first wedding anniversary.

6

⊶⟶

CHAIRMAN

Florida governor Jeb Bush was calling for County Chairman Mel Martinez. Mel's secretary, Linda Wright, relayed the call to Dan Murphy, the
chairman's peripatetic chief of staff. It was Tuesday, December 5, 2000,
and Mel was presiding at a county commission meeting. Governor Bush's
office wanted to pull the chairman from the meeting, but Murphy resisted,
thinking it would look bad at a televised meeting. Glancing at his watch,
he saw it was almost 11:00 a.m.; the commission would break for lunch at
noon. "He'll call back in an hour," Murphy told them.[1]

He figured from the governor's call that something important was up.
Maybe his promotion of Mel had succeeded. He took the elevator from
Mel's fifth-floor office down to the commission chambers and stood in the
back of the room, waiting impatiently as the commission meeting droned
on.

When the commission finally broke for lunch, he walked to the dais
and whispered to Mel. Together, they headed back to the fifth floor
and grabbed the first empty office to return the governor's call. Getting
through right away, Mel began an easy conversation with the governor
that belied his sense of excitement.

Ironically, he and Jeb Bush first met when he ran with Ken Connor—
against Jeb—in the 1994 governor's race. Since then, much had changed.
In recent months Mel had served as a statewide cochair of the George
W. Bush campaign, frequently standing on stage with the candidate, often next to Jeb. On October 31 he hosted former president George H. W.
Bush and his wife, Barbara, at a nonpagan alternative to traditional Hal-
loween, held at Orlando's First Baptist Church. During the vote recount
controversy he stayed in phone contact with the governor, offering support and advice, though without joining in the public brouhaha between
the two parties. Facilitated by Dan Murphy, who knew the Bush family

from working as a personal aide to Vice President Dan Quayle, Mel knew Jeb well.

As the two talked on the phone, Mel smiling, Murphy could hear only the chairman's side of the conversation: a string of yesses. Seeing Murphy's anxious face, knowing how hard he had worked the connections after the vote recount, Mel grabbed a legal pad and wrote in big letters HUD. Normally serious and restrained, Murphy had to contain himself. They had struck pay dirt: Murphy could return to Washington.

⟷

The events recounted in this chapter explain how Mel rose to such heights. Many people are encouraged to run for public office and never do. Had Mel not decided to run for county chairman, he would not have become a U.S. senator. Had he not won the chairman's race—and he almost didn't—his political career might have ended there. Had he not impressed the Bush brothers during his service as county chairman, he would not have become HUD secretary. Without their support, he might not have pursued higher office until 2006, following two terms as county chairman. Then he might have run for governor, his original goal. By then, with an unpopular Republican president in the White House, he might well have lost. Without luck on his side, his experience might have been like that of Linda Chapin, his predecessor as county chairman. After her service as county chairman, she ran for the U.S. House of Representatives and lost, ending her political career.

As we shall see, many factors—including luck and favorable social trends—conspired to put Mel on the fast track to higher office. Among these, Kitty's role was paramount. Mel was naturally risk averse, perhaps because his immigrant experience impressed upon him how much he had to lose. He therefore approached the decision to run for county chair with abundant caution. Kitty, his alter ego, was the one more willing to take risks, from all reports.

In an interview, Kitty could not recall a particular conversation on the topic.[2] For her, it was a foregone conclusion that Mel would run. She called it his destiny. Like her efforts to preserve his *cubanidad*, she was the keeper of Mel's flame. She sought to preserve and protect his story. In the cliché, she was the power behind the throne—not in the sense of whispering advice to guide his every move. Rather, she fortified his will.

Encouraged by Kitty, Mel committed to run for county chairman, contracting the services of two young political consultants whom he knew from previous campaigns. Catholic and Republican, John Sowinski and Tre' Evers had formed a consulting business, Consensus Communication, to combine their expertise. Sowinski had woven a successful career working on statewide initiative campaigns; Evers had served as Orlando mayor Glenda Hood's spokesman and managed her 1994 reelection campaign. They advised Mel in late 1996 to wait until the second quarter of 1997 to begin fund-raising. Raising money right after Christmas was too difficult, they told him, and a feeble effort might encourage others to run.[3] But once committed, Mel reared into action. He rejected their advice, opened his campaign account on January 1, and proved his consultants wrong—with their help—by raising an impressive $170,000 in the first quarter of 1997.

The object was to scare off the rest of the field. As Sowinski explained, Orlando had a history of coronations rather than competitive elections.[4] The pattern established by mayors Frederick and Hood was for "community leaders" from the downtown business community to coalesce around a candidate and raise enough money to deter a viable alternative candidate from running.

And for a while the strategy worked for Mel. Three local elected officials, state legislator Bob Sindler and county commissioners Mary Johnson and Bob Freeman, expressed interest in running but eventually withdrew, saying they could not match Mel's war chest. He had won support from the business interests—in banking, real estate, and the law—who wrote big checks and raised money from their friends and colleagues.

Mel's fund-raising prowess reflected his earlier success in penetrating Orlando's Anglo establishment. In his first month as a candidate, he held a fund-raiser in the boardroom of the Baker-Hostetler law firm. He told his campaign consultants he expected forty or more local notables to attend. Evers scoffed. "I told him he would be lucky to get fifteen, considering it was a year and a half before the election." Mel said, "No, they'll all come." In fact, almost fifty people packed into the boardroom. To Evers it indicated Mel's pulling power within Orlando's establishment. Then or now, he could not imagine another candidate, even an incumbent, attracting so much support so early in a race.

And yet, Mel parted company with his contributors on key issues. One was an increase in the county's sales tax. In November 1997 the county held a mail-ballot referendum on raising the tax a half cent to fund roads and schools. Virtually all of his finance committee supported the measure, perhaps because they would benefit from the growth it would fund. But Mel disagreed, not wanting to appear pro-tax. From a political standpoint his judgment proved sound: the measure failed two-to-one.

Another issue was authorizing a light-rail system. The train would run 14.7 miles from Orlando International Airport to the International Drive tourist sector and then to downtown Orlando. Enticingly, federal money would cover 55 percent of the construction costs, courtesy of the Clinton administration and Republican congressman John Mica of Winter Park, an ardent train proponent who served on the House Transportation and Infrastructure Committee. The state would pay another 35 percent of construction costs. After contributions from business and tourism interests, Orlando and Orange Counties would each pay 2 percent of the construction costs.

Initially Mel gave tepid support to the project, calling it an option worth considering. His weak support turned to outright opposition once John Ostalkiewicz entered the chairman's race in May 1998. A strong antigovernment conservative, Ostalkiewicz had opposed the sales-tax proposal, which had made Mel wary of supporting it, knowing that the state senator might join the chairman's race. When he did decide to run, Ostalkiewicz matched Mel's prodigious fund-raising by the simple act of writing his campaign a $500,000 check. Florida law limits campaign contributions to $500 per person or corporation but places no limit on candidates' contributions to their own campaigns.

Mel's turnabout on light rail put him opposite the *Orlando Sentinel*, which consistently supported the train. At a meeting with the editorial board, in which they badgered him with questions about the project, he said they could beat their heads against the wall but the political reality would not change: he could not get elected by supporting light rail, not with so many unanswered questions about its cost and alignment. Pushing his chair back from the table, raising his voice, he asked: "Do you think it's easy to run against light rail?" He was alluding to his campaign contributors, most of whom supported the train project, according to Evers.

As on the sales tax issue, his campaign finance people blamed his strategists, Evers and Sowinski, for Mel taking positions different from theirs. According to Mel, his finance people urged him to fire the consultants no fewer than five times. When the request was made at one finance meeting, Mel declared that Tre' and John had brought him that far, and he would continue with them. He was not only showing loyalty to staff, a pattern that would continue. He was also departing from the previous model for campaigns in the area, in which wise men from the local establishment advised candidates on strategy. Instead, Mel was embracing a modern, consultant-driven, media-savvy campaign, the first in Central Florida and a forerunner of future campaigns.

One change was in the use of media, as Evers and Sowinski were big believers in TV advertising. For cost reasons, they planned to delay their media campaign until two weeks before the election. Three factors changed their timetable. One was their polling, which showed Mel's name recognition in single digits. He would need more TV exposure, and sooner. The second was their fund-raising success, which enabled them to buy more ads. The third and most important was Ostalkiewicz's entrance into the race, as he could afford TV ads too. After the senator announced, Mel's campaign made several media buys, which the diamond merchant quickly matched, commencing a media war between them.

By July 1998, seven persons vied for the nonpartisan chairman's post. Only three were viable candidates: Martinez and Ostalkiewicz, both Republicans, and Democrat Fran Pignone, who had mounted a weak campaign against incumbent Linda Chapin in 1994. All three candidates were multimillionaires; Martinez, with assets of $3 million, was the least wealthy of the three. Yet Pignone lacked Ostalkiewicz's willingness to self-fund her campaign. She had joined the race because, in her opinion, neither Martinez nor Ostalkiewicz knew enough about county government. "If they were going to go around the county debating the issues," said the two-term county commissioner, "I wanted to be there to lecture them on the issues."[5]

In May 1998, the three candidates scored nearly identical favorable ratings among voters who knew them, according to Martinez's polling. Evers and Sowinski did not worry about Pignone, figuring she would not have money. Martinez's strategy was to pull Ostalkiewicz down and raise his own rating, explained Evers. Eventually that happened, although Ostalkiewicz surged during the summer, only to decline in late August as Mel's negative advertising kicked in. Politically, Evers and Sowinski wanted to position Mel as a "center-right" candidate: more centrist than Ostalkiewicz but right of the liberal Pignone.

The first-round qualifying election was September 1. If no candidate won an outright majority, the top two vote-getters advanced to the November 3 general election. In the September election, Evers and Sowinski figured they would come in second, thereafter pulling support from Pignone's supporters, mostly Democrats. Ostalkiewicz's best hope for winning, as his campaign manager Cheryl Moore affirmed, was a knockout win in September.[6]

One wild card was Alex Lamour, a Puerto Rican and perennial candidate, who would pull Hispanic votes from Mel in the first round. (In the event, he won 5 percent, nearly all from Puerto Rican precincts.) Orlando and Central Florida were experiencing large-scale in-migration of Puerto Ricans from both New York and the Commonwealth. Yet despite vigorous voter mobilization efforts, mostly by Democrats, Puerto Ricans' registration and voting lagged behind their population numbers. Mel's ethnicity was essentially a "wash," according to polling his campaign conducted: roughly equal numbers of voters (approximately 7 percent) were attracted and turned off because he was Hispanic, said Evers, a figure supported by newspaper exit polls on the day of the election.[7]

Cubans had long since become a minority within Orlando's Hispanic community. But their political prowess compensated for their lack of numbers. The Cuban leaders, Mel's figurative Cuban Mafia, actively participated in his campaign, having become savvy politicos since their introduction to electoral politics in Bill Frederick's 1980 mayoral campaign. Their involvement ran the gamut from hosting fund-raisers to canvassing neighborhoods to driving Mel to events. Even better for him, they were self-starters.

Said architect Ernesto Gonzalez-Chavez: "Mel told us not to bring him problems. If something needed to be done, if we saw that a neighborhood or group needed canvassing, we did it."[8] As one example, attorney Armando Payas learned at the Cuban-American Club that some Hispanics, even Cubans, saw Mel as a rich attorney who hobnobbed with the Anglo elite and cared little about people like them.[9] So he recruited Mel to make more appearances in Hispanic neighborhoods, introducing him around, letting his personal charm work, to counter those concerns.

Still, the Hispanic bond proved strong in the election, even among Democrats. Evelyn Rivera, a Puerto Rican political activist and vice chair of county Democrats, had grown frustrated with Mel in the late 1980s. Coleader of an effort to unite Cubans and Puerto Ricans politically, she had sought his advice and support; to her chagrin, he brushed her off, telling her that Puerto Ricans and Cubans would never agree politically. But she supported him against Ostalkiewicz, working to bridge the Puerto Rican–Cuban divide in Mel's behalf.[10]

So did Puerto Rican attorney James Auffant, who served with Mel on the first Hispanic Advisory Committee in 1980. Back then, he chafed at the "insider game" played by the committee's Cubans, who refused to share their connections to benefit non-Cubans like him. Still, he supported Mel for chairman "absolutely and without question," despite his long involvement in the county Democratic Party.[11]

Rivera's and Auffant's common response to Mel's campaign demonstrated the power of ethnicity to trump nationality (Cuban vs. Puerto Rican) as well as party and ideology. While the Hispanic vote was only marginally important in 1998, more Puerto Ricans were migrating to the area—realizing, said Rivera, that Miami was a Cuban city and Orlando was up for grabs—and the importance of ethnic voting would increase.

Mel's campaign headquarters, located on a side street west of downtown close to where his parents lived when they first came to Orlando, reflected his diverse appeal. On any given day, one could find Anglo country clubbers and Mel's country cousins from Cuba working side by side, getting out mailings, assembling yard signs, and performing the diverse tasks of electioneering.

One of Mel's first full-time volunteers was Holly Stuart, a seasoned public relations pro and the wife of Orlando's Chamber of Commerce president. As she wryly commented, the experience taught her about "Cuban time." In helping to coordinate events, she tried to keep Mel punctual. But old friends, frequently Cuban, would drop by the headquarters to chat, throwing the candidate off schedule. When she tried to intervene, Mel would tell her: "No, this is important." For Stuart, who would work in Mel's administration, it was a lesson about Cuban culture as well as about Mel—namely, that personal relationships were all-important.[12]

On the issues, Mel advocated putting one hundred more sheriff's deputies on the street, strengthening fire protection, lowering property taxes by 5 percent, and negotiating the county's release from court-ordered school busing to support building community schools. Reaching out to Democrats and environmentalists, whose support he would need in the November second-round election, he called for purchasing environmentally sensitive land and improving stormwater controls. His reference to school issues prompted some derision, as education issues are the province of a county school board, not the county commissioners whose board he would chair if elected.[13] But Mel declared he would not be limited by his formal job description. He would use his office as a bully pulpit to address vital issues affecting the county, recognizing, as his campaign polling supported, that education ranked high among voter concerns.

To introduce Mel to voters, the campaign produced a seven-minute feel-good TV spot that told his immigrant story, showing him with his family and their dog, walking through a field in soft amber light. Despite promising to run a positive campaign, his TV ads made questionable charges against Ostalkiewicz. One ad claimed the senator was "on record against tax cuts." The "on record" was a newspaper quote in which Ostalkiewicz called Mel "irresponsible" for proposing a tax cut without specifics. In contrast, the senator's own TV ads before the September 1 primary did not mention his opponent. But Senator O (or Senator No, as his detractors called him) sent out mailers that played the ethnic card none too subtly, saying his mother "traces her roots and values" to America's founding.[14]

On primary election day, Evers met with Mel at his house. There, in the quiet of the attorney's study, Evers offered his prediction: Martinez would place second, ten points behind Ostalkiewicz, who would not win a majority. As they spoke, Kitty walked into the study and sensed something amiss. "What's wrong?" she asked. Mel turned to Evers and said, "Tell her what you just told me." When Tre' did, she responded: "Didn't you tell us at the beginning that Ostalkiewicz would place first in the primary? And didn't you say that we would make it to the second election and win in November?" Tre' answered yes to both questions, and Kitty turned and walked out of the room without saying another word.

Commenting on this story, Evers said that some campaign spouses are "accelerators" who intensify the highs and lows of the candidate. He described Kitty as the preferred opposite, saying she kept an even keel and exercised a calming influence on Mel, suppressing any excitability that might come from his Cuban background.

As Evers predicted, Ostalkiewicz failed to score a knockout punch. But Mel did better than the consultant expected, taking 41 percent of the vote to Ostalkiewicz's 40 percent—a margin of 586 votes. Immediately, a new round of fund-raising began, as the $500 contribution limit (excepting a candidate's personal contribution) applied "per election." Consistent with Ostalkiewicz's description of Mel as pro-development, the attorney's campaign coffers swelled with checks from major growth interests in banking, construction, real estate, and law.

Ostalkiewicz won support from developer interests in both rounds of the election, too. As gleaned from interviews, many companies and individuals who did business with the county regarded the race as too close to take a chance, so they wrote checks to both sides. Still, Martinez won the lion's share of developer dollars. In the end, the campaigns raised roughly equal amounts—$1.3 million for Martinez and $1.5 million for Ostalkiewicz—triple what was raised in the 1994 chairman's race. In all, Ostalkiewicz contributed $1.3 million of his own money.[15] The remainder of his contributions came mostly from outlying rural areas and the I-Drive tourist corridor.

With Pignone gone from the race following the primary, both candidates solicited her endorsement. They also sought support from Orange County Democrats. At a meeting of Democratic precinct captains attended by the author, Mel presented himself as a political moderate who would rise above partisanship as county chair. He won Pignone's endorsement along with a $500 contribution from her. Helped by sign-waving Hispanics, he also gained support from the Orange County Democratic Executive Committee, but asked them not to advertise their endorsement for fear it would cost him Republican votes.[16] The county GOP head and most of the party's rank and file supported his opponent.

The two candidates bought more than $200,000 worth of TV ads before the last two weeks of the campaign. Ostalkiewicz's ads featured actors portraying developers, drinking fine wine and smoking cigars as they bragged about having Mel in their pocket. Mel's ads offered feel-good shots of him and his family, alternating with attacks upon his opponent as an extremist.[17] His most effective spot criticized the state senator for his lone vote against the current state budget. That budget, which other conservative Republican legislators had supported, included funding for roads and education; so in the syllogism of campaign advertising, the thirty-second spot said Ostalkiewicz opposed roads and education.

In the final balloting, Martinez polled better than Evers predicted, winning 60–40, largely because of Democratic support. A *Sentinel* exit poll showed that more than 70 percent of Democrats voted for him.[18] A common postmortem was that Ostalkiewicz defeated himself—by playing into the extremist description, by speaking in his odd-sounding Rhode Island accent in his own TV ads, and by his demeanor during the campaign, in which he frequently seemed disorganized and sometimes grew angry with questioners, even shouting at them.[19] Other factors were Mel's considerable personal appeal and his resolve to run a modern political campaign relying upon experienced political pros, extensive use of television, and attack ads against his opponent.

⟷

Orange County's lame duck period is short. Mel took the oath of office, in both English and Spanish, on November 17, just two weeks after the election. Invoking the American Dream metaphor, he told the assembled audience: "I stand before you today as a living testament to the promise of America." He made a special effort to reach out to Hispanics, saying, "Hoy es un día especial tanto para ustedes como para mí"—this day is as much yours as mine.[20] Changes for Mel and the county would come swiftly.

Winning office with a million-dollar media blitz made Mel's name and face recognizable throughout the county. Kitty realized the change when she persuaded Mel to go Christmas shopping with her at Florida Mall, a megamall south of Orlando, close to several Hispanic neighborhoods. In her words, "It was a complete disaster." People kept coming up to meet Mel and wish him well, making shopping all but impossible. "I sent him home and decided I would do the shopping after that," she said.[21]

At the county administration building, the change was also swift. County Attorney Tom Wilkes observed a difference at senior staff meetings. A friend, neighbor, and fellow congregant at St. James Cathedral, he was asked to continue as the county's chief legal officer, having served in that post for seven years under Linda Chapin. "Mel brought a more businesslike approach to staff meetings," said Wilkes.[22] The meetings were shorter, focused on decision making, and staffers were told to be succinct.

At a meeting with holdover department heads, one senior executive proposed an initiative requiring new funding. "Listen," Mel said with emphasis. "I campaigned on a platform of reducing taxes. Don't be bringing proposals for additional spending." The message to staff was clear: there was a new agenda, and Mel was in charge.

The same was not true at commission meetings. Mel's first meeting was little short of disastrous. The five commissioners quarreled with him and with each other.[23] It was clear that Mel's political skills would be sorely tested by the unruly board. Controlling the board was complicated by Florida's Sunshine Law, which forbids officeholders from conferring about agenda items outside public meetings. In this open-meeting environment, Mel's well-honed interpersonal skills had little application.

Besides keeping Wilkes as county attorney, Mel made two other key appointments. The first was Dan Murphy as chief of staff. In selecting Murphy, a former aide to Vice President Quayle with a law degree but little legal experience, Mel chose a political adviser rather than a policy wonk. He also chose someone who knew the federal legislative process, with strong links to the Republican Party and the Bush family, who could ply the political process at higher levels in Martinez's behalf. Bright, energetic, at times brusque, Murphy was completely loyal to his boss. He took care of his back, alert to possible missteps or miscalculations, but also took charge of his future, facilitating what would come next.

The other key appointment was Agit Lalchandani as county administrator, in charge of the county's 6,058-person bureaucracy. A civil engineer born and educated in India, the bright, affable, nonpolitical Agit (pronounced a-JEET) had risen through the hierarchy of county government in the previous ten years, becoming director of public works under Linda Chapin and thus the county's point person on the light-rail issue.

As Agit acknowledged, his immigrant background created a common bond with Mel.[24] He told, for example, of going to lunch with Mel at Medina's, the Cuban restaurant and bodega. There, over obligatory beans and rice, Mel asked him: "What are a couple of immigrant guys like us doing running Orange County?" For them it was the fulfillment of the American Dream. When they left, Mel told him not to try paying for their meal. "It's family here. You'll offend them if you offer to pay," said the chairman, reflecting the ties of family and ethnicity that aided his rise to power.

⬌

Soon after Mel's election, the *Orlando Sentinel* editorial board invited him for lunch to discuss his proposed agenda. Both symbolically and practically, it was an important meeting, because the *Sentinel* sets forth a local agenda too. And sometimes its agenda is bolder and more responsive to the long-term interests of the community, taken as a whole, precisely because the editors do not need to sell their agenda to voters in an electoral process in which short-term interests predominate and some groups exert more influence than others. At least, that is how the editorial board sees it.

Wanting a neutral location, the editorial board chairman, Manning Pynn, arranged for lunch in the boardroom of CNL, a real estate investment firm and one of Orlando's largest local companies. As editorial writer Marianne Arneberg related, Pynn asked board members in advance not to raise the light-rail issue, saying the meeting was for Mel to discuss *his* agenda.[25] At the lunch, Dan Murphy and Holly Stuart sat at Mel's side, looking at him admiringly as he expounded upon his plans. Arriving late, *Sentinel* publisher John Haile took a seat at the table, sized up the situation, and immediately asked: "Has anyone asked about light rail?" Arneberg looked at Pynn with a shrug of her shoulders that said, it wasn't me. Evidently Pynn had not explained the game plan to Haile, his boss.

To Arneberg, Haile's bluntness conveyed a valuable message. During the campaign, Holly Stuart had criticized Arneberg to Pynn for writing editorials that accused Martinez of waffling on light rail. Arneberg wanted Martinez and Stuart to see that the whole editorial board, as well as Haile, stood foursquare behind the project. In endorsing Martinez, the board accepted that he could not win by supporting light rail. With the election over, however, they wanted to make sure he understood the case for the project, hoping he would move it along.

For Martinez, light rail was the project from hell; there was no winning on the issue. Because his predecessor Linda Chapin had secured a symbolic county commission vote favoring the project in August, just before the first round of the election, and because of the pressing timetable for federal approval of the project, the issue fell in his lap immediately after he took office.

To Dan Murphy, Mel's political alter ego, light rail was especially troubling. It was not an issue that his boss could take hold of and manage. Other actors—Mayor Hood, Congressman John Mica, and Gordon Linton, head of the Federal Transit Administration—were driving the issue. It arose too early in Mel's tenure, before he mastered the levers of power. And Murphy disagreed with the project philosophically. For him it was a boondoggle in the making, a paternalistic attempt to give citizens the mass transit that federal bureaucrats and media elites thought they should have, instead of the roads they wanted.

On the other side stood the *Sentinel*, whose support Mel needed in the future. As Arneberg's editorials made apparent, they saw the issue in stark terms. Orlando was sprawled, having been designated by the Sierra Club the previous summer as the number one "most sprawl-threatened" mid-size city in the nation. Rail transit, not more roads, was the antidote to sprawl, the editorial board thought. Sure, there were unanswered questions about routes, construction and right-of-way costs, ridership, and more. But faced with these imponderables, the community needed "leadership" with a "big-picture vision" to cut through the chaff and embrace light rail, just as the editorial board had done.[26]

In fairness, the light-rail proposal was a classic example of the kind of multilayered project, characteristic of the American federal system of government, that political scientists have written about endlessly. So many favorable decisions are needed, from so many different actors with so many different interests, timetables, and constraints, that failure seems inevitable. And if such projects do gain approval, the results are seldom as positive as the advocates predicted. To succeed, political leaders must "manage the politics"—easier said than done for a new county executive.

Caught between the conflicting demands of good policy and good politics, between the *Sentinel* and Dan Murphy, Mel resorted to a timeworn practice: he created a commission to study the problem. The commission was headed by former Orlando mayor Bill Frederick, a light-rail supporter, but also included a few critics of the project. To cynics, it was an attempt to resurrect light rail despite Mel's campaign promises—just as Ostalkiewicz predicted he would do. The truth is probably more prosaic: Mel was genuinely undecided. The study committee would give him time.

On issues more in his control, the chairman made progress in his first hundred days, earning the newspaper's praise.[27] He had pledged during the campaign to wring $28 million from the county's budget by 2002, enough to reduce taxes by 5 percent. Doing so was more of a challenge, because he had also pledged to spend more for law enforcement, storm-water facilities, and environmentally sensitive land. Accordingly, he moved quickly to cut seventeen top executive positions and eliminate the county's Community Affairs Department, which Chapin had used to empower low-income communities. The need for additional cost savings would constrain his hand on light rail.

As many expected, the Frederick Commission found more questions than answers. They criticized Lynx, the regional transportation agency spearheading the train project, for failing to nail down construction costs and finalize land-purchase agreements. The total cost, the commission said, might rise to $685 million from $600 million, pushing the county's share from $11 million to $20 million. They also concluded that the project would neither improve air quality appreciably nor relieve congestion on Interstate 4, the area's main transportation artery.[28]

The cost and alignment issues identified by the commission were not just policy problems. For each problem there existed a constituency of train opponents. On the alignment issue, local officials in Winter Park and Maitland opposed running the train through their cities, responding to citizen concerns about noise and road blockages. As well, many county residents living outside Orlando opposed paying for a route that served the city. Concern about cost overruns and overstated ridership figures prompted additional taxpayer opposition. A perennial antitax group, Axe the Tax, led by local talk-radio host Doug Guetzloe, succeeded in coalescing much of this anti sentiment.

Nonetheless, the Frederick Commission recommended approval of the project, accepting the *Sentinel* line that exercising leadership and vision was more important than having good answers to all the policy questions they identified. The new county chairman, who stayed in contact with Frederick during the commission's work, agreed to vote for light rail. It was thus his third position on the issue, having progressed from tepid support early in his campaign, through downright opposition once Ostalkiewicz entered the chairman's race, to renewed support once in office. Though he continued to worry about the cost, he offered his qualified support after learning, he said, that the county's contribution would be covered primarily by tourists, through an existing 7 percent tax on hotel bills.

In all, the county commission voted five times on the project. Except for the final vote to commit funding and enter contracts, none of the votes was legally binding. Rather, the votes were driven by the exigencies of federal funding. Congressman John Mica, Federal Transit Administration head Gordon Linton, and Orlando mayor Hood felt local support was essential to secure congressional approval for Orlando's funding request. In the opinion of County Attorney Tom Wilkes, these claims were spurious—and the multiple votes doomed the project locally. Lalchandani agreed: each time the commission voted, the opponents got one more opportunity to confront the commission with the unresolved issues concerning costs, alignment, and ridership.

At the final vote, on September 8, 1999, Mel tried to have it both ways. In announcing his vote, he took pains to distinguish himself from commissioners who had continuously opposed the project, as well as from Commissioner Mary Johnson, the board's other Hispanic, who had always supported it. Though voting yes, he sought middle ground. Clarence Hoenstine, who had previously voted yes, cast the deciding "no" vote, saying, "There were too many unanswered questions."[29]

In the frank assessment of Skip Dalton, Mel's law partner who would later serve as his general counsel in the Senate, it was his biggest policy failure as county chairman. "He didn't make light rail happen and could have," said Dalton.[30] To County Commissioner Bob Sindler, who consistently opposed the project, Mel fell victim to his lack of resolve. "He was stuck between Dan Murphy, who hated the project, and the *Sentinel*, so he waffled and broke his pledge to voters." Sindler added: "On this issue, like others, he had too much fluidity."[31]

Sentinel editorial writer Marianne Arneberg agreed with Sindler, describing Mel as a political animal, too dependent on his staff. "He has too many masters," she said. As her newspaper would editorialize: "His reactions come after options have been run through a committee of weather vanes that measure the political winds."[32] Said Mary Johnson, "I hope he outgrows changing his mind. As someone new to politics, he was overly reliant on staff."[33] Orlando mayor Glenda Hood, a friend and supporter of Mel's, attributed the county's action to "a real lack of leadership on the Orange County Commission."[34]

On another issue, school concurrency, Mel did exercise leadership, taking a position sharply at odds with the development community, which had solidly supported him against Ostalkiewicz. His stance here, as on light rail and the sales-tax hike, demonstrated independence from his financial supporters. More, his innovative response to the schools issue came impressively early, in his second year of office. Most elected officials take longer to learn the levers of power.

As background, in 1984 Governor Bob Graham pushed the Florida legislature to address the downside of the state's mushrooming population growth: overcrowded public facilities. Florida was then receiving 800 new residents a day, straining the state's infrastructure, especially roads and schools. The signal provision of the state's 1984 Growth Management Act was its "concurrency" requirement, which said that public facilities and services must be upgraded "concurrent with the impact of new public or private development."[35] Thus, if a new shopping mall brought additional traffic, affected roads would need to be expanded accordingly.

Significantly, the concurrency provision applied to a long list of public facilities, from roads to wastewater to parks and recreation—but not to schools. This exclusion was politically driven: the development community feared that extending concurrency to education would enable school boards to stop development by refusing to build or expand schools. They did not want to empower school boards to halt the growth engine. So "school concurrency" was made optional in the 1984 law.

But that was not enough. In 1997 the Republican-controlled legislature responded to fears in the development community that Orange County would adopt a school concurrency provision. In a bit of legerdemain outstanding even by Florida standards, the legislature essentially "reformed" the school concurrency option out of existence, requiring that every last municipality of a county agree to the school provision—a practical barrier that no Florida county has ever surmounted.

Upon entering office, Mel learned that county government was part of the school overcrowding problem, even if it was not the builder of schools. Every time the county rezoned property to allow more development—for example, by changing the classification for a tract of land from agricultural to residential—it impacted schools. Permitting new housing developments, as the county frequently did, put more children in surrounding schools, many of them overcrowded already.

When rezoning requests came before the county commission, school parents would pack the meeting in opposition, complaining, often noisily, about schools so strained that children were scheduled for lunch at 9:30 A.M. Again and again Martinez and Tom Wilkes, the county attorney, tried to explain to these parents that their hands were tied legally. Florida law, as they understood it, did not permit them to deny a rezoning request because of its impact upon schools. To do so would violate the property rights of the petitioning landowner, who could take the matter to court—and win.

County Commissioner Teresa Jacobs, who in 1998 was president of the Orange County Home Owners Association, believed the county could legally deny such rezonings, giving parents and schoolkids the relief they sought. On the advice of attorneys, she maintained the county possessed the requisite authority even without going through the state-prescribed—but now virtually impossible—procedure for adopting school concurrency. The county, she said, possessed the authority to deny rezonings in such cases, without infringing anyone's property rights, through its inherent "police powers." She had advocated this position during Linda Chapin's administration, winning support from Commissioner Clarence Hoenstine, who encouraged her to press her argument with Wilkes, the county attorney. But Wilkes rejected her argument, temporarily ending the matter.

Enter Mel, who had an advantage over Chapin and Hoenstine, neither of whom was an attorney. As a personal injury lawyer, he knew the law was sometimes ambiguous and subject to interpretation. Maybe there was legal wiggle room for the county to deny rezonings that would harm schoolkids. So he asked his friend Tom Wilkes to research the issue anew. Taking several weeks, the county attorney concluded his earlier judgment had been wrong: the county could do as Jacobs and Hoenstine urged. He inscribed his new reasoning in a legal memorandum, which became the subject of debate among Mel's senior staff—namely, Lalchandani, planning head David Heath, and Wilkes himself.

Lalchandani opposed the idea, saying it would inflame the development community. "I had observed from my service in government that the development community usually got what it wanted," he said in an interview. Said Wilkes, "I was losing the debate two-to-one until Bruce McClendon joined us." McClendon, the head of growth management and an innovative, nationally regarded planning expert, tipped the scales in Wilkes's favor. Mel, wanting staff support, went with him.

"I told them we would be sued, but I thought we could win the lawsuit," said Wilkes. Mel wanted the incipient policy to pass the "smile test," he added. "We knew we would be sued over the policy. He wanted us to be able to argue our position straight-faced. I told him we could."

Wilkes's legal memo was presented as the opinion of staff in a rezoning case that arose in August 2000. The case was a request by a property owner, Betty Jean Mann, to rezone eleven acres to build 40 units of housing where existing zoning permitted only 20 units. At the county commission hearing on the Mann petition, lively debate ensued (in the course of which Wilkes apologized to Hoenstine for reversing his opinion on the county's authority in rezoning matters). Commissioner Sindler, who took pleasure in opposing Mel, said a denial was a violation of property rights. But the commission rejected the rezoning in a split vote.

In the aftermath the *Sentinel* reanointed Mel, discovering that, despite his blundering on light rail, he was a leader after all. But the response was not all rosy. In a meeting with a delegation from the county home builders association, one representative told Mel he would be "flipping hamburgers" after the dust settled. Robert Mandell, a financial supporter of Mel's and the president of Greater Homes, a large residential home builder, told Mel the policy was "ludicrous" because it hurt the development community without creating a corresponding public benefit. "Mel was just dismissive" of his view, Mandell said. Yet he added: "Everybody knows he is still my friend."[36]

It was like Richard Nixon, the arch anticommunist, recognizing mainland China as a legitimate sovereign state. Martinez, the consummate friend of developers, was taking the side of schoolkids against developers. As Mandell suggested, Mel could commit this liberal heresy precisely because he was no liberal.

As Wilkes predicted, the courts at both the local and appellate levels upheld the county's position, which jurists dubbed the Martinez Doctrine. That may have settled the legal issue, but debate continues on a different question: whether the policy is beneficial. Developers maintain that it promotes urban sprawl by discouraging "in-fill development" in favor of shifting new-home construction to places farther out, where schools are less crowded. McClendon defends the policy, saying it forces developers to do "up-front planning" with the school board.[37] Since the county commission approves rezonings only when the school board agrees, developers must negotiate with the school board; typically, they make up-front donations to pay for additional classrooms, thus privatizing part of the cost of school construction. As Agit and Mandell agree, what one thinks of the policy comes down to a matter of belief—about where new residential development would have occurred without the policy.

The ink was scarcely dry on the Martinez Doctrine before Mel left for Washington. There he would earn plaudits for his innovative response to the school overcrowding issue—despite the interesting fact that, a decade later, no other county in Florida has adopted the policy. Nonetheless, before Mel went to HUD, Governor Jeb Bush appointed him head of a statewide Growth Management Commission. This appointment was criticized by the American Planning Association, which said he would be beholden to developers. The association apparently failed to appreciate how much developers disliked the Martinez Doctrine. In fact, the state growth commission he chaired recommended developer responsibility for school overcrowding, an idea that Governor Bush and the Florida legislature walked away from, suggesting that they, more than Mel, were beholden to developers.

⟺

A problem for Mel in moving to the next level was finding appropriate issues. Local government, in which he was enmeshed as county chairman, typically provides things that people want: police and fire protection, water and sewer service, and the regulation of building and land use. That is why ideological debate between liberals and conservatives seldom descends upon local government as it does upon state and national government. Local politicians wishing to advance themselves to these higher levels need to be creative.

Wanting to distinguish himself, Mel talked during the county chairman campaign about using his office as a bully pulpit to address broader issues affecting the community. As Tom Wilkes would tell him, county commission meetings were his bully pulpit in part because the meetings were televised via the county-owned cable channel, Orange TV. But Mel was bored by the minutiae of most county issues and put off by the back-and-forth on a commission where his powers as presiding officer were limited. He needed a starring role. Indeed, his finest moment as county chairman came, some said, away from the county commission dais when Hurricane Floyd bore down on Orlando in September 1999. At the county's Emergency Operations Center, Mel spoke calmly and reassuringly to TV viewers, alternating between English and Spanish, urging precautions before the storm. According to people around him, his presence and instinct in knowing just what to say made them realize that something larger awaited him.[38]

Mel would find a bigger pulpit on Thanksgiving Day 1999 when a six-year-old Cuban boy, Elián González, was plucked from an inner tube off the coast of Fort Lauderdale. His mother and stepfather had died when their overloaded boat sank after leaving Cuba. Mel's role in the ensuing media melee, while driven by passion, was not totally removed from political considerations. That role began in the strategic mind of Dan Murphy.

Several weeks after Elián's arrival in the United States, Murphy and Holly Stuart were enjoying an alfresco lunch at the Signature Plaza, two blocks from the county administration building. Young Elián had become the subject of a custody battle, with the boy's relatives in Florida seeking asylum for him, while millions of protestors in Cuba demanded his return to his father there. Over lunch, Murphy said to Holly: "What would you think if Mel brought Elián to Disney World?" Outwardly it would be a humanitarian act, removed from the custody brouhaha. It would give the six-year-old a respite from the media circus surrounding him in Miami. At the same time it would burnish Mel's own immigration story, a story of youthful courage but also of fear and loss.

In fact, Elián's Disney World visit on December 12 offered him little respite from the media circus. As his family caravan wended its way from Miami to Orlando, a three-and-a-half-hour drive, a motorcade of TV trucks followed. Once at Disney, reporters were not allowed to accompany Elián's entourage through the park. For pictures of the boy—and Mel—a Disney photographer was supplied. After the tour, a press conference was scheduled at Disney's Contemporary Hotel, where Mel and a family representative spoke, as arranged by Stuart, a former Disney PR executive.

At the park, Elián and his family pulled up to a designated parking area, where they were met by Mel and Kitty and their six-year-old son Andrew. The two boys smiled at each other, their interaction limited by the language barrier. As they walked through the park, Elián readily took Mel's hand. Surrounding them was a phalanx of police officers, most of them Hispanic, backed by Disney security. As incredible as it sounds, they had information that Castro's agents might try to grab the boy.[39]

The cathartic moment came when the entourage entered Disney's classic It's a Small World attraction. The ride, originally produced for the New York World's Fair in 1964, is a low-tech affair. Small boats holding twenty people glide through a flume that takes passengers through the various regions of the world, with stylized animatronic dolls in national costumes singing the title song, "It's a Small World," in numerous languages. More whimsical than exciting, the ride evokes smiles rather than thrills and chills.

Mel's father, Melquiades Sr., and his father's mother, Graciela.

Mel and his mother, Gladys.

Mel's grandfather Melquiades Martínez, ca. 1940.

Above, right: Mel at age two or three.

Above, left: Mel at age three with his pet goat Pancho in Cuba.

Below: Mel and Ralph with their pet dog in Cuba.

Above: Mel and his father, Dr. Martínez, on a fishing trip.

Right: Mel and Ralph with their father in Cuba.

Below: Mel (center) and Ralph (right) with a schoolmate in Sagua.

Mel's father's mother, Graciela (center), Ralph (left), Mel (right), and assorted cousins.

Ralph (left) and Mel.

Mel (left) and his brother, Ralph.

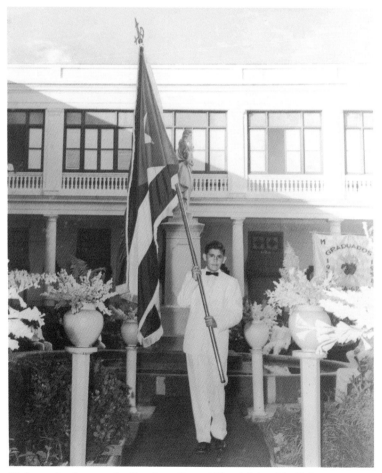

Mel, age twelve, graduating from Sacred Heart School in Cuba.

A day at the beach with teachers/priests from Sacred Heart School, 1959–60.

Mel and his sister, Margarita, just before he departed from Cuba.

Above, left: Mel's first foster parents, Eileen and Walter Young.

Above, right: Mel's senior picture at Bishop Moore High School.

Below, left: Mel in his Bishop Moore uniform in front of the Youngs' house, 1962.

Below, right: Mel in his American Legion baseball uniform in the Youngs' backyard.

Left to right: Ralph, Kitty, and Mel at Florida State University in 1969, with Kitty's VW in the background.

Newlyweds Mel and Kitty at his parents' home in Gainesville.

Mel's swearing-in ceremony as HUD secretary in the Oval Office of the White House.

Mel's swearing-in ceremony as HUD secretary.

Above: Secretary Martinez at the HUD building in Washington.

Left: Kitty Martinez at the time Mel was HUD secretary.

HUD secretary and President George W. Bush in the Oval Office.

HUD event promoting minority homeownership in Washington.

HUD secretary and President Bush building a house for Habitat for Humanity in Waco, Texas.

HUD secretary with President Bush at Camp David.

Karl Rove and Secretary Martinez.

Left to right: Senator Bob Graham, HUD secretary Martinez, President Bush, and Senator Bill Nelson on Air Force One.

President Bush announcing the appointment of the HUD secretary and Secretary of State Colin Powell as cochairs of the Committee for Assistance to a Free Cuba in October 2003.

Mel and his family visiting President George H. W. Bush and Barbara Bush in Kennebunkport, Maine.

HUD secretary Martinez, Laura Bush, and President Bush celebrating Cuban Independence Day in the East Room of the White House on May 20, 2001.

Rudy Giuliani with Mel during his 2004 senate campaign.

Mel campaigning for the Senate in Miami.

Mel and Kitty after his Senate victory in 2004.

Mel and his mother, Gladys, during his 2004 Senate campaign.

For young Elián it drew a different response. As he approached the boats, the child suddenly froze, leaning back against his uncle, not wanting to board the eighteen-foot craft. "¿Se va a hundir?" he asked worriedly—will it sink? Immediately the adults understood his fear. "We felt embarrassed about not anticipating his anxiety," said Kitty. The adults offered hurried assurances of the boat's safety and the scant depth of the water, only about three feet. Bravely the boy continued on, his mind soon captivated by the cavalcade of sounds and sights along what Disney calls "the happiest cruise that ever sailed around the world."[40] Among the adults on board there were no dry eyes.

At the press conference afterwards, Mel refused to discuss his views on where the boy should live, saying the day was designed for Elián's enjoyment, not for political debate over his future.[41] He explained that he was helping pay for the visit by the boy and his family. And in response to questions, he recounted his Peter Pan experience, saying he knew about being displaced from parents.

As Murphy expected, Elián's visit catapulted Mel into the national limelight, returning him to his Cuban roots, to his Peter Pan experience, to when his refugee story began. Yet much had changed. Mel was a leader now, an elected official; he had proved himself in America, doing right by his adopted country, as his father had encouraged him to do. Thus credentialed, he had the opportunity to take up the anti-Castro cause in the national media.

His first such opportunity came on Chris Matthews's *Hardball* show on MSNBC. He appeared along with three others, including Miami congressman Lincoln Diaz-Balart. As Mel waited to join the discussion, the garrulous host finally turned to him, asking what it was like taking Elián to Disney World. Mel answered that he recognized himself in the boy—and they broke for commercial, ending his national TV debut. He was disappointed, though at least he shared billing with leaders of the Cuban community. It put his name and face in front of them for the first time since the 1994 governor's race.

Then in mid-January he appeared on CNN's *Larry King Live*, where another panelist accused him and other Republicans of using young Elián as a political pawn. King asked Mel, "Weren't you parading him around?"[42] As the custody battle wore on, Mel also appeared the following month at a hearing of the U.S. Senate Judiciary Committee, where he reminded senators that "the Cold War has not ended between Mr. Castro and the rest of the free world."[43]

Mel had found the bully pulpit he needed. As he spoke on these issues, his personal story grew in amplitude. The *cubanidad* he kept compartmentalized came to the fore. It became his identity, his hook for media attention. In acting from passion, he facilitated his transition to the next level.

Two passions drove Mel in these events. One was his identification with Elián's cause. Some said there was a physical resemblance between Elián and the young Melquiades. The other was his passion for the Cuban community. At the time, "there was a lot of hollering and arm-waving" among Miami Cubans, said Mel's chief of staff, Dan Murphy. In fact, full-scale riots erupted in the Little Havana section of Miami after Immigration and Naturalization Service agents took the boy, in the middle of the night, for repatriation to Cuba where his father awaited him.

Mel, according to Murphy, did not like the portrait the news media was drawing of Cuban Americans. "It helped their cause to have a non-Miami Cuban speak on the issue," the aide added, "someone in a Brooks Brothers suit, who was articulate and well spoken, who could hold his own with the most fervent advocate for the cause." He might have added, someone who had learned to speak unaccented English from being sent as a Peter Panner to Orlando rather than Miami.

To his Cuban friends, Mel courageously did the right thing in embracing Elián's cause. George Rodon, whom Mel had made economic development director for the county, said it best. "Let them send the boy back only if his father comes to the United States and says, free from coercion by Fidel Castro or his agents, he wants to take Elián back."[44] For Cubans who fled Castro, it was inconceivable that the father would freely choose to remain in Cuba. Or that he would want to repatriate his child to the island nation, which they regarded as a communist prison.

Yet few of Mel's Anglo friends and supporters seem to have agreed. When asked in interviews, many just shook their heads in silence. Others spoke more overtly, even to Mel. Holly Stuart, frustrated by the ordeal because of her own child custody experience, told Mel she would not work with him on the issue. Her husband, Jacob, the veteran of a similar experience, called Mel and asked him: "Doesn't even someone who is a bad father"—as Elián's father was characterized—"have the right to his child?"[45] Still, the husband and wife continued to support Mel politically.

Through the Elián affair, Mel gained notice as an articulate Cuban American politician, appealing to Hispanics and Anglos alike—at an opportune moment. No one could have predicted the 2000 presidential vote recount squabble in Florida. But the importance of Florida's increasingly diverse Hispanic vote for winning this contested state was clear. Bill Clinton won the state's vote in 1996, including Orange County, buoyed by the in-migration of 200,000 Democratic-leaning Puerto Ricans to Central Florida. And the Clinton-Gore administration had made inroads in winning support from Miami Cubans, capitalizing on policy and generational divisions. But that was before Elián came ashore, before Janet Reno ordered the boy repatriated to his father, before the ensuing melee in Miami.

＝

Having gained attention through these events, Mel soon formed a personal relationship with presidential candidate George W. Bush. On March 23, 2000, the Texas governor made his first of many campaign visits to Orlando. It was the eve of Super Tuesday, when Florida and five other states held presidential primary elections. Bush was assured of Florida's GOP vote, but his campaign was focused on the general election, knowing Florida would be a pivotal battleground, even with his brother being the governor. The key to statewide victory was winning the Interstate-4 corridor, the belly of the state extending from Tampa to Orlando to Daytona.

In planning the candidate's visit, the Bush campaign contacted Dan Murphy in the county chairman's office. He was their go-to guy, a seasoned political operative known to the Bushes from when he worked for Dan Quayle. Bush strategists wanted to use the Orlando visit to tout the Texas governor's education initiatives in Texas, which prefigured the No Child Left Behind plan subsequently adopted at the national level.

Initially the campaign wanted to go to Winter Park, a wealthy suburban enclave with high GOP registration. But Murphy demurred. "He needs to be where students otherwise wouldn't get to meet him," said the media-savvy aide. Miguel Pagan, Mel's driver and security chief, remembers the conversation in Mel's nominally nonpartisan office.[46] As a sheriff captain on loan from the sheriff's office, he knew the Orlando community well, especially its Hispanic community. He suggested to Murphy that Bush go to Colonial High School. It was about 60 percent Hispanic and 30 percent black—the right demographics for Bush's speech. The school was also a direct shot from the airport, making access for the candidate and his media entourage easy.

Pagan, who accompanied his boss to the event, said Mel and the Texas governor enjoyed immediate rapport. And Bush seemed taken by Mel. When the county chairman took the microphone to introduce the governor, the mostly Hispanic audience erupted in applause—for Mel. He and Bush both spoke some in Spanish, but Mel got a better response from the crowd, said Pagan. "Looking back, you could see then that Mel was going somewhere," he added. The crowd energized Mel, and his presence as a Hispanic in a position of power, standing next to a possible future president, moved the largely Hispanic student body.

At the event's end, after ceremonial photographs of Bush and Mel and Kitty, the county executive accompanied the Texas governor to his waiting limousine. As they walked down the sidewalk, students approached Mel, in front of Bush, to ask for the county chairman's autograph. Taking it all in, Bush said to Mel with a wry smile, "You're pretty popular around here, aren't you?"

Later, as they talked in his limousine, Bush said he was confident about winning the election and becoming president. "Stick with me," he told Mel, "and you'll go places."

7

SECRETARY

Matthew Hunter was only twenty-six, but he had worked on Capitol Hill and for various GOP entities before he came to Orlando, in early 2000, as field director for the Bush-Cheney campaign, responsible for the nine counties of Central Florida. His first day in town he met Mel Martinez at a political fund-raiser for Florida's Speaker of the House, Tom Feeney. Mel was one of the state's eleven cochairs for the Bush-Cheney campaign, several of whom were present at the event. Said Hunter: "Most of the others said, 'Hi, nice to meet you. I guess I'll hear from you.' But Mel was different. He said, 'Tell me what you need.'"[1]

Hunter explained he needed an office, and the county chairman put him in touch with Dan Murphy, who helped him secure space. This experience encapsulated Mel's relationship with the Bush juggernaut. Though elected to a nonpartisan post, and though a political moderate as county chairman, he would become a proactive Bush Republican, dedicated to advancing George W.'s conservative agenda in Florida and, as HUD secretary, in Washington and the nation.

During the campaign, Mel and Kitty regularly invited Matthew over for dinner or just to relax and watch television on Sundays. In turn, Matthew recruited Mel to emcee four Bush campaign rallies in Orlando, enabling Mel to become "real familiar" with the future president, said the campaign aide. Matthew knew the younger Bush from interning in the White House under Bush 41, and he observed a personality similarity between Mel and George W. "They're alike in their approach to people and how people respond to them," he said. "Both are approachable and put people at ease."

In May of 2000, Mel played "attack dog," according to the local media, when Vice President Al Gore came to Orlando for an AARP gathering at the Orange County Convention Center. Relying upon notes the Bush campaign gave him the night before, he criticized Gore at a press conference held in a side room of the convention center. Before members of the national media, he called Bush the true candidate of the elderly and accused the vice president of flip-flopping on issues. Then, in August, Mel stood next to Jeb Bush as he introduced his brother at the GOP convention in Philadelphia. There, according to media reports, he was among a group that hectored Ralph Nader when he came onto the floor. As part of the convention's focus on diversity, Martinez was sent to talk to TV crews about Republican momentum. It was a new role for a county chairman elected to a nonpartisan post on the strength of Democratic voter support.[2]

On election eve Hunter watched the vacillating vote count with Mel and other local Republicans at Orlando's downtown Marriott Hotel. At 6:30 the next morning the campaign aide received an emergency phone call from Bush headquarters telling him to "get lawyers on the ground immediately." He hurriedly called Mel and Dan Murphy asking for help. "Mel assisted us by recruiting local lawyers and by advising on local strategy," said Hunter. For Mel the thirty-day recount controversy was a stroke of luck, as it kept all eyes on Florida. His aid to the Bush effort during this period would be remembered once the Supreme Court settled the election.

When Jeb Bush called Mel on December 5, he told him to wait for a follow-up call. In fact, Mel and Kitty nervously waited two more days before Mel received a call from Clay Johnson, a Bush friend from Texas and the assistant to the president-elect for presidential personnel. Arriving in Washington a day later, Mel met with Johnson in the transition office on G Street, two blocks from the White House. The Texan took Mel upstairs to meet with vice president–elect Cheney, who told the county executive to go home and assemble his financial records for an FBI background check. Keeping his accountant busy in the interim, he returned to Washington on December 18 to meet with Bush.

When Mel entered the president-elect's suite in the Madison Hotel, Bush was sitting with Andrew Card, who would become his chief of staff. The two men were in shirtsleeves and George W. was making coffee. Despite the casual atmosphere, Bush got right to business, saying he wanted Mel to serve in his cabinet. "Would you take the job of HUD secretary?" The Cuban American said he would be honored to serve. Bush continued by saying that the department had been historically troubled, adding that he imagined the first scandal of his administration would come from HUD. That was why he had selected Mel, knowing his background was squeaky clean. He thought Mel possessed the ethical compass to keep the ship at HUD upright.[3]

The county chairman was soon off to Austin, where president-elect Bush announced him as his choice for HUD on December 20. Bush, who got HUD's name wrong, calling it the "department of housing and human development," described Mel as someone who "understands American values," adding that "there is no greater value than owning something— owning your own home." In his own comments, Mel evoked the American Dream theme. His nomination, he said, "is the fulfillment of the promise of America, the promise that regardless of where you come from, what language you speak, the color of your skin, or your economic circumstances, all things are possible."[4]

Except in Cuba, the media showed little reaction to Mel's selection. The nonpartisan *National Journal* praised other cabinet choices while calling Mel simply "a friend of W's." The *Washington Post* attributed his selection to "cronyism."[5] The Cuban press, however, reacted virulently. Prensa Latina, the official Cuban news agency, described Mel as "a rabidly anti-Cuban Republican" who was "one of the political hacks in Florida's Cuban communities" and "an unconditional ally of the Bush family." They said his nomination settled "Bush's debt of gratitude toward [Florida Cubans], the only Hispanics who voted en bloc against Gore because the Democratic administration authorized the return to Cuba of the kidnapped boy Elián González."[6]

Immediately after the announcement, Mel acquired a "shepherd" to guide him through the confirmation process. That person, assigned by the White House Office of Presidential Personnel, was Sean Smealey, who had worked as a special assistant to Bush 41. Smealey also knew the Senate Banking, Housing, and Urban Affairs Committee, which would vote on Mel's confirmation, as he had worked for its previous chair, Senator Alfonse D'Amato (R-N.Y.). Smealey believed Mel would do well in the confirmation process, he said in an interview. "He was a very genuine guy, serious and smart, without errors."[7] On top of that, he had a "compelling story" that would trump what the *Washington Post* called his "slender record" on housing.[8]

Mel took direction from Smealey, who told him not to talk to the press. "I told him there was nothing to gain from saying anything to the media until his confirmation." Aided by his courtroom experience, Mel did well at "murder board," a mockup of the confirmation hearing in which Smealey and others played the part of Senate interrogators, peppering him with questions. A veteran of the DC scene, Smealey thought Mel and Kitty would be popular there. "Washington gets a lot of self-important people, some of whom spiral and fall," he said. "Mel and Kitty were different. They seemed real."

Dan Murphy, who accompanied Mel to Washington, was surprised by their sparse office accommodations. The transition building on G Street was down the street from the Executive Office Building, adjacent to George Washington University. Walking along the hallway, he passed the no-frills offices of Donald Rumsfeld, Colin Powell, and other cabinet nominees. Mel's office was a twelve-by-twelve affair with a cement pillar in the center. Because of the pillar, a person sitting opposite Mel's metal desk had to turn sideways to see him. Down the hall was a bullpen where each nominee had a staff person at a desk. In this open atmosphere—people moving back and forth, phones jangling, transition documents piled high—newly appointed aides worked feverishly to overcome the thirty-day delay caused by the recount.

Following protocol, Smealey took Mel to meet with the twenty-one members of the Senate Banking Committee, starting with chairman Paul Sarbanes (D-Md.) and ranking minority member Phil Gramm (R-Tex.). (Until the inauguration, the Democrats controlled the Senate; after January 20, Gramm became the committee chair and Sarbanes the ranking Democrat.) Like the Peter Panner who sought to avoid making waves, Mel did well in these encounters, listening to senators' concerns, taking notes, saying he would check on their issues, searching for common ground, acknowledging he knew little about HUD programs, said his shepherd. A problem did surface with Senator Gramm, however.

Smealey and the White House hoped to obtain a confirmation vote on inauguration day. Senator Sarbanes said he was ready to move, but Gramm dragged his feet on scheduling a vote. Smealey asked Mel whether Gramm might have a problem with him, and Mel said no, they had always been friendly. He added that the Texas senator asked him to serve on his presidential campaign committee during an Orlando visit in 1996. Mel had declined, saying he was already committed to Bob Dole.

Worried by this report, Smealey called a friend on Gramm's staff to ask whether the chairman might hold something like that against Mel. "Absolutely," came the response. It was Mel's introduction to big-ego politics,

Washington style. As Smealey said, "Gramm was making him pay for his sins."

Once convened on January 17, the three-day confirmation hearing proved a love fest. Mel was glowingly introduced by Florida's two Democratic senators, Bob Graham and Bill Nelson. Both had enjoyed Mel's past political support. Before his county chairman campaign, Mel made several political contributions to Graham, and he and Kitty walked precincts for Nelson when he first ran for Congress.

By custom each senator makes a statement regarding a nominee. At Mel's hearing several senators submitted statements for the record and left, explaining they had other hearings to attend. When Mel got to speak, he began by introducing his family, saying here is my wife, Kitty, my brother Ralph, and so forth. His youngest son Andrew, then six, had become restless, and his aunt had taken him outside. So when it came to introducing Andrew, the nominee improvised, saying to laughter, "My son Andrew was here, but I guess he had another hearing to attend."

In their comments the senators kept returning to his compelling personal story, now more of an asset in the realm of national politics. In his own comments he called himself a "living testament to the promise of America." He added: "I came to America with a suitcase in the hope of a better life. I know the value of home ownership because I have witnessed its great power throughout my entire life."[9] Substantively, he promised to strengthen HUD, an agency some Republicans had sought to eliminate, and make it more responsive to housing needs.

The former Peter Panner was unanimously confirmed, not on inauguration day as the White House wished, but three days later. His easy confirmation contrasted with the treatment accorded his Hispanic counterpart Linda Chavez, a firebrand opponent of affirmative action nominated to run the Labor Department. Her selection was vigorously opposed by labor unions and affirmative action proponents. Following contentious hearings, the new administration withdrew her nomination after it came out that she employed an illegal immigrant in her home.

Immediately following his confirmation, on January 24, Mel took the oath of office in the vice president's office. With a handful of his staff watching, he swore to uphold the Constitution of his adopted country. Reflecting HUD's recent vintage, he ranked thirteen in the line of presidential succession, though the Constitution he swore to support denied him that opportunity: by Article II, Section 1, as a naturalized citizen he could not be president—the only Bush cabinet member so excluded.

Kitty had returned to Orlando with Andrew and could not get back for the ceremony. A repeat swearing-in ceremony for her and their family occurred in the White House on March 8. After Vice President Cheney administered the oath, President Bush turned to Kitty and asked whether she and Mel would join Laura and him at Camp David the following weekend. Kitty graciously declined, saying they had friends and family visiting in Orlando that weekend. Mel tried to interject: "Honey, I'm sure we can reschedule—" but the president moved on. This incident would become legendary among friends and family, told to gales of laughter. As Kitty says good-naturedly, "I didn't know . . ."[10] Even the president joined in the teasing, asking Mel whether he realized his wife "had turned down an invitation to Camp David from the president of the United States."

In Kitty's telling, the story exemplified Mel's good humor and tolerance of others' mistakes. In Sean Smealey's rendition, it signified how Mel and Kitty differed from other Washington couples. "They were grounded," he said. "They were real people with friends and family obligations to meet, and not that enamored of the Washington power game."

⮞

They called themselves the parachutists. On January 22, the Monday after the inauguration, the seven of them "parachuted" into the executive conference room at HUD. Unlike his counterparts at State and Defense, Mel lacked a retinue of former aides to assist him at HUD, but he moved quickly to assemble a team. As he was a delegator by nature, choosing the right staff was important.

Seated around the table for the 8:30 A.M. meeting were the ever-present Dan Murphy; Terry Couch, Mel's scheduling secretary from Orange County; Phil Musser, who had observed Mel's star power while working for a lobbying group that represented the county; Sean Cassidy, a Hill veteran and housing expert; Matthew Hunter, the Bush-Cheney field coordinator who had latched onto Mel; Oscar Anderson, who was Orange's in-house lobbyist in Tallahassee; and Robert Woodson Jr., a HUD veteran who assisted the Bush-Cheney campaign on housing issues.

In the division of labor, Murphy was chief of staff, as in Orange County. Couch moved up to executive assistant. Musser became deputy chief of staff, traveling with Mel constantly. Anderson, drawing on his lobbying experience, ran the congressional affairs office until an assistant secretary was appointed there. Woodson, who would die in an auto accident two years later, was another deputy chief of staff. Building on his ties to the Bush-Cheney team, Hunter worked as White House liaison, and Cassidy was deployed to the Federal Housing Administration.

Sitting in the conference room, the parachutists pondered what to do. Mel was busy with the confirmation process and not present, so Murphy presided. They quickly decided on two goals. The first was getting the agency staffed. HUD had approximately 9,000 employees, down from 13,000 a few years earlier. About a hundred were Schedule C political appointees; the most critical of these for exercising control of the professional bureaucracy (regarded as strongly Democratic) were the deputy secretary and seven assistant secretaries. The second goal was raising the profile of HUD within the new Republican administration. These objectives were related, as means to ends, because promoting the department with the White House would attract good appointees.

As congressional relations aide Oscar Anderson explained, housing policy traditionally scores low on the Republican agenda. Hundreds if not thousands of Republican policy experts seek jobs at Treasury, Commerce, and especially State and Defense, "but only about a dozen Republican TBs [true believers] do housing policy."[11] The 2000 Bush campaign had nonetheless released three statements on housing policy, authored by Woodson, while the Gore team issued none. By connecting HUD to the GOP political agenda, Mel would capture White House attention and bring good TBs to the department.

His biggest success was luring Alphonso Jackson as deputy secretary and chief operating officer for the department. A.J., as he was known to his friends and associates, was a longtime housing administrator, African American, a former housing-authority chief executive in Dallas, St. Louis, and Washington. More pertinently, he was a backyard neighbor to George W. Bush in Austin, where he was president of American Electric Power–Texas. He and Governor Bush met regularly for lunch, and Jackson had been a senior adviser in the 2000 campaign.

When first George W. and then his father urged the utility executive to join the administration, A.J. had demurred. But Clay Johnson, in charge of presidential personnel, persuaded him to stay in Washington an extra night after the inauguration to talk with Mel. Before leaving his hotel room for dinner with Mel—just the two of them, at Washington's Market

Inn, a popular seafood restaurant—Jackson told his wife not to worry about relocating. "I'm not taking the deputy job at HUD. I want to keep running the utility company."[12]

In fact, the two men clicked personally right away, said Jackson. Mel picked him up before 7:00 P.M., and they were still discussing the deputy job after 9:00. The cabinet nominee kept asking him: "What will it take for you to accept?" Finally, looking at his watch, Jackson said: "What do I need to do to get you to drive me back to my hotel?" Mel deadpanned: "You'll need to take the job." At last Jackson agreed.

Despite differences in personality—Jackson is more deliberate and managerial, Mel more big-picture—the two made a good team, an important feat because cabinet secretaries and their deputies often clash, fighting turf wars. Aided by his long history in public housing, Jackson knew how to operate within HUD. "HUD is a culture, and he knew how to manage it," said Phil Musser.[13] "We," he said, referring to the political staff around Mel, "didn't understand that culture or know how to manage the department. So we relied on Jackson while we promoted the president's agenda." This division of labor worked because the two got along personally, and because Murphy as chief of staff kept Jackson in the loop on what Mel was doing.

As Jackson said of the relationship: "We didn't let them divide us, as often happens in cabinet agencies." By "them" he meant the department's professional staff. "Anytime there was a potential issue between us, we talked about it. We had disagreements but never debates. And no one in the agency knew about our disagreements. Our disagreements stayed behind closed doors."

Other strong hires for the department were John Weicher, a University of Chicago–trained economist with experience in two previous HUD administrations, as assistant secretary for housing, and Roy Bernardi, the first Republican mayor of Syracuse in twenty-four years and a people-person like Mel, as assistant secretary for community planning and development.

During the transition, Mel met with Andrew Cuomo, Clinton's last housing secretary, who recommended he focus on the budget. Press for more Section 8 money, said Cuomo, referring to the rental vouchers that consumed two-thirds of the department's budget—advice the former secretary trumpeted in the media.[14] During his tenure, the son of New York's ex-governor made high-profile tours of Indian reservations, public housing projects, and urban ghettos, to spotlight the nation's housing shortage. According to Martinez staffers, New York State fared well in Cuomo's push for affordable housing—because of his own gubernatorial aspirations, they thought.

The new secretary rejected the negative role model of his predecessors. Cuomo's answer—spending more—was not Republican thinking. Jack Kemp, under Bush 41, had freelanced on urban policy issues and become a thorn in the president's side. Samuel Pierce Jr., the African American HUD secretary whose name Ronald Reagan famously forgot, presided over scandal. And former secretary Henry Cisneros, the great Hispanic hope of the Democratic Party, resigned during the Clinton years after revelations that he paid hush money to a former mistress.

Mel's first task was avoiding scandal. That was the charge given him by the president-elect. As a Hispanic, he felt that responsibility with special force: a scandal on his watch would reflect not just on him but on all Hispanics. He could not run a Miami-style housing agency. As a fiscal conservative, he could not define success as spending more. And not having a constituency with the urban poor or the housing, realtor, or mortgage-banking industries, he would not be their advocate within or against the administration.

To the contrary, having come to Washington without an agenda, he was prepared to dance with the person who brought him to the party: George W. Bush. That was why from the beginning he assigned Deputy Secretary Jackson to run the department, freeing himself for political work assisting the president. And one of their first acts was to ask the department's Senior Executive Service for assistance, telling the SES, in Jackson's words, "We can't do this without your support. We didn't come here thinking that all the answers were on the [administrative level] tenth floor."

One of Mel's first trips as HUD secretary was to Kansas City. As would become standard practice, his staff organized a "Hispanic outreach" event following his official business. Appearing before a Hispanic Chamber of Commerce, speaking *en español* the whole time, Mel earned rave reviews from the predominantly Mexican audience, according to the ever-present Dan Murphy. Soon afterward Murphy accompanied Mel to a White House meeting with Karl Rove, the president's political director.

"Rove was ecstatic," said Murphy. The adviser to the president displayed a Spanish-language newspaper reporting on Mel's talk in Kansas City, under a banner headline that translated as "Bush Keeps His Promises."

That was when the White House began really appreciating Mel, said several of his staffers. He was not just a Hispanic emissary or a housing guy. He could help the administration on a variety of topics. And he had assembled a staff who knew how to work with Rove's Political Affairs Office and Margaret Spellings's Domestic Policy Group. Woodson, Hunter, Musser, and Murphy had all worked with the White House previously; like Mel, they were proactive about helping the administration. Under Mel, HUD would be an asset to Bush rather than a source of scandal.

In eight years under Clinton-Gore, no housing events involved the president. During Mel's tenure, however, the White House "gave" President Bush to HUD numerous times. One was a whole-day affair in Tampa— in electorally important Florida—where Mel and the president pounded nails, sweating in shirtsleeves, as they helped frame a Habitat for Humanity house for a single Puerto Rican mom with several children. At the end of the day, the two handed a welcome mat to the grateful young mother. As Dan Murphy commented, "That photo helped to counter the image of an administration devoted to tax cuts and helping the rich."

But the president's interest in housing policy ran deeper, going back to his governor days. His longtime friend Jackson said that Bush "realized there was a home ownership gap for blacks and Mexican Americans" and that stabilizing neighborhoods by extending home ownership would support his No Child Left Behind education program. "His interest in home ownership came hand in hand with the education initiative in Texas that he was talking about in the [2000] campaign," said Jackson, who would succeed Mel as secretary.

Diane Tomb, Mel's assistant secretary for public affairs, welcomed the connection. "We were pleased to discover that the new president had talked about housing in the 2000 campaign."[15] Mel began advancing minority home ownership in his second month in office. Citing statistics showing that 72 percent of white households owned a home, compared to 45 to 46 percent of African Americans and about 50 percent of Asian Americans, he told the *Washington Post*: "I'm not sure we can improve a whole lot on that 72 percent, but in that 45 to 46 percent, we darn sure can do better."[16]

It was an old idea, going back to Otto von Bismarck's social initiatives in nineteenth-century Germany. Home ownership is a conservatizing force, as Bismarck recognized. Since it gives potentially disruptive groups a stake in society, home ownership (properly understood) is appropriate policy for a conservative Republican administration. Oversimplified, four approaches define housing reform. One is public housing—the construction approach, which officially ended in the Reagan years. A second is rental assistance, an alternative that President Richard Nixon promoted as a pro-market because voucher recipients rent from private landlords at market rates. A third is affordable housing, encouraged through tax incentives and regulatory rollbacks. Fourth is extending home ownership, promoted through consumer education, down-payment assistance, and real estate settlement reform.

Rental assistance, known as Section 8, posed a dilemma for the GOP administration. Though Republican in origin and not officially an entitlement program, it grew like one. Rental vouchers respond to market forces: as rents increase, the cost of rental assistance rises. HUD needed to spend more on Section 8 each year just to stay in place, without benefiting additional families. Of the department's $32 billion budget, the program consumed $16 billion when Mel arrived, growing to $18 billion during his tenure. That increase was scarcely evident from press accounts, however, in part because of the new secretary's focus on expanding minority home ownership.

It was an ideal cause for Mel. Home ownership and the American Dream go hand in hand, both as aspiration and as reality. As aspiration, home ownership equates with making it in America—overcoming immigrant origins, joining the mainstream, achieving a better life for oneself and one's children. As reality, home ownership is an American success story: more Americans own their own home than do citizens in any other country. But Mel wanted to spotlight the cracks in the Dream—namely, the ownership gap between whites and minorities.

And who could advance this cause better than someone who escaped from Castro's Cuba at fifteen, whose parents bought their first home with an FHA-backed mortgage, who appreciated that buying a home was more than a financial transaction, more than gaining a roof overhead? As he knew from his parents' experience, buying a house meant putting down roots. "It meant this is our new country. We are going to stay here."

No previous HUD secretary had such credentials. As happened during his Orange County campaign, he sometimes complained about speechwriters overplaying his personal story. "We would tell him, 'No, you can't leave that out. People want to hear that. It's your cachet,'" said Phil Musser, his deputy chief of staff. Because of Mel's story, the department also made liberal use of the American Dream concept. Said Diane Tomb, the department's publicist, "We developed the theme with him in mind."

On June 7, 2002, Martinez and Jackson traveled with the president to Atlanta for a speech on housing at St. Paul AME Church. During the flight on Air Force One, the president summoned them to his onboard office to say he was announcing a new goal: 5.5 million new minority homeowners by 2010. They drank sodas and talked with him about it. When they returned to their seats, Mel said to Jackson, "A.J., how are we going to do it?" Jackson responded: "I don't know, but if the president summons us like that, we'd better make it happen."

To execute the president's directive, the department took several initiatives: organizing a public-private partnership with housing stakeholders, creating a homeownership month, launching a bilingual informational bus tour of the nation, and proposing new regulatory and funding measures to Congress.

The stakeholder meeting, held on October 15, 2003, at George Washington University, included mortgage giants Fannie Mae and Freddie Mac, major banks, mortgage companies, community groups, and faith-based organizations. President Bush spoke, calling on the assembled groups to reduce the barriers to homeownership faced by minority families. As an outgrowth, HUD created the Blueprint for the American Dream Partnership to harness federal resources with those of the housing industry to accomplish the president's goal. The banks and other lenders agreed to offer mortgages with special terms that Fannie Mae and Freddie Mac would buy and that several mortgage insurance companies would insure.

To frame the initiative, HUD working with the White House created a housing month by presidential proclamation. Previously there had been a housing *week* in June, but the department needed more time for its publicity campaign, Diane Tomb explained. To help reach first-time home buyers, she and Phil Musser conceived the idea of an "American Dream bus"— a Greyhound-type coach with "American Dream Express" emblazoned on its side. The bus traveled to almost forty states, stopping at ethnic affairs, Indian reservations, and sporting events to provide bilingual consumer education on finding affordable housing, getting down-payment assistance, securing credit, and managing the real estate closing process.

In addition to the public-private partnership with Fannie Mae and Freddie Mac, the administration proposed a limited program for down-payment assistance. President Bush requested $200 million in his 2002 budget to help low-income families become homeowners. Unveiled at a news conference at which Mel stood with two low-income black families from Maryland, this American Dream program would help 130,000 first-time home buyers make down payments. For every dollar provided by a third party, the program would provide three dollars, up to $1,500 per family.

This "gift" was not greeted with open arms, however. Housing advocates noted it was not new money. Funding would come from an existing $1.8 billion Home Investment Partnership program, which already allowed states and local governments to use money for down-payment assistance. Some Republican lawmakers as well as the U.S. Conference of Mayors complained that it was an unfunded mandate that obliged them to drain money for down-payment help from the more flexible HIP funding, which could be used for a variety of other services, from building and renovating low-income apartments to providing rental assistance.

"It's worse than the traditional unfunded mandate—it's an Indian giver's mandate," said John T. McEvoy, executive director of the National Council of State Housing Agencies. "It takes money that you already have and violates the premise on which you were given it. It says, 'We're now going to tell you how to use money that up until now has been for your own use and your own discretion.'"[17]

Despite press reports that the initiative was "dead on arrival" in Congress, it did win lawmakers' approval, though not easily or quickly. Bush requested $200 million annually for the initiative, but received only $50 million from Congress in 2002 and $75 million in 2003. In December 2003, only weeks after Mel resigned to run for the Senate, Congress authorized the full $200 million for 2004. President Bush signed the legislation in a ceremony at HUD with Mel and then acting secretary Jackson present.

In fact, minority homeownership did improve significantly. Between 2002 and 2006, an additional 2.6 million minority families purchased homes; for the first time, a majority of minority Americans owned their own home. Of course, this gain occurred in a booming real estate market abetted by easy credit and low interest rates. During the Clinton years, minority homeownership also rose. Still, HUD Secretary Jackson described the rise in minority homeownership during Mel's tenure as "a proud legacy that no one can take away from him."

In fact, it *was* taken away, a victim of the Great Recession of 2008. According to a 2009 report issued by the Pew Hispanic Center, the gains made in homeownership by African Americans and native-born Latinos fell more sharply in the economic downturn than those of whites.[18] The Pew report found that the gains that minority groups achieved from 1995 to 2004 were disproportionately tied to relaxed lending standards and subprime loans. After peaking at 69 percent in 2004, the rate of homeownership for all American households declined to 67.8 percent in 2008. For African Americans, the rate fell to 47.5 percent in 2008 from 49.4 percent in 2004.

Pew reported that blacks and Hispanics were more than twice as likely to have subprime mortgages as white homeowners, even among borrowers with comparable incomes. These loans, which typically require little or no down payment and are meant for borrowers with low credit scores, made homeownership possible for many black and Hispanic families during the boom years, but also led to high rates of foreclosure. There were dangers, it seemed, in tying the American Dream to homeownership.

◁────▷

The new secretary could also be tough.

In his first year, he marched to Capitol Hill to defend zeroing out the Public Housing Drug Elimination Program, which cost $309 million. It was essentially a discretionary grant program with an appealing name—the funds could be used for almost anything, making the nominal drug-elimination program popular with housing agencies and Congress. As a cue to Mel's team at HUD, Fox News profiled the program as a classic example of WFA—waste, fraud, and abuse. In one case noted by Fox's Bill O'Reilly, funds were used for "god and goddess" counseling, a so-called creative wellness program for public housing tenants. Appearing before Congress armed with a poster board filled with headlines from articles detailing spending abuses in the program, Mel successfully defended the program's elimination.

In his second year, he again showed his conservative colors by attacking the Hope VI program, which leveraged private capital to revitalize public housing properties. Drawing upon an internal performance-outcome review, he told a congressional hearing the program had no quantifiable output.[19] One liberal Democrat, Congresswoman Stephanie Jones, an African American from Cleveland, became almost apoplectic, stopping just short of swearing at the housing secretary. In fairness, the $20 billion backlog in public housing made any housing program worthwhile for some members of Congress. Nonetheless, liberal congressman Barney Frank, the ranking member of the committee, rebuked her.

Yet Mel held no grudge against Jones. Said his aide Matthew Hunter: "I asked whether he wanted to take the American Dream bus to her district after her outburst at him, and he said, why not." It was an example of what Sean Smealey, his shepherd during the confirmation process, saw in Mel from the start. "He's conservative," said Smealey, "just as he's devoutly religious and Catholic. But he's not awash in it. You don't feel like he's proselytizing all the time." Or as others commented, he was easy to disagree with. It was the same temperament observed by his law partners: Mel was a good negotiator because he didn't put other people's hackles up.

In his appearances before Congress, Mel proved a quick study. Though initially unfamiliar with HUD programs, he defended the HUD budget with ease. John Weicher, the assistant secretary for housing who had served under two previous HUD secretaries, was impressed. "I sat with him when he testified on the HUD budget, but he never needed my assistance."

Phil Musser remarked similarly on Mel's verbal skill. "You could brief him on something before we went to the Hill, and, getting out of the car, a reporter would ask him a question. He could always explain things in simple and uncomplicated terms." Another deputy, Oscar Anderson, once asked him how he could do this. Mel said it came from being a trial attorney, where the parties in a lawsuit could ask the court reporter to read things back from the record. "You had to speak knowing that your remarks might be read back," said the secretary.

⟷

Another example of Mel getting tough was RESPA reform. HUD has regulatory and enforcement power under the federal law that governs much of the home-sale process—the Real Estate Settlement Procedures Act. Every settlement sheet used in a closing was developed by the department. The "good faith estimates" of fees and closing costs that lenders give home buyers early in the mortgage process are mandated by RESPA. So too are the antikickback rules that prohibit title companies or lenders from slipping money under the table to a realty agent for referring business to them.

When Mel arrived, HUD had not taken a major enforcement action against a large lender or title firm in nearly a decade, "leading many in the real estate industry to return to the free-flowing kickbacks that caused Congress to pass RESPA back in 1974," wrote real estate columnist Kenneth Harney.[20] Martinez responded by tripling the RESPA enforcement staff, from fourteen investigators to forty-five, and hiring outside specialists including former FBI agents to assist in investigating violations of antimarkup and antikickback regulations.

He also promoted an overhaul of the Real Estate Settlement Procedures Act itself. RESPA reform was part of the struggle to promote minority homeownership. As Mel stated in congressional testimony, "The mortgage finance process and the cost of closing are major impediments to homeownership."[21] Simplifying the process and reducing up-front closing fees would enable thousands more families to buy homes. But RESPA reform proved highly controversial. As Phil Musser explained, "We were moving on two parallel tracks." On one track, HUD was "moving with an industrywide train" to expand minority homeownership. On the other track the realtors, title companies, and mortgage brokers all opposed reforming RESPA. "It was an indication that all was not well in Camelot."

The reform effort had multiple origins. One was Mel's personal experience. On coming to HUD he bought a house in McLean, Virginia, his first home purchase in twenty years. That experience proved daunting, with unexpected closing costs and forbidding legal documents. He said about the papers presented at his closing, "If you are a lawyer, you can get through it. But John Q. Public doesn't have a shot at understanding what they are doing."[22]

Another source was internal staff work. There had not been a RESPA review in ten years, and assistant secretary John Weicher, who promoted a similar reform under Bush 41 only to be rebuffed by the White House, was eager to try again. Soon after his appointment in 2001, the housing economist briefed the new secretary on the issue, and Mel said something like, "I see." Said Weicher: "I figured that was the last we'd hear of that issue."[23] But that was before Mel took up the cause of minority homeownership, and before he realized the impact of unexpected settlement costs on first-time home buyers.

The trigger event was a decision by the 11th Circuit U.S. Court of Appeals, shortly after the Bush administration took office, that called into question the legality of "yield spread premiums," or payments to mortgage brokers from lenders based on the interest rates of individual loans. The court's decision ran counter to HUD's view that such payments were legitimate if they went for a real service to consumers, such as lowering upfront settlement costs. Formulating a response presented an opportunity to devise new rules governing the settlement process.

RESPA is complicated, and so was the attempted reform. Essentially, HUD proposed two rule changes, both aimed at simplifying the mortgage closing process and reducing settlement costs to consumers. The first was to require a Good Faith Estimate settlement disclosure—to guard against predatory lending practices and provide consumers with full disclosure about the various fees charged in the mortgage lending process. The second allowed for the packaging of settlement services and mortgages—to increase competition among settlement service providers and enable consumers to compare one package with another.

Under the proposals, consumers would get guaranteed interest rate quotes packaged with fixed closing costs when they applied for a loan. This would enable them to "shop" the package with competing lenders, potentially bidding down prices. The theory was that lenders eager for business would put pressure on appraisers, title agents, and others to deliver services for less. With a package system, lenders could press for lower prices more effectively than consumers could under the piecemeal system.[24]

HUD's proposals went into the Federal Register on July 29, 2002. Receiving an avalanche of comments, the department extended the public comment period for the rule from the usual sixty days to ninety. They asked for comment on thirty specific questions to ensure that all major issues were fully considered. By the end of the period, on October 29, 2002, they had received a record number of comments, nearly 43,000. Of these, about 400 were substantive responses, coming from a broad range of industry, consumer, and government representatives. At that point the department could submit a final rule to the Office of Management and Budget, revise their proposed rule, or solicit more input. After internal debate, HUD officials decided on this last course, conducting more than sixty meetings with interested groups and parties over eighteen weeks. Mel found the slow pace of consultation under Weicher frustrating and wanted to move more quickly.

The proposal to create a legal "safe harbor" for the packaging of closing costs excited the most controversy. Martinez maintained from analysis done at HUD that the average home mortgage settlement bill would decrease by almost $1,000 under the packaging plan. Realtors, title companies, appraisers, and mortgage brokers opposed the idea, fearing the savings to consumers would come from them. The proposed rule, which was an option, not a requirement, enabled any party—whether a title company, mortgage broker, or lender—to assemble the package. But the opponents worried that mortgage bankers, being more powerful, would take the lead in packaging and pressure them to accept lower fees. Consistent with those fears, mortgage bankers initially supported the option. So did all the major consumer groups—the Consumer Federation of America, AARP, Consumers Union, and the National Consumer Law Center.

Yet the opponents had powerful allies in Congress. The most controversial was Senator Richard Shelby (R-Ala.), chairman of the Senate Banking, Housing, and Urban Affairs committee, who called Martinez's reform plan "significantly damaging to small business." Along with chairing the banking committee, Shelby was board chairman of the Tuscaloosa Title Company back home in Alabama. His investment in the company was between $1 million and $5 million and his earnings between $115,000 and $1,050,000 a year, from his federal financial filing at the time.[25]

In the House of Representatives, the reform proposal's chief opponent was Representative Donald Manzullo (R-Ill.), chairman of the House Small Business Committee, who was a real estate settlement attorney before coming to Congress. In his previous campaign he received a $7,000 contribution from the American Title Association, the title industry's principal lobbyist on Capitol Hill. According to real estate columnist Kenneth Harney, Manzullo pledged to introduce legislation to kill the settlement-cost reform if it was adopted.

At HUD, Frank Jimenez became chief of staff following the departure of Murphy, who left for a government-relations law practice to help support his growing family. Jimenez was a Yale-educated attorney, plucked from the staff of Governor Jeb Bush just as the fight over RESPA got under way. In his view, the fight revealed the barriers to minority homeownership. "There was no win-win-win solution," he said. "To get real reform, someone had to lose."[26] In the end, the reform advocates would lose, though not without concerted effort.

Mel refused to cave to congressional and industry pressure on the issue. In appearing before the Senate Banking Committee, on March 20, 2003, he went toe to toe with the chairman, Shelby, a Democrat turned Republican who repeatedly and deceptively called Martinez his "good friend." Following the secretary's prepared testimony, the courtly southerner asked him, "How do you explain the unprecedented controversy surrounding your proposed rule?" Mel responded: "I would say, Mr. Chairman, that if it was easy and uncontroversial, it would have been done a long time ago. The fact that it does shake up the marketplace does not deprive the proposal of merit."[27]

In their back-and-forth, Shelby defended a piecemeal approach, so consumers would know the separate cost of title work, appraisal, and so forth. While not opposing such disclosure, Mel argued it was far more important to know the total closing cost. That was what major consumer groups advocated, he said. By analogy, when consumers buy a new car, they don't care what the transmission costs; they want to know the bottom line, so they can compare competing makes and models. Likewise, "If you were to go purchase a home and you knew your closing settlement costs were going to be $1,500, and that was the bottom line, [isn't] that more important than knowing how much the title insurance was, how much the bug inspector cost?"

At the end of the hearing, Shelby implored Mel to delay submitting a final rule until more comment could be heard from business. The secretary reminded him that 43,000 comments had already been received, a HUD record. "I am reluctant to just delay for the sake of delay," he told the committee, adding, "It bothers me greatly, frankly, to have groups that we have been closely working with to try to accommodate their concerns continue to act as if nothing was being done to help them."

On RESPA, Mel had returned to his populist roots, to his experience as a personal injury attorney, to defending the little guy. It was reminiscent of his stand against developers on the issue of school overcrowding in Orange County. As he told the banking committee, he did not tackle the issue because it was fun—it clearly wasn't. He did so out of a "desire to make a difference, to do something right to help people." It aroused his passion.

The experience "showed why Mel was a good choice for HUD, and why he was different from other cabinet secretaries," said Ron Kaufman, a close Washington observer who managed George H. W. Bush's 1996 presidential campaign.[28] Kaufman explained from his experience as a presidential adviser that in selecting a cabinet member you want to "keep the family happy," referring to the family of interests surrounding that department. "But if you make them too happy, you lose your effectiveness." The department secretary "goes native" and can no longer be trusted by the administration, he added.

And the White House supported Mel on the real estate closing issue. In June 2002 the administration released a white paper titled *A Home of Your Own: Expanding Opportunities for All Americans* calling for RESPA reform. This policy statement meshed with the rule changes under way at HUD. It said that current policy was ambiguous about when fee disclosure was required and did not "promote competition so that cost savings can be realized."

The language was a victory for Mel and his staff, who kept the White House domestic policy staff apprised of their work on RESPA. They were aided by the president's support for extending minority homeownership, which he mentioned in his 2002 State of the Union address, and his interest in the concept of an "ownership society," a term that was percolating through the White House at the time. Karen Hughes, the president's communications director, was particularly taken by this concept, and she and Mel had many simpatico conversations about their mutual interest in faith-based initiatives, minority homeownership, and compassionate conservatism.

As events unfolded, the Mortgage Bankers Association eventually changed its position. It did so after smaller mortgage bankers, fearing that in smaller markets the large realty firms would assemble packages and dictate prices to them, pressed the MBA to change its stance on packaging. Kurt Pfotenhauer, the MBA's chief lobbyist, made an appointment with Jimenez to deliver the bad news. "It was not a happy meeting," Jimenez recalled. "We were both civil and polite, but there was little need for discussion. I thanked him for his time and that was it."

Sean Cassidy, who worked under Weicher, said the lesson was that "to do reform, you had to do it right and do it quickly."[29] By moving slowly, they enabled their opponents to coalesce against them. Yet Jimenez, the chief of staff, maintains that reform was still possible after the mortgage bankers reversed their position. HUD submitted a final rule to OMB in mid-December 2003, just as Martinez was leaving the department to run for the Senate. They did so with White House support, yet knowing that Congress could kill the rule.

In the end, the reform became a casualty of Mel's resignation. Alphonso Jackson did not have Mel's commitment to the cause, and the stakes proved far higher for him. When President Bush nominated him to replace Martinez, Senator Shelby threatened to block his confirmation unless the rule was withdrawn. Jackson complied, generating hard feelings in the transition between secretaries. He rubbed several of Mel's staff the wrong way by declaring, in withdrawing the rule, that industry groups had insufficient time to respond.[30]

A.J.'s tenure at HUD would end badly, with him resigning in late May of 2008 amid a criminal investigation of alleged favoritism in awarding HUD contracts.[31] His own words prompted the initial investigation: in 2006 he stated in a speech that he revoked a HUD contract with a vendor who said he did not like President Bush. (He later claimed he made up the story.) At his resignation, the FBI was investigating charges of cronyism in awarding contracts—precisely the kind of bad news that President Bush had told his first housing secretary he wanted to avoid at the agency. But these problems did not occur on Mel's watch, attesting to his ethical compass and his abundance of caution not to commit errors that reflected unfavorably upon other Hispanics.

———

Mel enjoyed a special relationship with President Bush. After Kitty declined the president's first invitation to Camp David, they received several more. On their first visit to the Maryland retreat, the president wanted to practice with Mel before throwing the first pitch to open the baseball season. In turn, Mel wanted to practice before catching for the president, so he and his aide Oscar Anderson tossed a baseball back and forth on the plaza atop the HUD building. Mel and Kitty also celebrated her birthday at the White House, and they spent a weekend at the president's ranch in Crawford, Texas, something not all cabinet couples get to do.

For Mel these presidential invitations were a power boost—a highly public demonstration of his close relationship with the president—in a town in which power is the coin of the realm and the reputation for power is indistinguishable from power itself. As Mel said in an interview, "In

Washington it all comes down to your relationship with the guy down Pennsylvania Avenue. That's what gives you power."[32] Oscar Anderson, a newcomer to Washington, explained how Mel's stature affected him. "In Washington you have all these Schedule C political appointees climbing over one another, looking for their next job. They left me alone, knowing I was one of Mel's guys."

The secretary's close relationship with George W. also stemmed from their kindred personalities. They are both jocular men, comfortable in their own skins. Said Ron Kaufman, the Bush 41 political affairs director, "Mel is the kind of guy you'd like to be with playing cards in the backyard, smoking a cigar and swapping stories. He has a big personality, and the president collects personalities, especially men." The president also liked Mel because of his manifest values, said Kaufman. "You only have to know Mel for twenty-nine seconds before you know about Kitty and his children. He projects the same family values as the president."

The two men shared a philosophy of personal responsibility and voluntarism, a philosophy reinforced by their religious faith, as evident in their mutual support of Habit for Humanity. The president participated with Mel and Kitty on Habitat projects in Tampa and Waco in 2001; Kitty and Alma Powell, the wife of Secretary of State Colin Powell, got their fellow cabinet wives to work on a Habitat project; and the parent organization, Habitat for Humanity International, was part of the Blueprint for the American Dream public-private partnership to address minority homeownership. HUD's involvement with Habitat was facilitated by the housing agency's Office of Faith-Based Initiatives, created under Mel, which participated in numerous programs at the department.

No one could seriously think that individual acts of voluntarism, as evident in Habitat projects, could make an appreciable dent in America's $20 billion housing shortage. For Mel and Kitty, such acts signified what individuals owe their fellow man. As public policy, stimulated by the president's directive to encourage faith-based initiatives, the push for voluntarism is more questionable. Kevin Phillips, author of a 2004 book on the Bush "dynasty," described these efforts in both Bush administrations as cynical attempts to curry favor with white evangelical Christians. University of Pennsylvania professor John DiIulio, the first director of the younger Bush's Office of Faith-Based Initiatives, seemingly agreed. He complained, in resigning his post, that everything in the administration, "and I mean everything," was "being run by the political arm."[33]

Mel also gained favor by collecting frequent flyer miles for the administration. At his resignation Barney Frank, the ranking Democrat on the House committee overseeing HUD, called him "a hands-off secretary."[34] The description was apt—to a point. Martinez did rely upon Deputy Secretary Jackson to run the department while he concentrated on broader issues and worked to assist the White House. The *National Journal,* in a report card on Bush's first cabinet, gave Martinez a C on policy and an A for carrying out the president's agenda.

All of which meant frequent flying for the housing secretary, his six-feet-three frame crammed into a coach seat when first class was not available on short notice. He flew with the president seven times on Air Force One and was a frequent stand-in for Bush at political fund-raisers, bringing in more political dollars for the president and his party than any other cabinet member, according to records kept by his staff. Between March 27, 2002, and September 30, 2003, he traveled to Florida twelve times on government business, in addition to making seven nonbusiness trips to the state in 2001. He visited Miami five times; Orlando, Tampa, and Tallahassee twice each; and St. Augustine once. He made additional trips to Miami, Orlando, Sarasota, and Tampa for which the costs were split between the government and Republican groups. Besides traveling to Florida, he visited New York eight times, followed by California (five), North Carolina (four), Arizona, Illinois, and Ohio (three each), and Texas (once).[35]

Following Mel's resignation to run for the Senate, the *Post* suggested he trekked to Florida at taxpayer expense so many times to raise his profile with Florida voters. Perhaps. But his trips to Florida, on which he frequently spoke to Cuban American and Hispanic groups, also benefited the president and the GOP. He often appeared on the road with Bush, who repeatedly told his Peter Pan story about coming to America as an unaccompanied teenager. "I love his story—it's a story of America," the president said at an Orlando event in November 2003.[36]

One special trip came soon after 9/11. Airports were not yet fully opened, so Mel and his travel staff received authorization to fly by military aircraft. When they arrived at Andrews Air Force Base, the colonel in charge said there was a problem with their plane, an executive jet. After a delay, he asked whether they would mind flying in a 747 from the Air Force One fleet. So they did, five of them in the cavernous aircraft, which Phil Musser dubbed Air Force 13 in reference to Mel's place in the line of presidential succession.

Many of Mel's trips involved speeches to Hispanic groups. As Matthew Hunter said, the staff always sought opportunities for "Hispanic outreach." It was here especially that Mel's evolution as a politician and public speaker was evident. He would ignite crowds whether they were Cuban, Mexican American, or Puerto Rican, demonstrating his capacity to bridge differences of nationality in describing his immigrant experience. His staff tell of audience members wanting to touch him after an electrifying bilingual speech, and of older Hispanic women swooning over him. Travel aide Phil Musser began calling him L.J. for Latin Jesus.

Further evidencing his value for the Republican administration, he would go on Univision and Telemundo after a State of the Union address to praise the president's message in Spanish. Diane Tomb, HUD's publicist, marveled at his coverage in the local and national Latino media, noting that he always gave Spanish-language reporters equal time, something many politicians fail to do. "Watching him," she said, "I became aware of how untapped the Hispanic audience was. There was no one on the Democratic side doing what he did—no Latino who could speak to such a variety of issues."

His willingness to serve the administration gave rise to an irony. He had come to the cabinet in a special way: as a surprise choice, as someone without cabinet aspirations, as a newcomer to national politics without an agenda for his self-advancement in Washington. Yet in selflessly serving the administration, he created a groundswell of interest in his own political future, a groundswell aided by the electoral significance of Florida and the growing importance of the Hispanic vote.

During his tenure as county chairman, his aides speculated about him running for governor after serving two terms in the county post. His interest in the governor's job was whetted by his run for lieutenant governor with his college friend Ken Connor in 1994. Even with his cabinet service, a bid for governor still made sense for personal and family reasons. He complained of the cold in Washington. His disliked the posturing and self-promotion there; they conflicted with his humble nature. And above all, he missed his extended family in Orlando.

In an interview, he said he always imagined that after one term as HUD secretary he would return to Orlando, make some money, have a Washington presence, but regain his private life. His mother, brother, and sister-in-law all spoke of how they missed Mel and Kitty. Though his Orlando family visited him frequently in Washington, and though Ralph and his mother talked with him many times a day, the absence of Mel and Kitty created a hole in their family life, all reported.

Mel, however, was getting continual pressure from Karl Rove and others to consider running for the Senate. Republicans needed a strong candidate to oppose incumbent Bob Graham in 2004. In 2003, Graham was a declared Democratic candidate for president. As the chairman and later ranking member of the Senate Intelligence Committee, he was well versed on matters related to the war in Iraq, the looming issue in the coming presidential race, and he was an outspoken critic of the administration's war policy and the flawed intelligence underlying it. Many political analysts thought Graham would make a good vice presidential candidate, especially considering the electoral importance of Florida, where he was a proven vote getter, though no candidate starts out running for vice president. But prior to October 2003, Graham had not said whether he would seek reelection to the Senate in 2004.

Ron Kaufman, a veteran of candidate recruitment, had talked with Mel about the Senate race. From the first time he saw Mel in action as county chairman, at a time when Kaufman's firm was lobbying for the county, he knew the Cuban American had a special talent. He maintained that Mel possessed two important qualities that political candidates often lack in combination: the "retail ability" to sell himself and the "wholesale ability" to talk convincingly about public policies. As county chairman he also had the third important requirement: ambition for higher office. Kaufman worried, however, whether Mel had a burning desire to serve in the Senate. "I told him, don't do it if you're not really committed."

On June 13, 2003, Mel announced he would not run against Bob Graham for the Senate. Instead, he would serve through 2004 and then consider whether to run for governor when Jeb Bush's tenure ended in 2006. His decision cleared the way for former congressman Bill McCollum, who was defeated in a Senate bid in 2000, to pursue the GOP nomination. Mel would concentrate on helping the president and would put his own electoral plans on hold.

8

CANDIDATE

Secretary Martinez was in Russia in late October 2003 when he received a hurried phone call from Matt Schlapp, White House director of political affairs.[1] The housing secretary had flown to St. Petersburg following a bilateral Camp David summit between President Bush and Russian president Vladimir Putin. Little progress occurred on the key issue of nuclear arms reduction at the September 27 summit. To suggest progress on other fronts, the White House dispatched Martinez to confer with his Russian counterpart, Nicolay Koshman, chairman of the State Committee on Construction, on affordable housing and urban reinvestment strategies.

Schlapp's call followed an earlier conversation between Secretary Martinez and Pennsylvania senator Rick Santorum, a member of the Senate Republican Campaign Committee. As a favor to his college friend Ken Connor, Mel had arranged a lunch meeting between Connor and Santorum, both ardent abortion foes. Connor had just stepped down as head of the Family Research Council, an antiabortion group. Sitting in the Senate Dining Room on the day the secretary left for Russia, the three briefly discussed whether Florida senator Bob Graham would seek reelection. Martinez said he would and Connor predicted he would not.

Santorum had been urging Mel to run for the seat, but Mel had always demurred. In their conversation that day, the Pennsylvania senator asked whether he would consider running if Graham did not. Mel casually replied, "Well, sure, I would consider it. If he didn't run, it would be a whole different scenario."[2] When, later that same day, Graham announced he would seek the presidency rather than reelection, Santorum hurriedly phoned Schlapp, the White House political director, whose job included recruiting GOP candidates for congressional and Senate races.

Schlapp and other White House officials had talked with Mel numerous times about his future plans. It was a natural conversation with a cabinet secretary, said Schlapp; most high-level appointees begin considering their options after two years in office. It was especially appropriate in Mel's case because of the perception, widely held among party leaders, "that he would be a great standard-bearer for them." That's why he wanted to reach Mel right away after hearing from Santorum.

Tracking down the secretary in St. Petersburg, Schlapp first spoke to an aide, who said Mel's answer was still the same: "No, no, no." But when he got Mel on the line, he got a different response. Upon learning of Graham's announcement, Mel expressed genuine interest in running, saying he would seriously consider it. Feeling successful, the political director said, "Great. When will you get back to Washington? Let's talk again then." He added: "I know you'll need to talk to Kitty."

Walking into the dining room of his St. Petersburg hotel, Mel's head spun with the possibilities. Yes, it was late to join the race. Seven GOP candidates already sought the nomination. They were well advanced in their fund-raising. They had snatched up most of the state's top Republican campaign people. He would be giving up a cabinet seat to run. And he and Kitty had just moved into a new house with a pool in Virginia; they had just refinished the floors, for goodness' sake.

But it was a chance to become the nation's first Cuban American senator. Before the 2004 election, which also sent Mexican American Ken Salazar and Barack Obama to the Senate, the body had only three members of ethnic minorities: the two senators from Hawaii and Ben Nighthorse Campbell, an American Indian from Colorado. No Hispanic had served in that body for twenty-seven years. Nationwide, there were 6,000 elected or appointed Hispanic officials, mostly on local school boards. Although Hispanics numbered 13 percent of the population—the nation's largest minority—they could claim only one Hispanic governor (New Mexico's Bill Richardson), one Hispanic cabinet member (Mel), and twenty-four Hispanic members of the House, or less than 6 percent.

Getting elected to the Senate would give voice to Cuban Americans in particular and Hispanics in general. It would also help the GOP attract Latino voters, showing that the party was open to Hispanics, as Mel sought to do in his public appearances as HUD secretary. In 2000, President Bush won approximately 35 percent of the Hispanic vote nationwide. His 2004 campaign hoped to raise that figure to 40 percent to ensure his reelection. Mel could help in Florida, especially if he was a candidate.

It was a defining moment. To run would advance Mel one giant step further from *homo civicus*, private citizen, to *homo politicus*, political man.

Back from Russia and wanting another opinion from someone he trusted, he turned to his brother. Reaching Ralph at his office at 7:30 on a Sunday evening, Mel asked what he thought. Ralph, as he probably expected, implored him to seize the opportunity.

"Mel, this is your chance," his brother said. "You've got to do it. Think of the opportunity. You can vote on Supreme Court justices and influence Cuba policy. You would be the first Cuban American senator."[3]

"Yes," Mel said, "but it means spending thirteen months flying in a small plane between Key West and Pensacola." Mel was no fan of traveling in small planes or of being away from his wife and family. And he did not like missing meals, as would happen in the whirlwind of campaigning. As his aides knew, he grew cranky when he didn't eat.

"Do you think the generals in Iraq like being there?" Ralph responded. "Mel, this is your destiny. You have a place in history." Besides, he added, "You're probably the only Republican who can win."

In the end, Kitty's counsel was decisive. After all, she was the keeper of the flame; some said she *was* the flame. He told her, "I'm not deciding anything until I know what you want me to do." They agonized over the decision for a week. Then she awoke at four o'clock on a Saturday morning and made a list of pros and cons on a legal pad as Mel slept. When he arose at six she told him, "I've figured it out. You've got to run." They talked about it for the remainder of a cold, rainy November morning. He reached no firm decision, but the way was cleared: Kitty was in favor.

An unusual series of events followed. Two days later, his good friend and fellow Peter Panner Cesar Calvet hosted a fund-raiser for U.S. Senate candidate Bill McCollum. Loved by Republicans and loathed by Democrats for his role as a House manager in the impeachment trial of President Clinton, McCollum had run for Senate in 2000, losing to Democrat Bill Nelson. Like a fish out of water, the ten-term former congressman yearned to return to Washington. For the previous year he had traveled the fried chicken and mashed potatoes circuit, meeting with party leaders and raising money for another Senate run. Ralph had already sent checks from his wife and him for the Calvet fund-raiser. Mel suggested they not attend, however.

Three days later, November 13, President Bush came to Orlando for a GOP fund-raiser at Walt Disney World's Grand Floridian Hotel. As typically occurred when the president traveled to Florida, Mel appeared with him at the $2,000-a-plate affair. Naturally, Bill McCollum attended too. So did Congresswoman Katherine Harris, the controversial former Florida secretary of state; she stood a few feet from Ralph as the president spoke. Harris had contemplated running for the Senate in 2000, the year McCollum won the nomination, but party leaders coaxed her into a safe House run instead. At the president's visit, she was publicly flirting with joining the Senate contest.

In his onstage remarks, the president said in his Texas drawl, "Mel. He's done a superb job in my government. . . . I love his story—it's the story of America." He spoke Mel's name twenty-odd times, according to persons present, while giving a bare mention to Bill McCollum and Katherine Harris.[4] In Ralph's opinion, the president was not taking sides in the nascent Senate race; he was just that enamored of Mel and loved talking about his story. Knowing of Senator Graham's announcement, people at the event kept approaching Mel, encouraging him to run. McCollum could hardly have failed to notice. Marcos Marchena, a close friend and supporter of Mel's who had already written a check to McCollum, said to Ralph that night, "People are saying Mel is going to run for Senate. That's not possible, is it?" Grinning, Ralph responded, "Well, maybe."[5]

In the following days McCollum asked several of Mel's Cuban confidants about his plans.[6] Because Mel had not discussed his plans beyond his family, and because the federal Hatch Act prevented him from campaigning while serving at HUD, his Cuban friends were in the dark. So McCollum could not get confirmation. Though Mel resigned from HUD on December 9, 2003, he did not file paperwork to run for the Senate (enabling him to fund-raise) until January 5, 2004. Interestingly, in his last two months at HUD, he placed more than 170 phone calls to Florida on his government cell phone, suggesting a flurry of communication.[7]

In the 2004 Senate race, we can see the power of Mel's refugee story and how his political strategists exploited that story in his campaign. We also have an opportunity to assess whether he conducted a "mean" campaign, whether in that connection he relied too much on staff, and how his political views had changed since his arrival in Washington. As well, we see how his political career continued to benefit from the rising tide of Hispanic political influence.

In starting late, Mel's senatorial campaign faced several obstacles. His responses shaped the character of his campaign.

One challenge was finding a top-notch staff in a presidential election year, running against seven Republican contenders, two of whom would mount formidable campaigns. Mel (through Ralph) first turned to John Sowinski and Tre' Evers, who had run his campaign for county chairman in 1988. They had also worked in Bill McCollum's 2000 Senate campaign and, because of other business, were reluctant to mount another Senate bid. Sowinski at first declined, offering to recruit someone else as the campaign's general consultant. When Mel called and asked him directly, however, he could not say no. (Afterwards, McCollum called Sowinski to ask whether the rumor that he was joining Mel's campaign was true, and Sowinski confirmed that it was, reminding his former client that Mel was an old friend and a fellow congregant at St. James.)

As Sowinski explained, they did not follow the usual script in getting started.[8] Normally, a candidate hires a general consultant, then a few other people, and after that the campaign team gradually expands, giving the staff time to learn their roles and develop working relationships with one another. Owing to Mel's late start, that didn't happen; the team was assembled all at once. The result was a disorganized campaign that came close to spinning out of control. As Ralph said, the problem was that Mel needed to get on the road right away to raise money, "leaving no one at home to assure things were done right."

The second challenge was raising money. When they entered the race, McCollum had already harvested $2 million from Republican contributors. Johnnie Byrd, the powerful Speaker of the Florida House, employed political strong-arm tactics to raise another $1.6 million.[9] People told Ralph after Mel's announcement, "You're crazy if you think you can raise another drop of money for the Senate race. It's all committed." The money challenge was greater because Florida, with its ten media markets and diverse population, demands a large investment in TV advertising from candidates running statewide.

The challenge was overcome with Herculean effort. Mel quickly raised $1.7 million in the first three months of 2004, more money than any other Senate candidate in state history had collected in a single reporting period.[10] McCollum, who started the year with $815,408 in the bank, collected $524,000 in the same period, while Byrd brought in $770,000.[11] The Martinez team proved particularly successful in collecting checks from Bush Pioneers and Rangers—persons who supported the national ticket in amounts of $100,000 and $200,000, respectively. Mel's first quarterly report showed checks from forty-nine such persons, while McCollum got contributions from seven.

The *Tampa Tribune* wrote that many of these contributors believed media reports that the White House had recruited Mel to join the race.[12] In circular fashion, news stories calling Martinez the White House choice helped him raise money from the party's big contributors, whose financial support provided evidence for news reports that the party establishment favored him. That message was underscored when Senate majority leader Bill Frist and five other members of the Senate GOP leadership team— Mitch McConnell, Rick Santorum, Kay Bailey Hutchinson, Jon Kyl, and Ted Stevens—hosted a Washington fund-raiser for Mel. In all, eleven senators attended the event, at which $250,000 was raised.[13] As McCollum would say, he found it hard to raise money "inside the Beltway" after that.

The third challenge arose from Mel's minuscule name recognition. His meteoric career rise had left little mark on the average Floridian; at the race's start, only 6 percent of state voters knew his name. Sowinski adopted a twofold strategy: to link Mel with the president and to sell his personal story. The campaign knew from polling that the Bush connection would help with Republican primary voters but would hurt Mel in the general election. And his meager name recognition was also an opportunity. Sowinski reasoned that people would vote for a candidate if the first thing they knew about him was that he came to the United States as a teenage refugee seeking political and religious freedom, and that he succeeded in life through personal striving, religious faith, and commitment to family values.

The ethnic part was complicated, though. Mel's Cuban heritage would help with the state's burgeoning Hispanic population, but the campaign's "verbatim" surveys showed that Republican voters in North Florida would resist voting for "someone from Miami" (which their pollster interpreted ethnically). Yet Mel was no mere ethnic candidate. He was well assimilated, from Orlando rather than Miami, and married to a "southern belle" from Alabama. That would help to mitigate any possible anti-Hispanic bias in the Panhandle, or what Floridians call L.A., for Lower Alabama.

Mel was not the first Martinez to run—and win—statewide. Bob

Martinez, the grandson of Spanish immigrants and former mayor of Tampa, won the governor's race in 1986, becoming Florida's second Republican chief executive since Reconstruction and the state's only Hispanic governor thus far. Like Mel a former Democrat (he switched in 1983), Bob Martinez scarcely blazed a trail of glory. He won legislative approval for a sales tax on services, but when voters responded negatively, he called the legislature back into session to repeal the tax. This flip-flop wounded his credibility with Florida voters and his approval ratings dropped like a rock. He looked even more hapless when he unsuccessfully tried to pass antiabortion laws and waged a campaign, rejected in the courts, to prosecute the rock band 2 Live Crew for violating Florida's obscenity laws. In 1990 he was defeated in his reelection bid by former Democratic U.S. senator Lawton Chiles.

As Mel Martinez began his Senate race, the state had roughly 400,000 Cuban American voters in Miami-Dade County, representing about 10 percent of the GOP electorate. Mel's Republican opponents took extreme stands to win the Cuban vote, signifying its importance to the primary battle. McCollum proposed sending undercover agents disguised as tourists to destabilize the Castro regime, while candidate Larry Klayman, the head of a litigious conservative group, Judicial Watch, wanted the United States to invade the island nation.[14]

McCollum's tough anti-Castro talk earned him the gratitude of brother congressmen Lincoln and Mario Diaz-Balart, South Florida's leading Cuban American politicians. Unlike Mel's Cuban friends in Orlando, they did not switch from supporting McCollum when Mel joined the race. Some people around Mel speculated that the Diaz-Balart brothers saw him as a "yahoo" and an "upstart," because he was from Orlando and not part of the Cuban American establishment in Miami.

When the McCollum camp ran a Spanish-language radio ad in South Florida that questioned his loyalty to the anti-Castro cause, Mel was incensed, said media adviser Julio Rubell Jr., who taped the commercial and played it to Mel over the phone.[15] The candidate immediately dictated a response, which the media adviser recorded for radio play. "How can anyone question where I stand . . . when I have suffered in the flesh from what that regime has done . . . when I was separated from my family and lost friends," Mel declaimed in Spanish. He closed by saying the issue was too serious to play politics with.

The attack on Mel's anti-Castro credentials derived in part from his policy differences with some firebrands in the Cuban American community over whether Cuban exiles should be regarded as economic or political refugees. If the former, according to U.S. law, they did not deserve automatic asylum in the United States, a policy that Martinez defended during the campaign. Nonetheless, political analysts expected him to harvest the bulk of the Cuban vote.[16] The power of ethnicity—the opportunity to vote for a *compadre* for U.S. Senate—would trump policy differences, his campaign figured.

Rubell, after watching the campaign in South Florida, said, "As time went on, leading up to the primary and beyond, [Cuban Americans] started to realize that they as individual voters wanted to be part of this historic moment." For a whole generation that had put their aspirations for socioeconomic advancement on hold to come here, Mel's victory would validate their sacrifice. There was a sense among people of his parents' generation, especially the mothers, said Rubell, that he was their son too.

A further challenge lay in relating Mel's story to other "diaspora people"—Puerto Ricans, Dominicans, Hondurans, Mexican Americans, and even European Jews. After all, his story of humble beginnings, of coming to the United States in search of freedom and opportunity, of working hard and playing by the rules was not just a Cuban American saga. It was the classic American Dream story, one that plays especially well in Florida, as University of South Florida historian Gary Mormino observes, because so many people have come to the state in pursuit of a dream.[17]

To communicate Martinez's American Dream story, the campaign produced a nine-minute film on the candidate and his family. "It was expensive to produce," said Sowinski, the campaign's general consultant, "but worth it to introduce Mel to voters and overcome his name-recognition deficit." They drew their TV ads in the primary from the film and mailed a shortened DVD version to thousands of Republican voters.

The film, produced by Stuart Stevens, showed Mel discussing his Peter Pan experience with Kitty by his side, interlaced with photos of the young Melquiades at Camp St. John. Sounding the religious theme, his Orlando pastor, Father John McCormick, told of the Church's role in delivering him from Cuba. Emphasizing family, the film offered shots of his children and his foster parents, plus footage of his parents arriving from Cuba. One of his foster mothers, Eileen Young, told of Mel wanting to call her "mommy" and her saying he had only one mother and he should call her and her husband Tía and Tío instead. Underlining the Bush connection, the film showed Mel seated with the president in the Oval Office (suggesting trust and responsibility) and in casual clothes at Camp David (suggesting personal friendship). The film closed on a triumphant note with President Bush saying before a Hispanic audience: "The American Dream is alive and well and Mel Martinez represents it."

At a minimum, the film earned great media coverage. His story appeared over and over again in the state's seven major newspapers—in Miami, Palm Beach, Tampa, St. Petersburg, Jacksonville, Orlando, and Tallahassee—becoming almost tedious in its repetition. As one example, the *Palm Beach Post* wrote: "Mel Martinez has a misty-eyed American dream story that he plans on telling all the way to the U.S. Senate. He is, without a doubt, a man with such a great story to tell, that he can spare a decade or two of the details and still make it work for him."[18]

The strategy of associating Mel with President Bush proved "tricky"— the candidate's own word. He never publicly told audiences he was the president's pick, he says. He was not authorized to do so, not in a Republican primary, not when McCollum had been a faithful GOP stalwart in his twenty-year House career. In the closing weeks of the campaign, McCollum saw Karl Rove at a presidential campaign event and asked him directly whether the rumor of White House support for Mel was true. Rove said it was not.

There was also a legal complication. The 2002 Bipartisan Campaign Reform Act made it illegal to coordinate campaigns, preventing the Martinez team from running current photos of Mel with the president. Instead, the campaign insinuated a presidential endorsement by showing older photos of the two, quoting Bush that Mel "would make a fine U.S. senator," and planting the story that Rove had recruited Mel to run. As well, his formal endorsement in June by the National Republican Senatorial Committee— an unusual endorsement in a contested primary—telegraphed national party support for him.

Florida governor Jeb Bush proved a fly in the ointment, however. As Mel concedes, he erred in not consulting directly with Jeb before announcing his candidacy. He says he asked Karl Rove whether the Florida governor was okay with his joining the race and that a "miscommunication" occurred between Rove and the governor. The problem was, Jeb ran his own political machine in Florida, removed from the machinations of

Rove and the White House, and Rove and he did not always communicate well, an aide to Mel explained.

To pass his legislative agenda, the Florida governor needed to work closely with House Speaker Johnnie Byrd, an announced Senate candidate, and state senate president Daniel Webster, whom Jeb recruited to join the U.S. Senate race. (Webster announced his candidacy but withdrew before the filing date.) Hence, Mel's entrance into the race as the presumptive candidate of the White House created a political problem for Jeb, especially with the legislature about to convene. Expressing his chagrin, the governor told a Tallahassee reporter: "I know my brother has deep respect for Mel. They're friends, just as I am with Mel. But they're not endorsing him. . . . He's not the hand-picked candidate. . . . In this case, the campaign has already commenced. It would be completely inappropriate for the White House to be engaged, and I have been given every assurance by Karl [Rove] that that's the position of the White House."[19]

Still, aided by news reports based on inference, Martinez succeeded in presenting himself as the White House's candidate. Over and over, the state's major papers called him that. They did so without qualification or attribution, making it seem beyond dispute. Dating himself, McCollum was left to show pictures of himself—from the 1980s—with President Reagan.

McCollum, having campaigned statewide in 2000, did not need to introduce himself to voters. From the start he could run full tilt against his main rival, Mel.[20] In particular, he derided the former housing secretary as a "trial lawyer"—an irrefutable charge. On one hand, it represented standard Republican rhetoric. Since 1994, when Republican congressional candidates included tort reform in their Contract with America, trial lawyers have been a GOP punching bag. The terms "liberal" and "trial lawyer" (meaning plaintiff attorneys opposing insurance companies, corporations, and doctors) are used synonymously in Republican attack ads.

On the other hand, this kind of personal attack typified McCollum's high-priced campaign manager, Arthur Finkelstein. He excelled at the attack ad, as evident in his previous campaigns for Senator Jesse Helms of North Carolina and Governor George Pataki of New York. In the Helms race, Finkelstein skewered the African American opponent with an anti–affirmative action ad showing a white hand holding a pink slip. The anti-lawyer salvos thrown at Mel gained added force after Republicans began lambasting Democratic presidential candidate John Edwards in like terms. Ironically, McCollum himself was a former trial attorney, albeit the respectable Republican kind; he represented doctors and corporations against plaintiff attorneys such as Mel.

His anti–trial lawyer attacks against Mel began early, repeated constantly, and reverberated in third-party ads. Two weeks after Mel entered the race, McCollum placed an ad on his Web site—frequently cited by reporters—deriding Mel as a "liberal trial lawyer," language repeated in his joint appearances with Mel before Republican groups. In addition, the Florida Medical Association, which had endorsed McCollum, aired stealth ads against Mel through a 527 organization. Federal tax law exempts such organizations from normal campaign disclosure requirements. People for a Better Florida, the FMA offshoot, ran radio ads saying Mel supported "greedy trial lawyers." Later, in recorded phone calls to GOP households, they accused him of "stabbing our president in the back on tort reform."[21]

In his one departure from Republican orthodoxy, Mel opposed capping lawsuits at $250,000, as McCollum and Bush wanted, calling instead for a cap of $500,000 for noneconomic pain and suffering. His "reform" was a "loser-pays" provision requiring people who file baseless lawsuits to pay their opponents' legal costs.[22] This, he said, would deter frivolous lawsuits. Yet McCollum himself, while in the House, had departed from the Contract with America on tort reform, voting for a cap of $1 million instead of the Contract's cap of $250,000.[23]

McCollum also questioned Mel's Republican credentials, noting his service as president of the Florida Academy of Trial Lawyers, a pro-Democrat group, and his past contributions to Democratic political campaigns. Those donations included checks to Florida Democratic senatorial candidates Bill Gunter and Bob Graham, as well as support for Senators Fritz Hollings (D-S.C.) and Joe Biden (D-Del.). And, as head of the trial attorney association, he gave $20,000 to a group that successfully opposed an initiative to limit jury awards in medical malpractice cases.

Responding to McCollum's attacks, former U.S. senator Paula Hawkins criticized him in an open letter to the news media, saying he had violated Ronald Reagan's famous "11th Commandment" against speaking ill of another Republican. "He's launched bomb after bomb against Mel, implying he is in bed with trial lawyers, Democrats and anyone else who might want to destroy America," complained the former GOP senator. "My fax machine is practically smoking with those things," she said of his press releases.[24]

Otherwise the Republican primary was a race to the ideological right, as the candidates tried to outdo one another in condemning gay marriage, embracing the president's war on terrorism, and defending the invasion of Iraq. Mel called for a constitutional amendment banning gay marriage, opposed banning so-called assault weapons, advocated making the president's tax cuts permanent, and complained of media bias in reporting on U.S. military efforts in Iraq. To many Orlandoans, he seemed to have deserted the moderate stances he took as county chairman. People wondered, was this the same Mel? Some said he had been hijacked by the Bushies, others that Washington had changed him.

To judge from numerous interviews, neither was true. Mel was always a social conservative, fueled by his orthodox Catholicism and his experiences under Castro. Those views were masked in the county chairman campaign and garnered scarce media attention, because they mattered little in local government. And besides, his main opponent for the chairman job, state senator John Ostalkiewicz, was more conservative than he. Mel seemed moderate because of his temperament, as the *St. Petersburg Times* astutely noted.[25] Outside Republican gatherings, he was not in-your-face with his conservatism. McCollum's labeling him a *"liberal trial lawyer,"* in the context of a Republican primary, pushed him to sound more conservative.

The key issues in the Republican primary were embryonic stem-cell research and hate-crime protection for homosexuals. The research debate was punctuated by the death of Ronald Reagan on June 5, followed by Nancy Reagan's public statements defending embryonic stem-cell research as a potential cure for Alzheimer's, which afflicted her Ronnie. McCollum, returning from the Reagan funeral, said he agreed with Mrs. Reagan, putting him at odds with President Bush and much of the conservative movement. Martinez, following Catholic doctrine, hewed to the Bush policy against allowing additional lines of research, calling embryonic cell research "antifamily."[26]

The hate-crime issue also proved contentious. As a member of the House Judiciary Committee, McCollum had supported extending hate-crime law to acts committed against gays. As he said in an interview, he saw this as part of the political mainstream, noting that Florida had a similar law. Mel, on the other hand, opposed all hate-crime laws, saying they punished people differently for committing the same crime.

<hr/>

Just after midnight on August 13, Hurricane Charley, packing winds of 120 miles per hour, drove northward across Cuba just west of Havana before rapidly intensifying into a strong category-four storm. Later that day Charley slammed into Florida's west coast near Port Charlotte, in the midsection of the peninsula, and swept through Orlando before exiting into the Atlantic close to Daytona Beach, causing twenty-seven direct and indirect deaths and a staggering $6.8 billion in property damage. It also set the stage for a wild finish to the Senate primary campaign.

In the wake of Charley, the first of four hurricanes to pummel the state that season, Martinez's campaign office in Orlando got electrical power restored a few days before McCollum's office did. Still, the storm hurt Martinez more. He was behind in the polls when the storm struck on August 13, still struggling for name recognition, and the storm disrupted the two things he needed to close the gap: TV advertising and fund-raising. As Charley approached, his campaign's TV advertising was moving into high gear. Many of his ads were aborted, however, because TV stations were not operating, or because viewers lacked power or cable service, or both. He also canceled fund-raisers in the storm's path.

As the seven-person race contracted into a two-person contest between McCollum and Martinez, McCollum's campaign manager, Arthur Finkelstein, continued to produce anti-Martinez press releases at the rate of two per week. Meanwhile, the Martinez effort still suffered from its quick start. Disorganization and dissensus were rife in the campaign, creating an environment in which "things that shouldn't have could happen," said one consultant. But the campaign largely ignored McCollum's attacks, taking a high-road approach at Mel's direction, almost until the end.

Then, a week before the primary, a "gay war" erupted between the two campaigns. To emphasize Mel's support from Christian conservatives, his campaign arranged a conference call between reporters and leaders of several religious right organizations. Since both McCollum and Martinez opposed abortion under all circumstances and supported a constitutional amendment outlawing homosexual marriage, the debate turned on nuances. To the conservative leaders participating in the call, McCollum's support for additional stem-cell research violated his antiabortion stance, since it involved destroying a human embryo, and his support for granting hate-crime protection to gays was antifamily, since it would give special privileges to gays.

But then a reporter from the *Miami Herald* asked about gay staffers in Martinez's campaign. Earlier the *Washington Blade*, a gay publication in D.C., had identified two homosexuals working for Martinez, one a top staffer and the other a freelance political consultant. When the *Herald* reporter asked whether the call participants found this troubling, one of them cited McCollum's top adviser, Arthur Finkelstein, who is openly gay. At least Martinez's gay aides were not in policy-making positions, said John Stemberger, head of the Orlando-based Florida Family Policy Council, a state affiliate of Focus on the Family. Another call participant, Andrea Sheldon Lafferty, executive director of the Traditional Values Coalition, said Finkelstein had been "directing McCollum's votes all this time."[27]

In the aftermath, Mel condemned the *Blade* for outing his staff and disavowed Stemberger's statement about Finkelstein. Through their press spokespersons, both campaigns parsed their words about employing homosexuals, saying they practiced "don't ask, don't tell" in hiring staff. It was a curiously liberal hiring policy for campaigns jockeying to appear to the right of each other. Indeed, Mel's call participants were quoted as saying that he, unlike McCollum, would never compromise with centrist positions.[28]

During this same period, Martinez staffers were working on a final mailer and TV spot addressing the key issues of stem-cell research and hate-crime legislation. As initially prepared, the mailer included "third-party quotes" criticizing McCollum. One set came from Newswatch, a conservative Web site posted in Palm Beach, the other from the ultraconservative Traditional Values Coalition (TVC), a religious right organization opposed to homosexuality, hate-crime laws, pornography, and abortion. According to John Sowinski, he nixed the TVC quotes, finding them too vitriolic, and approved using only the Newswatch quotes.

Normally, as the campaign consultant explained, a PDF file for something as important as a final mailer would circulate among top campaign staff before the piece was printed and mailed. But that did not happen here, he says, because internal communication had broken down. Things were so bad that the campaign manager and campaign press spokesperson refused to speak to one another. In this environment, the mailer was sent with both sets of quotes, including those from TVC that Sowinski thought he vetoed.

TVC not only opposed McCollum on the hate-crime issue. They were furious about him appearing at a press conference with representatives from People For the American Way, a group they saw as ultraliberal, to publicize his stance on extending protection to gays. Mel's friend Ken Connor, the former head of the Family Research Council, agreed with TVC on this issue, saying in an interview that McCollum had forewarned him about appearing with representatives of the liberal group. Connor, who helped the former congressman in the 2000 Senate race but was supporting Mel this time, urged McCollum not to carry through, calling the staged appearance with representatives from People For the American Way a "cynical political move."

Of course, Sowinski and others in the Martinez camp knew how Finkelstein operated from working with him in McCollum's 2000 campaign. In particular, they knew he liked to use a "man-bites-dog strategy" to position his candidates. Having the conservative McCollum support something gay-friendly fit that strategy, making the stodgy former congressmen seem more interesting. Never mind that it fit with Finkelstein's lifestyle too.

The campaign piece was mailed, according to Mel and Sowinski, without the candidate's knowledge. Mel first heard about it from a reporter aboard the campaign's chartered plane. When the *Palm Beach Post*'s Brian Cowley read him quotes from the mailer, the candidate was clueless, according to travel aide Tomás Bilbao.[29] "Tomás, find out about this right away," Mel barked. When the plane landed, they learned about the mailer and its message through a hurried series of phone calls to the campaign office. From all reports, Mel was fuming.

Interestingly, McCollum knew about the mailer before Mel did. Someone in the post office sent him one as a favor, he said in an interview. "Apparently the person was a supporter of mine," he said, adding: "I guess his actions were probably illegal." The next day, McCollum also learned of a companion TV ad running in North Florida. He and former U.S. senator Connie Mack, his honorary campaign chair, were incensed about him being called antifamily. Sitting in Mack's car in Jacksonville, McCollum listened as Mack called Governor Bush to complain about the ad. Mack also sent a public letter to GOP activists saying that Martinez had "sunk to a new low" by engaging in "hate speech" that could "doom the party in November."[30]

At a televised debate just four days before the election, McCollum responded to Mel with righteous indignation. According to the Martinez camp, their opponent received coaching on how to display anger for maximum impact.

"That is just despicable. It's nasty. It's an absolutely incorrect characterization," he said, waving the mailer. "I would like to ask you, first of all, if you would condemn this publication that you are putting out right now. And number two, if you would apologize to me for these accusations that are wrong and nasty and incorrect."

But Martinez refused to budge in the debate. "For about ten months, I have been the subject of continuing attacks by you on me," he said. "I have been victimized, over months and months. I was attacked on the Internet. I was compared to one of the most liberal senators in the Senate [John Edwards]. I was attacked by mail. I was attacked on radio in Miami where my commitment to a free Cuba has been questioned by Mr. McCollum's campaign."

After the debate, McCollum said that if he lost the primary, he would not vote for Mel unless he apologized for his tactics. Martinez acknowledged that he had not seen the mailer in advance, but continued to defend the mailer after the debate, saying it raised issues that were "fair game" and sought to "draw distinctions." He added: "All I can tell you is that when you dish it out, you ought to be able to take it."[31]

The brouhaha over the charge against McCollum earned it more attention than it would have received otherwise. It was a good gambit on McCollum's part: he turned a negative into a positive as Martinez's campaign advertising became the issue. His biggest success was in getting the liberal *St. Petersburg Times* to rescind its earlier endorsement of Martinez. The paper condemned his "hateful and dishonest attacks on McCollum" and called the former housing secretary "an ambitious politician who has resorted to unprincipled tactics to get elected."[32]

When Governor Bush, at the behest of McCollum, asked Martinez to pull the TV spot that had aired in the Panhandle making essentially the same charges as the mailer, he immediately did so. Martinez also quietly reassigned his campaign manager, Scott Bernhardt, to managing media buys, making Sowinski and Evers the de facto campaign managers. Yet he continued in the waning days of the primary to defend the contents of the mailer, while still denying advance knowledge of it. Even his supporters were unhappy with this stance. Typical was the comment of the Cuban American attorney Marcos Marchena, who called the mailer a blunder. "It was not only unfair to McCollum, who didn't deserve something like this. It was also unnecessary, because Mel was winning, for heaven's sake." By now their campaign was running 10 points ahead in internal polls and winning by 6 points in the published Mason-Dixon poll. As many would say, you don't need to go negative when you are well ahead.

For his part, McCollum describes the attacks years later as a "low blow." His own salvos against Mel—calling him a liberal trial lawyer and worse—were different, he maintains. Those negatives related to legitimate policy differences, namely, their marginally different views on tort reform. Moreover, in his view, Mel's attack ads probably made the difference in the election. As evidence, he points to his victory in the market area of the *St. Petersburg Times*, which rescinded its endorsement of Mel. Yet Mel won by 14 percentage points statewide, defeating McCollum in every other region of the state. Says Sowinski, "No mailer has ever moved an electorate fourteen points."

In some quarters, continuing to this writing, Mel earned a reputation as mean-spirited. That impression was strengthened by how the brouhaha played in the media. In its second and third iteration, the story was that Martinez himself accused McCollum of being antifamily. In fact, his ad retailed third-party quotes making that accusation, an important distinction. Reinforced by subsequent events, Martinez also acquired a reputation for relying too much on staff and for blaming them when things went awry. The first charge is valid, the second more questionable.

On election eve, a visibly angry McCollum refused to endorse the election victor as defeated candidates normally do in primary battles. Doing so conveys that you are a team player, desirous of future support from your party. He did not endorse Martinez for ten more days, not until the two met behind closed doors at his request. There Martinez, the bigger man, apologized for the mailer.

To the Martinez campaign staff, the apology was unnecessary—yet defining of Mel. Their out-of-state consultants had said, "What's the problem?" Hate-crime legislation and stem-cell research were fair issues, and the statements in the mailer were factually correct. Even if Mel did not know of the mailer in advance, he could have persisted in defending its message. Doing so would show courage and backbone. Though he would take heat for standing firm, mostly from liberals who opposed him anyway, the alternative of apologizing was worse. It made him look weak, the consultants thought.

But that wasn't Mel. He was not mean enough to engage in acceptable campaign practice. As he later said of the anti-McCollum ads: "They were completely inappropriate and out of bounds. They shouldn't have happened. I have been made to pay a price for all this. I hope that someday I will be forgiven." The issue weighed on him at the GOP convention in New York, where he raced immediately after the primary. Convention planners had penciled his name on the speaker roster, pending his victory.

＜────＞

The light shined brightly on Mel at the convention. His presence there was all-important for party strategy. He personified the new, less stereotypically white and Anglo face of the party that Rove and other strategists wanted to project. As a candidate for one of seven open Senate seats— called the "string of seven pearls"—he was essential to the party's strategy for winning a Senate majority. And not least, his presence on the 2004 ballot in Florida would boost the president's support among Latino voters, helping him to carry the state.

Once again, the stars lined up for Mel. It was the right time to run on the Florida GOP ticket as a Hispanic.

＜────＞

To win the state, both Martinez and Bush needed to do well with the state's Hispanic voters, who comprise 14 percent of the Florida electorate. Among them, 36 percent are Cuban, 32 percent Puerto Rican, and 21 percent Central or South American in heritage. The Hispanic vote is especially important in South Florida. That part of the state, consisting of Broward, Palm Beach, and Miami-Dade Counties, is normally a Democratic stronghold, because of the large concentrations there of black, elderly, and Jewish voters, many of them transplants from New York and New Jersey. Mel's strategy, as outlined by Sowinski, was to hold down the Democratic vote totals in South Florida by turning out the Hispanic vote in larger than usual numbers and cutting into the normally Democratic Jewish vote. In addition, they hoped to win the I-4 corridor through the belly of the state, in which 30 percent of voters are Independents, and to win by a large margin in North Florida and the Panhandle, a rural, agriculturally dependent region with large numbers of military retirees and Old South social conservatives.

⟵⟶

Observing from 2000 census data that the nation's Hispanic population had surged to 38.8 million, Republican strategists crunched the numbers and concluded that if Bush won the same percentage of minority votes in 2004 as in 2000 he would lose by 3 million votes.[33] Accordingly, the new administration had made high-profile Hispanic appointments, including Mel at HUD and Alberto Gonzales as White House counsel. The White House also carefully architected its policies: the president halted controversial navy bombings on Vieques Island off Puerto Rico, he announced a proposal for a "guest worker" program, and he traveled to Mexico on his first foreign trip. And Karl Rove tailored the party message in Spanish-language ads, fine-tuning their use of idioms and accents to win support from the different Latino nationality groups.

⟵⟶

In Florida, the president's best allies were his brother Jeb, who speaks Spanish and whose wife is Mexican-born, and Mel. On the Democratic side, party critics complained that when their candidate John Kerry came to Florida there was no discernible Hispanic focus. He had no visible Latino staff and seldom appeared with Hispanic politicians at his side. Nor did he lend much support to the Democrats' senatorial candidate, Betty Castor. A telling example came when folk singer Jimmy Buffett performed a tribute concert for the Democratic presidential candidate in Miami. Kerry's people did not include Castor in the program. Rather, Buffett saw her sitting in the audience and brought her onstage in the middle of his performance.

By May 2004, the Bush campaign had spent $500,000 on Spanish-language TV and radio ads in Miami, Tampa, and Orlando. In this effort the New Democratic Network, a minority-oriented offshoot of the DNC, matched them dollar for dollar. But the party of Jefferson and Jackson had no Hispanic messenger. Where the Republicans had Jeb Bush as a spokesman and Mel as a candidate, both speaking in Spanish, the Democrats ran commercials with actors and slogans and music. One ad relied on images of past presidents—Franklin Roosevelt, John Kennedy, Jimmy Carter, and Bill Clinton—to forge a bond with Latinos.[34]

And Mel proved a good bridge candidate for Hispanics, using his language skills and political savvy to span the gap between Latino voter groups, such as Cubans and Puerto Ricans. He made two campaign appearances in Puerto Rico, where he promised he would be "Puerto Rico's senator too." It was an important promise, as Puerto Rico has a nonvoting member in the U.S. House but no voice in the Senate. And, as the Martinez campaign knew well, Puerto Ricans living and voting in Florida remain closely identified with the island commonwealth, frequently traveling back to visit family there.

Mel's outreach to Hispanic voters was "high touch." He achieved a "palpable level of contact with his audiences," according to travel aides. With Latino audiences, especially with these audiences, he achieved "rock star" status. Traveling in his American Dream bus with former New York City mayor Rudy Giuliani, he gave one of his most electrifying performances outside GOP headquarters in Miami. Afterwards he worked the crowd of one thousand people who had waited in a parking lot in hot sun just to see him. "That was the most impressive thing," said his media adviser Julio Rubell Jr. "He didn't do it because he was supposed to. He enjoyed it. He soaked up the love, and needed to give it right back."

According to his travel aide Tomás Bilbao, who worked in the same role at HUD, such occurrences were common. Whether Mel was talking to three hundred people outside an ice cream shop in Sarasota or speaking alongside Mayor Giuliani in Miami, "he felt an amazing reaction from people." It would sometimes get dangerous when Mel worked a Hispanic crowd, said Bilbao. "Dangerous because of all the people pushing and shoving just to touch him or shake his hand. They saw him as a symbol that they had made it." The only way Bilbao could stay with Mel as he worked the crowd was to hold on to the candidate's belt.

Mel's personal story was also a bridge to normally Democratic Jewish voters.

In appealing for their vote, Mel could take advantage of the fractious primary fight between Betty Castor, the victor, and her pugnacious opponent, Peter Deutsch. A five-term member of Congress, Deutsch was the wealthiest candidate in the race, accustomed to bankrolling his own campaigns. He was running against Alex Pinellas, the Cuban American former mayor of Miami, and Castor, who had served in the state Senate and twice been elected statewide as education commissioner. For the previous nine years she was nominally out of politics, serving as president of the University of South Florida.

In incessant attacks, Deutsch pilloried Castor for her handling of allegations regarding a Palestinian computer science professor, accused of supporting Islamic jihadists. In the pre-9/11 environment, prior to the expansion of federal investigative powers authorized by the Patriot Act, Castor maintained she had done all she could in suspending—but not firing—the professor in question, Dr. Sami Al-Arian. After she left office, her successor would fire Al-Arian, though not until he was indicted on the basis of Patriot Act–established government powers.

In his attack ads, Deutsch used a sly argument, effectively saying: "I'm raising the issue that the Republicans will raise; if Castor wins the primary, they will destroy her on this issue in the general election campaign." In the view of Sam Bell, Castor's husband and a former state senator, Deutsch's attacks were always a "sordid appeal for the Jewish vote." He added that Deutsch "made it seem that Betty was anti-Semitic."[35] The Jewish vote is important in state elections, because the state's Jewish population, at 500,000, is the second largest in the nation.

But Mel's appeal to Jewish voters also arose from his personal story. They could relate to someone who, like them, came to the United States seeking political and religious freedom. As he explained to audiences in the Jewish community, the Peter Pan program evolved from something called Kindertransport that spirited children out of Nazi Germany. "I tell Jewish audiences that I know there are bad people in the world," he said in an interview.[36] "The Yasir Arafats of the world run in the same circles as Fidel Castro and Saddam Hussein. I know the price of tyranny, what it means to be religiously persecuted, and to yearn for freedom."

He was frequently asked by Jewish voter groups whether he had been to Israel. Knowing the symbolism of such trips, he promised he would go if elected. (It was a kept promise; he traveled there soon after the election, before his swearing in.) Mel was frequently told at his appearances in the condo towers of Broward and Palm Beach Counties, home to large concentrations of Jewish voters, "We will vote for you but not for Bush." In fact, Bush improved his performance among Florida's Jewish voters in his reelection race, from 4 percent in 2000 to 22 percent in 2004. His performance was aided by the efforts of the Republican Jewish Coalition, an ally of the Republican Party of Florida, which sent direct mail to Jewish voters asserting that Bush, not Kerry, was the best president to continue the War on Terror.[37]

◁══▷

Martinez and Castor both raised a mountain of money for their campaigns, with a slight edge to Martinez, though not enough to explain the outcome. Altogether he raised $1.4 million more than she did, but the totals were huge. According to the Federal Elections Commission, he collected $12.8 million compared to her $11.4 million, his support coming mostly from PACs and hers from individuals.[38] She received more help from advocacy groups than from the Democratic Party, whereas he got more assistance from his party and from groups such as the National Rifle Association and the National Right to Life Committee.[39] The National Republican Senatorial Committee spent $1,672,810 on television and radio advertising supporting Mel Martinez, while the Democratic Senatorial Campaign Committee spent $1,622,963 on Castor's broadcast advertising. Furthermore, EMILY's List spent more than $316,000 and the AFL-CIO roughly $350,000 on television advertising for Castor.[40]

The more important difference was in how the candidates used their money. Castor spent more on the "ground war," Martinez on the "air war." Castor favored direct mailings targeted to specific audiences, while Martinez used the airwaves to aim at larger broadcast audiences, telling about his relationship with the president, his refugee odyssey, and his strengths over Castor. As one example, he ran an ad using his mother and foster mothers to support his proposal for privatizing Social Security. "They depend on Social Security, and one thing, I'm someone who will go to Washington prepared to defend and fight for Social Security to make sure there's no reduction in their benefits," he said in the ad.

By October, after the ad wars had turned nasty, Castor offered to pull hers if Martinez would too. She was angered by a National Republican Senatorial Committee ad claiming she would raise taxes if elected. She called the ad despicable. The basis for it was her support for repealing President Bush's tax cut that benefited the wealthiest 1 percent of the population. When she requested, in a televised ad, that he pull his offending ads and address other topics, Martinez refused, saying, "I've been victimized by repeated negative attacks." He saw a trap: if she ceased her negative pieces, EMILY's List would continue their attack ads against him.

"If I were to say I'm going to take down my negative ads, it would be uni-lateral disarmament."[41]

Castor was not the only one pleading to halt negative ads. On Mon-day, October 11, she launched an ad containing a photo of President Bush together with Sami Al-Arian in 2000. The photo was from a fund-raiser cochaired by Martinez. This ad was created in response to an earlier Mar-tinez ad featuring Bill West, a former federal immigration agent who be-gan the Al-Arian investigation in 1994. In that ad, West claimed Castor had shown a "lack of strong leadership" in her handling of the matter. Responding in her own ad, Castor questioned why, if Al-Arian was so dan-gerous, Martinez and the White House allowed him near the president. Complaining, her opponent called the ad "completely outrageous, errone-ous and wrong. . . . The ad leaves a clear impression that I was actually with or somehow knew or had a connection with Mr. Al-Arian. I'm outraged by that. It's kind of reprehensible. I've never seen that man in my life."

Martinez's good-guy image took a hit from his negative TV ads.

WFLA–Channel 8 in Tampa accused him of "egregiously" using a snip-pet of Castor out of context from a TV debate it sponsored. Yet, overall, Martinez had a stronger ad campaign. Castor neglected to reach out to the Hispanic community, to highlight her opponent's faults, and to gen-erate an overall theme as Martinez did so well. He consistently portrayed himself as a survivor of communism, a shining example of middle-class success, a defender of moral values, and a friend of President Bush's.

Castor's best opportunity to tarnish him was on raising the state's min-imum wage. Voters in 2004 could approve or reject hiking the state's mini-mum wage by one dollar. In possibly his saddest hour, Martinez opposed the proposal, saying it would hurt job creation. Meanwhile Castor sup-ported the measure, saying it would help the state's Hispanic and female populations. Though Martinez tried to avoid the issue, Castor cleverly said about him: "He wants to deny them the American Dream."

In an interview, Martinez said his stance on the measure was influ-enced by his relationships with Governor Bush, who opposed the increase, and the governor's brother. For Castor, the issue was an opportunity to damage his popularity among the Hispanic demographic that represents a large proportion of low-wage workers. She might have purchased Spanish television ads in Miami-Dade highlighting his uncompassionate stance on this issue. Not doing so was a missed opportunity. Although many His-panics took pride in electing one of their own to the Senate, many also questioned how he could call himself a "compassionate conservative," as he frequently did, if he opposed raising the minimum wage.

For the Martinez campaign, the Al-Arian issue posed a dilemma after he and Castor won their respective primaries. His strategists had wanted him to attack her for mishandling the Al-Arian case, just as Deutsch predicted her GOP opponent would do. Mel initially said no. He was smarting from the backlash against his anti-McCollum mailer, and he feared the "ugliness that would be heaped upon us" for doing what Deutsch predicted. According to aides, he also feared the appearance of attacking a female opponent too forcefully.

Then Castor went on the offensive with the Al-Arian issue. She opened her general-election TV campaign by saying she had proved she was tough on terrorism by her decisive handling of the Al-Arian case. Her husband, Sam Bell, who played a key role in the campaign, said of this salvo: "We thought she should try to immunize herself on the issue. It was no secret [to Republicans] that Deutsch had attacked her on this. We figured we had to get out front on it."

For the Martinez camp, the commercial provided an opening to attack. The night before her ad started, his senior campaign staff had met with Mel at his home. There, in the privacy of his study, Mel decided over opposition not to attack her on the Al-Arian issue. The next day his staff came to him saying, "We have to respond." He told them, "There's no argument from me anymore." As he explained, "I went into my trial attorney mode. Once she opened the door, it became admissible evidence. I was very comfortable going with the issue after that." The breach she opened enabled them to do what otherwise seem impossible: to accuse a nonincumbent with no national government experience of being soft on terrorism.

The ad war over which candidate was better prepared to respond to the terrorist threat proved decisive, allowing Martinez to win in a squeaker. His victory margin was small enough that no winner was declared until Castor conceded the following day. President Bush won the state by 52–47 percent, Martinez by 49–48 percent with about 70,000 votes separating Castor and him. The ballot presence of third-party candidate Dennis Bradley prevented Martinez from cracking the 50 percent mark. Yet Mel did win 3.6 million votes, more than any other winning Republican candidate in the nation, incumbents included.[42]

The terrorist issue evoked particular concern in Florida, because the state economy had suffered when tourists were afraid to fly after 9/11. Accordingly, Florida voters ranked the terrorist issue differently than voters elsewhere did. National exit polls showed that concern about moral issues was the most often cited reason voters chose Bush over Kerry. But in Florida, it was terrorism over moral issues, 24 percent to 20 percent.[43] Castor understood that, in order to win the election, she had to shift voters' attention from terrorism and homeland security to domestic issues. Unfortunately for her, as political scientists Robert Crew, Terry Fine, and Susan MacManus have written, national media coverage concerning missing explosives and the Osama bin Laden tape released in October refocused voters' attention on terrorism and homeland security issues, aiding Bush and Martinez.[44]

Martinez consultant John Sowinski explained their victory in terms of geography rather than issues. They won, he said, because they accomplished their three strategic objectives. First, they edged out Castor in heavily Hispanic Miami-Dade County, preventing a Democratic sweep of South Florida. Second, they won the Interstate-4 corridor in the middle of the state, home to the largest concentration of Independent voters, many of them recent migrants to Florida. Third, they scored big in conservative North Florida, winning 55 percent of the vote.

Having Mel on the ticket was a boost to President Bush in South Florida, where he invariably campaigned with his cabinet appointee by his side. Mel won Miami-Dade County by 2,400 votes, running well ahead of President Bush, who lost there to Senator Kerry by 42,000 votes. In losing this Democratic bastion, the president nonetheless won a larger percentage of the county's vote than he did in 2000, enabling him to win the state by 381,878 votes, or 5 percent. This compares with his 537-vote margin (as judged by the U.S. Supreme Court) in 2000.

Recognizing the importance of the Hispanic vote to the future of the GOP in Florida and elsewhere, Mel saw his Senate victory in ethnic terms. In South Florida his ethnicity worked for him. His strong support and high turnout from Hispanic voters was pivotal in the election. As he said in 2008, "I won Dade County. Jeb [Bush] never won Dade. You only win Dade by winning the Hispanic vote by an overwhelming margin and getting a disproportionate turnout from Hispanics."

In North Florida, home to military retirees and Old South social conservatives, it was a different story. Since the Martinez camp knew from the beginning that Republican voters there were averse to "someone from Miami," meaning a Cuban American, they understood that selling a Hispanic politician there would be difficult.

To Mel it was a "strange thing," as he said in a 2008 interview. "During the Senate race my views were the same as George Bush's, yet Bush was running at sixty-four percent in the Panhandle, I'm running at fifty-five percent, and I'm losing statewide to Betty Castor by four, five points." In his view, the problem came down to ethnicity—his. "If my name were Jones instead of Martinez, I don't think it would have been the same problem."

What he confronted was the two Floridas. "For much of its history," writes University of Florida historian David Colburn, "Florida has been two states—one that extends south from the Georgia border to Ocala and that has identified with the South and its racial and social traditions and another south of Ocala whose heritage has little association with the South and that views the state as part of a national and, indeed, international economy."[45]

In the end, Mel's antiterror stance as conveyed in his Sami Al-Arian ads proved decisive with North Florida voters, deflecting attention from his ethnicity. To win their support he offered assurance on the immigration issue, declaring in words that would come back to haunt him: "I came here legally and learned English and I expect other people to do the same."[46] In addition, his campaign Web site said that he opposed giving amnesty to illegal aliens and supported a plan that "matches workers with needy employers without providing a path to citizenship." Those words, aimed at trying to reassure social conservatives, prefigured future struggles. For after Mel joined the Senate he would advocate for immigration reform that granted amnesty to some people who came here illegally.

9

SENATOR

Their odyssey began in Sagua la Grande, Cuba. They arrived in the United States by various means, some by plane, others by boat, still others in rafts made of inner tubes and timber. Most settled in Miami, where they worked initially in the garment district and in commercial establishments such as restaurants serving other Cubans. They had weathered the Bay of Pigs fiasco, at least the older ones had, and watched the Cuban population of South Florida grow in numbers as well as political strength.

The tipping point for their political involvement came in 1980, as sociologists Alejandro Portes and Alex Stepick wrote in 1993.[1] Before that, South Florida's Cuban population had negligible political input. Their wake-up call for political involvement was the Mariel boatlift debacle, a race riot in Miami, and a proposal for an English-only amendment. In 1990 and 1992, they witnessed the election of Cuban Americans to the House of Representatives in congressional districts designed to favor them.

Now they had special reason to rejoice. It was not just a fellow Cuban American who was becoming a United States senator. It was a *compadre* from their hometown in Cuba. They shared the expense, hiring a bus to drive straight through from Miami to Washington, D.C., there to watch the inauguration of Melquiades Martínez as a member of this august body.

Protocol prevented their viewing him take the oath of office in person. Instead they watched on a large screen in the ballroom of the Rayburn Senate Office Building, along with five hundred other supporters of the state's new junior senator. It was a diverse crowd consisting of Anglos and Hispanics, bankers, attorneys, and housewives, along with middle-class evangelical Christians and Cuban Americans like themselves. Looking at them, they seemed to have little in common save their support for Mel and his smiling wife, Kitty.

On the big screen, they watched as Mel and Kitty walked down the aisle with three other new senators and their accompanying spouses and sponsors. One of the new senators being sworn in was Barack Obama. In addition to spouses, the freshmen senators were permitted to bring one sponsor each. Mel chose former senator Paula Hawkins, frail but still feisty, whom he assisted down the aisle. He had asked her to accompany him, telling her "it was your seat." Senator Hawkins won the seat in 1980 and quickly became a favorite of President Reagan's. In the end she joined her predecessors Richard Stone (1974–80) and Edward Gurney (1968–74) as a one-termer. Martinez hoped to be different.

In 1986 Hawkins lost the seat to Bob Graham, who would serve three Senate terms following his two terms as governor. He was part of a dying breed—a moderate southern Democrat—and he enjoyed such political stature that Martinez's Democratic opponent in the Senate race, former education commissioner Betty Castor, ran a TV ad questioning whether Mel Martinez could fill Bob Graham's big shoes. For Graham was a man of gravitas, chairman of the Senate Intelligence Committee and a sharp critic of U.S. intelligence failures in Iraq. His criticisms proved prescient when no weapons of mass destruction were found, but Graham had bombed in his 2004 presidential bid. (Had he been selected as the vice-presidential nominee, the Democrats might have at least carried Florida.)

But even Graham could not excite crowds the way Martinez could. Over the course of his Senate campaign, he had become a dynamic stump speaker, easily switching from English to Spanish. He was much improved over his campaign performance running for Orange County chairman only six years earlier. During his stint as HUD secretary, the White House had sent him to speak to Spanish-language audiences across the country as the administration's liaison to Hispanic America. As he said of the experience, "It's amazing how you find Hispanic people all across this country."

He was not only their representative in the cabinet; he symbolized that Latinos could make it in America. This Hispanic support had been evident during the Senate campaign as well. Marching in a Puerto Rican parade in Orlando, where most of the crowd would have been Democrats, since Puerto Ricans vote approximately 70 percent Democratic, he was saluted with signs saying, "Martinez Sí, Bush No." That is why he promised during the campaign to be a senator for Puerto Rico, too.

Of course, Democrats claimed their own Hispanic senator. Ken Salazar, the former attorney general of Colorado, also won election to the Senate in 2004, defeating a well-financed Republican opponent, Pete Coors. Reflecting the different ethnic bases of the two parties, Salazar was Mexican American, a group that votes 75 percent Democratic in national elections. Though competitors for the loyalty of Hispanic voters, Salazar and Martinez enjoyed a friendly camaraderie. In the formal environment of the Senate, however, they refrained from conversing in Spanish.

Earlier, the Democrats had pinned their hopes on Henry Cisneros, who served as HUD secretary during Clinton's first term. Like Salazar a Mexican American, Cisneros was the three-term mayor of San Antonio and a popular and effective vote-getter. Blessed with good looks, credentialed with a Harvard degree, he moved easily between the Anglo and Hispanic worlds, and received mention as a possible vice-presidential candidate on the Clinton ticket in 1992. But Cisneros's fortunes plummeted after an FBI inquiry revealed that he had paid hush money, during his service as HUD secretary, to a former mistress. The disclosure forced Cisneros to leave office in 1997, ending his political career.

Preparing to take the oath of office, Martinez put his left hand on the Bible and raised his right hand. Standing tall, looking like the former high-school basketball center that he was, wearing his perpetual navy suit, pale blue shirt, and red tie, this Jesuit-educated son of a Cuban veterinarian repeated the words after the president of the Senate, Vice President Dick Cheney, "I do solemnly swear . . ." Among the senators milling at the back of the chamber, one was heard quieting the others. "Shh, this is historic," he said, as Mel became the nation's first Cuban American senator. Retreating to the Senate cloakroom, Mel and Kitty were greeted by a cluster of admiring senators. As Hawkins would say later, "Mel has lost no time. He seems to know everyone already." In Martinez's own words, "I had a head start working with senators from my HUD service." He was in his element.

⸺

Looking back, Mel's Senate career began auspiciously. He was no stranger either to Washington or to Capitol Hill. As HUD secretary he had testified before congressional subcommittees on numerous occasions and met frequently with GOP House and Senate members. Of course, he still needed advice. He had attended "Senate school," a bipartisan affair with sitting senators serving as faculty, for the nine new members elected in 2004. It was an opportunity to bond with members of his Senate class, learn about Senate procedures, and get advice on running their offices. As Mel recounted, that advice included admonitions to hire Hill veterans rather than "political types" from their campaigns for their Senate staff.[2] It was advice Mel followed to the chagrin of some of his campaign people, he reported.

As a freshman, his star seemed to shine brighter than other members of his class. In part this was due to his close association with President Bush and his previous cabinet service. It was also because of his immigrant background and his difficult passage to America, which intrigued the media and his new Senate colleagues, just as it had the president. "So tell me about how you got here," they would say. In the media attention he received, he was more like the newly elected African American in his class, Barack Obama.

Before his confirmation Mel was a senator in transition, inundated with office seekers, caught between the euphoria of his new status as U.S. senator and the reality of working from a converted trailer, with three longtime aides to handle a huge flow of paper, sift through applications from newfound admirers, and hire staff. One such favor seeker was the author, hoping to secure Martinez's participation in this book project. Though he sought to hire Senate veterans rather than staff from his campaign, he quickly discovered how the D.C. job market works. There are two kinds of staffers: Democrats and Republicans, the former as liberal as the latter are conservative, all of them young. Rather than finding sober-minded policy specialists, he was besieged by "young Republican types"—something he, at the same age, was not. For them, as for their Democratic counterparts, Washington was a place to attend think-tank lectures, steel for battle against the ideological opposition, and settle scores. Inevitably, Mel would make mistakes in staffing.

His first media sortie was positive. Being true to his origins, he was quick to work the Spanish-language media, building upon relationships developed while HUD secretary. Just as Michael Jordan and Nike developed a symbiotic relationship, each nurturing the other, Mel developed a relationship of mutual support with the capital's nascent Hispanic news media. They needed a star, someone who was one of them, who understood the immigrant experience and could talk about pertinent issues *en español*. And Mel needed a way to honor his immigrant experience as a Peter Panner who came to these shores without parents, looking for refuge, before adopting this country and earning political office. It was a perfect match.

Cementing that relationship, Mel made his first Senate speech (always a big step for a new senator) in Spanish, marking one of the few occasions when a language other than English was spoken on the Senate floor. Or at least it was reported as "a speech in Spanish," probably because the Spanish-language news media were alerted in advance and were there to cover his remarks, in stories that ricocheted in the English-language media, including the *Washington Post* and *New York Times*. In fact, Mel's remarks were mostly in English—how else would his colleagues comprehend?—save for about two paragraphs.

The occasion was Senate confirmation of President Bush's nominee for attorney general, Alberto Gonzales. Gonzales, who had been Bush's personal lawyer before joining political forces with him, had two obvious commonalities with Mel: both were Hispanic and both owed their political career to the forty-third president. One of eight children of migrant workers, Gonzales was a Harvard Law graduate appointed to the Texas Supreme Court by then governor Bush. What complicated Gonzales's cabinet confirmation was his service as White House counsel during the president's first term. In that role he drafted legal memos saying that U.S. soldiers were exempt from the Geneva Convention in their military role in Iraq. He was also responsible for legal memoranda on the treatment of prisoners that, critics said, condoned acts of torture. Coming after John Ashcroft, who famously authored the Patriot Act, his legal opinions generated stiff opposition from opponents of the administration's policy in Iraq.

During debate over Gonzales's nomination, Democratic critics sought to link him to the Abu Ghraib scandal, while Republicans played up his status as a minority. Senator Salazar of Colorado took a position that seemed ironic at best, hypocritical at worst. Martinez's rival for the allegiance of Hispanic voters, he introduced Gonzales during his testimony before the Senate Judiciary Committee—an apparent act of ethnic solidarity, since Salazar is a Democrat. Yet he criticized Republican senators during floor debate for defending Gonzales on ethnic grounds, a criticism that clearly applied to Martinez.

In his maiden Senate speech, the Florida junior senator began by addressing those who came to America to make a better life for themselves, saying "Gonzales es uno de nosotros. El representa nuestros sueños y esperanzas para nuestros hijos. . . . No podemos permitir que la politiquería nos quite este momento que nos enorgullece a todos." The *Congressional*

Record included the translation "Gonzales is one of us. He represents all of our hopes and dreams for our children. . . . We cannot allow petty politicking to deny this moment that fills us all with such pride."[3]

The implicit message was clear: Mel Martinez had arrived in the Senate. Only it was not the old Mel Martinez who ran for Orange County chairman in 1997 as someone who was incidentally Cuban. This Mel was loud and proud about his Hispanic heritage. And it seemed to be working for him. Alerted by the senator's office, Univision, the most popular Spanish-language cable network, and CNN en Español carried the speech live. Telemundo interrupted afternoon soap operas to broadcast the speech live as well.

Asked about the response to his speech, Martinez said his Orlando office received some unfavorable calls. Some people had said, "This is America, we speak English here." He figured these people probably did not vote for him anyway. The response from his Republican colleagues was uniformly favorable, however. "The leadership was giddy about it. They thought it was great," he said.

Mel's choice of his top staff would cause him deep embarrassment in the Terri Schiavo matter, marring his first hundred days in office. Theresa Schindler Schiavo was a forty-one-year-old Tampa Bay woman who had lived since 1990 in what her doctors termed a "persistent vegetative state." She was the subject of a long legal battle between her husband, who sought to have her feeding tube removed, and her parents, who wanted to keep her alive. Florida courts consistently sided with the husband. Hours before the court-approved removal of her feeding tube, the House of Representatives sought to intervene at the urging of Majority Leader Tom DeLay, an ardent abortion foe and "culture of life" defender. The House Government Reform Committee issued subpoenas to Schiavo and her husband, Michael, to attend a March 25 hearing. They also subpoenaed two doctors treating Schiavo, as well as the director of the hospice where Terri Schiavo resided.

Going further, the subpoena instructed Michael Schiavo and the hospice director to maintain the medical equipment used to care for Schiavo in its "current operating state," in an attempt to prevent the feeding tube's removal. Prefiguring the partisan battle to follow, Henry A. Waxman of California, the ranking Democrat on the Government Reform panel, reacted angrily to the move, saying, "Congress has no authority to use subpoenas to tell doctors what treatment they can and cannot provide to any individual under their care."[4] Then on March 16, as Congress prepared for its Easter recess, the House passed a bill authorizing the transfer of the Schiavo matter to federal courts after all state remedies were exhausted.

Reflecting its calmer demeanor, the Senate took a more restrained approach. Led by the freshman senator from Florida, the Senate passed a bill similar to the House bill, except that the Senate bill left federal court review to the discretion of a federal judge, rather than mandating a federal court review as the House bill did. The nation watched as Senate and House members delayed their spring vacations to engage in a war of words over which was the right approach to take. Meanwhile, antiabortion activists blamed both chambers for the stalemate.

Mel's leadership in winning bipartisan support for the Senate bill was an impressive accomplishment for a freshman legislator. If only the story ended there. Unfortunately for him, he committed a serious blunder during Senate consideration of the bill. While he was working to get support from Senator Tom Harkin (D-Ia.), he pulled a piece of paper from his inside coat pocket and handed it to him. He thought he was giving Harkin a list of bullet points on the bill, he would later say. That evening, Democratic senators told the media that a GOP strategy memo on the Schiavo matter had fallen into their hands. The memo outlined how Republicans could appeal to their conservative base with the issue and use it against Florida's Democratic senator Bill Nelson.

In the ensuing donnybrook, Democratic senators uniformly denounced the memo, while GOP legislators led by Tom DeLay in the House and Senate majority leader Bill Frist denied knowledge of it. Some Senate aides— possibly Mel's, it was rumored—accused the Democrats of authoring the memo, a charge picked up by conservative bloggers and talk-radio hosts, including Rush Limbaugh. In a poll of Senate offices by the *Washington Times,* no office on either side of the aisle claimed responsibility for the memo.

Then Senator Harkin announced how he received the memo, after first calling Mel. He reached the freshman senator as he was preparing to fly to Rome for the pope's funeral as an official representative of the United States, an honor granted him by the president. But Harkin's call destroyed any sense of honor Martinez might have felt. As the Iowa senator would explain to the media, Mel had given him the now infamous memo on the Senate floor. Mel quickly assembled his top staff and asked them how the memo got into his pocket. His staffers denied knowledge of the memo at first. Several hours later his counsel, Brian Darling, confessed to authoring the memo. In most Senate offices, as Hill veterans remarked in news stories covering this episode, such a memo would pass from the legal counsel to the chief of staff before going to the senator. Its contents would also be shared with the legislative aide and the press assistant. None of these staffers claimed knowledge of the memo, however, and Darling alone was fired.

In his press release Martinez said:

> It is with profound disappointment and regret that I learned today that a senior member of my staff was unilaterally responsible for this document. It was not approved by me or any other member of my staff, nor were we aware of its existence until very recently. This type of behavior and sentiment will not be tolerated in my office. As the senator, I am ultimately responsible for the work of my staff and the product that comes out of this office. I take full responsibility for this situation.[5]

Mel received a torrent of bad press. He was criticized for blaming his staff—once again—for a major political blunder. Scant months had passed since Mel's Senate campaign, when he blamed an unnamed aide for the campaign flyer calling primary opponent Bill McCollum a darling of the homosexual lobby. He was criticized too for hiring a staff of right-wing politicos. (Darling had previously served as general counsel to New Hampshire senator Bob Smith, regarded by some as part of the loony right, and after that worked for the Alexander Strategy Group, closely linked to Tom DeLay, where he lobbied for gun rights.) That charge, in turn, led to criticism that Mel was a Bush-Rove puppet. News stories pointed to his near-perfect voting record in support of President Bush's agenda, despite barely winning election from a strongly bipartisan state. The partial exception was Mel's negotiating with the White House before voting with the president in favor of drilling for oil in the Arctic National Wildlife Refuge on Alaska's northern coast. In return, the senator got the president to agree to extend the moratorium on drilling off the Florida coast.

One of the most stinging rebukes came from Florida congressman Dan Wexler, a Democrat from Palm Beach County, who said of Martinez: "I see him as someone with very few scruples. Say anything, do anything as long as it advances his political interests. He's humiliated himself and our state."[6]

This criticism assumes Martinez knew the memo's contents when he handed it to Harkin, one of the Senate's most outspoken Democrats—clearly a dubious assumption. Harkin himself was quick to defend the freshman senator, calling him "a very decent guy to work with." A more likely interpretation is that Mel didn't know what he was giving Harkin—still a mistake, a gigantic faux pas given the tidal wave of negative publicity it created, but a mistake of the bumbling variety rather than the failure of character that Wexler alleged.

As for Mel assembling a partisan staff, that too was the result of inattention and inexperience rather than his own partisanship. And Mel's support for the president's agenda was because he believed in the agenda and felt loyal to the president who had brought him to national politics. His staff, Brian Darling in particular, might have been motivated on the Terri Schiavo issue by partisan zeal, but Mel's zeal was more personal. Rightly or wrongly, he connected the Schiavo issue to his sister, Margarita, who had died from brain tumors that left her comatose. That experience profoundly affected both Mel and Kitty, who left her job to help care for her sister-in-law. As with the abortion issue, Kitty's views were as important as Mel's.

When the Schiavo case broke into the news, Kitty told Mel they should do something. She urged him to call his old friend Ken Connor, the person with whom he ran in the 1994 Florida governor's race on the Right to Life Party ticket. Kitty joined Mel on the phone when he called Connor. Together they asked, "What can we do?"[7] It was that phone conversation, according to Mel, that sent him back to Washington dedicated to crafting a solution that would win Senate support and not go to the drastic length of the House bill. In the end, none of this was successful: there was no federal court hearing, the state court decision allowing Terri Schiavo's intravenous feeding tube to be removed was executed, and she died twenty-two days later. A subsequent autopsy revealed that she had irreversible brain damage and that she was blind, contradicting claims that while comatose she was able to respond to visual stimuli.[8]

In the beating that Mel took in the press over the Schiavo memo incident, the question arose repeatedly: Who is the real Mel—is he the centrist politician who served as Orange County chairman or the passionate conservative who ascended to national office? The question poses a false dichotomy, however. It was not Mel who changed but rather the issues. As he said in an interview, "I am really only passionate about two issues, Cuba and abortion, and abortion is really Kitty's issue more than mine." He seemed moderate in Orange County because his job responsibilities did not extend to either issue—except when the Elián González controversy erupted, focusing attention on U.S.-Cuba relations.

Part of the embarrassment over the Schiavo memo was that Democratic senator Frank Lautenberg of New Jersey brought ethics charges against Mel, saying that he had broken a Senate rule against distributing anonymous memos on the Senate floor.[9] The Senate Rules Committee considered the case and dismissed it on less than comforting grounds. The person responsible, Darling, no longer worked for Mel, they declared.

In the aftermath, Mel turned to his old friend and law partner, Skip Dalton, to serve briefly as his legal counsel. The arrangement was modeled after one used by Bob Graham, who employed a rotating general counsel when he was governor, putting friends whom he trusted in that position. It was something Mel needed, too. As Dalton explained: "Mel went to Washington without legislative experience, without [many] of his own people. It made sense to turn to me because I had no skin in the game, no agenda. I was not looking to move from this job into some other job, but to see that everything was done in Mel's interest."[10] Translated, his job was to keep Mel from getting into any more trouble. He would supply judgment, as needed, to balance Mel's passion.

A committed Democrat, Dalton did not view himself as a policy advocate but as someone responsible for seeing that procedures were followed. It was a message he brought to Mel's staff as well. Their job, he stressed, was not to advocate for policies but to process information and present the pros and cons of legislation for the senator. In short, their first loyalty was to Mel, not to the conservative movement or the GOP. Dalton's initial assignment was to learn about Senate ethics rules and make sure Mel's office was complying—a response to the Darling-Schiavo affair.

Soon Mel's focus switched to immigration, an issue on which his office staff had no expertise. "It sort of fell to me," said Dalton. He worked with Nilda Pedrosa, the head of Mel's South Florida office, who had served during his Senate campaign as chief political director after working previously for Mel's Republican predecessor, Connie Mack. A Cuban American, she had also worked for the State Department and was familiar with the immigration issue from that experience.[11]

This focus on immigration grew out of conversations that Pedrosa, Dalton, and other staffers had with Mel after the Schiavo affair about what kind of name he wanted to make for himself in the Senate. Every member can't be an expert on every issue, they told him, not when you cast more than three hundred votes a year. "You have to decide what interests you, what's important to your state, and where you can be most effective in terms of playing a role and shaping policy," said Dalton. Immigration was one of those issues, but only one; others included foreign relations, specifically relations with Latin America and Spain, where Mel was a natural because of his background, and even Africa, since he sat on the Foreign Relations Subcommittee on Africa.

The immigration issue was a natural for Mel too, said Dalton. "It was a confluence of the planets lining up at the right time, of being in the right place at the right time, of having the background and interest, of being the natural person to support the administration's initiative in this area, and having the wisdom to realize what role he could play." As well, it was an important issue to the state, and Mel had the ability to influence policy because of his background—an ability that extended to the "other side of the aisle," as Democrats also knew and respected his background. He was someone who could both carry the administration's message to the Senate and carry the Senate's message to the administration. And, said Dalton, the Senate GOP leadership saw him as someone they needed in their fold to succeed on this issue.

In 2005 there were two competing immigration bills: Kennedy-McCain and Cornyn-Kyl. The differences between them centered primarily on border enforcement and amnesty, issues that mattered to Mel in a personal way. Though he came to the United States legally, he knew people who had not. He found their plight worrying, as Dalton explained, not just from the standpoint of security, so we could know where they were, and not just because agriculture and tourism in Florida depend on immigrant labor, but also because he wanted a way for them to become enfranchised as Americans. That was where his ethnic identity stretched from Cuban to pan-Hispanic (or "pan-American," as Dalton put it). Because federal laws advantage persons who are fleeing political persecution, Cubans have no immigration problem—on the U.S. side. But this Cuban boy, who struggled to integrate himself into American life and become a citizen, could relate to the plight of undocumented workers, primarily Mexican, who could not do what he did because U.S. law prevented it.

Mel could have taken a different tack. He could have said—as he did during his Senate campaign—"I came here legally and I expect others to do the same." It would have been the politically expedient thing to do, earning him points with the base of his party, both nationally and in Florida. However, his own experience made the politically expedient route hypocritical, once he won election. He could not be the person he was and do that.

That was why Mel, from the beginning, wanted a comprehensive immigration bill, one that addressed not only the border security and guest-worker issues but also the conundrum of what to do with the estimated 12 million undocumented workers in the country. He knew, as he said in an interview, that "if you didn't address the problem of the undocumenteds, you couldn't go back and do it later."[12] The only way to address this issue was to use the ferment over border security to move action on the undocumented issue. So Dalton was assigned to monitor action on both the Cornyn-Kyl and Kennedy-McCain bills, to see whether there was some middle ground that he could help negotiate, to make possible a compromise bill that would clear the Senate and become law. The monitoring was easy at the staff level, said Dalton, because both groups of sponsors wanted Mel "on their bill." But he wisely chose to avoid a sponsorship role, which freed him from having to defend one bill over the other and allowed him to play a broker role and display the negotiation skill he honed as a young attorney in Orlando.

His middle-ground role led to conversations with Barack Obama's office. Obama, with his immigrant father from Kenya, coming from the big state of Illinois with a large immigration issue, wanted to play a role in the immigration debate, too. In the end Mel's role eclipsed Obama's, in part because Mel played a more centrist role in focusing on what was doable, and also because Republican control of the Senate made that role easier for Mel. The 2006 session also provided an opportunity to work with Ted Kennedy's office. Mel was impressed, Dalton recalled, with Kennedy's legislative acumen—his knowledge of Senate rules and his strategic sense of what was doable and what was not. It was a lesson in leadership, and Mel learned to appreciate that Kennedy was no mere ideologue, as he once thought, but a political realist who knew how to tack into the wind.

A positive step, Mel hired Brian Walsh, an experienced Senate staffer who knew immigration policy cold—knew the players, knew the issues, and knew how to move the legislation along. (Walsh was no relation to the priest and social worker named Bryan Walsh who assisted a young Mel in the Peter Pan program.) After internal staff discussion involving

Walsh and Dalton, Mel concluded that the Kennedy-McCain bill failed as a vehicle for reform. "There was too much Kennedy in it, and too little Mc-Cain," he said. His assessment was tactical rather than ideological. He and his staff thought Kennedy-McCain might pass the Senate but would not win support from the chamber's GOP leadership, dooming the legislation in the House, where Republicans possessed a larger majority and where GOP leaders opposed legislation granting any kind of amnesty to illegal aliens.

Mel's shift away from Kennedy-McCain corresponded with advice he received from Laura Reiff, an attorney-lobbyist for an association named Essential Worker Immigration Coalition (EWIC). Her organization was run from the Washington office of the Greenberg-Traurig law firm. EWIC represented major employers who were essentially hiding behind this trade association, their CEOs fearful of coming out publicly in favor of anything that smacked of amnesty. They feared, as Reiff and other participants in immigration reform noted, that border patrol agents would swoop down on their plants if they testified in favor of easing regulations. Or, worse, that they would get a shellacking in the news media from the likes of CNN's Lou Dobbs, a rabid immigration foe, if they spoke publicly in favor of what Reiff called "workable enforcement." So EWIC was formed and Reiss, wanting to secure passage of a bill, met with Mel, urging him to push for a middle-ground position, something to the safe right of Kennedy-McCain that might have a chance in the House.

"Mel needed to step up" was Reiff's message. She had contacted him through a fellow Greenberg-Traurig attorney, Cesar Alvarez, who was a friend of the senator's. Mel was perfect for the role of negotiating a middle-ground position, she said, because his state had a large immigrant population, because he had all that credibility as an immigrant himself, and because he could speak so passionately on the issue. Mel's response, she said, was "Sure, I'd love to do it." The role corresponded with his instinct as a bargainer and enabled him to make an impact as a freshman.[13]

Skip Dalton explained how significant that was. As a freshman, he said, you don't feel in control, a feeling reinforced by the sheer difficulty of getting around the labyrinth of Capitol Hill offices. You have an aide walking you everywhere just to get from point A to point B, said the friend and former law partner, who kept Mel company and joined him for dinner on evenings when the senator had no official function to attend. Despite being unsure of himself, here was a chance (in the baseball metaphor) to "play in the bigs" and be an impact player, not just by putting points on the board in some partisan competition but by actually moving a bill toward passage, making a difference for people back home. It was the reason he had come to Washington in the first place, the senator told himself. In doing so he was taking a risk. Most party leaders tell a freshman senator to concentrate on securing his seat—doing constituency service, answering the mail, and avoiding controversial stands that might come back to haunt them at reelection time. Mel Martinez would be different.

Mel stepped up to the plate in the spring of 2006 by collaborating with Nebraska senator Chuck Hagel. Through his aide Brian Walsh, Mel learned about an earlier immigration bill filed by Hagel, a maverick Republican, and South Dakota Democratic senator Tom Daschle.[14] Their proposal was shelved for lack of cosponsors, and pieces from it were incorporated into other bills. What was left was not a comprehensive bill, but one that responded to a key question—namely, which illegal aliens should be allowed to remain in the United States?

What attracted Mel to the Hagel-Daschle bill was its three-tiered approach to determining who could stay. Undocumented workers who had resided in the country for less than two years would be sent home. Mel liked this provision because it enabled the immigration reformers to say they were being punitive with at least some immigrants. A second category was for those who had been here more than five years; they could stay, provided they had no criminal record and met other requirements. In between was a third category that intrigued Mel the most. It was for workers who had been in the country for two to five years. They would be required to "touch back," which meant returning to their port of entry and requesting to come back through a temporary-worker program. As Steve Taylor, an aide to Hagel, explained, Mel liked the three-tiered approach but wanted to make the touchback symbolic. The Cornhusker senator's own version required that workers win approval from the U.S. consulate before returning to the United States. Mel's contribution was to remove that procedural hurdle.

Taylor gives Mel credit for seeing that the three-tiered approach could work and winning agreement on it. "If he had not recognized that the approach was something we could move" during the first week of debate on Kennedy-McCain in March 2006, when various senators were scurrying to find a compromise to Kennedy-McCain that could win passage with the support of the GOP leadership, "it wouldn't have happened." For a freshman told to keep his head down by party leaders, "that was a huge risk," said Taylor. "Fortunately, he didn't listen to the advice he received. He knew this was the time to pass a bill that was important to his state. He chose not to take a pass."[15]

To this point Mel had been meeting with a core group of senators who supported the Kennedy-McCain bill. As Tamar Jacoby, a writer and immigration reform advocate who lobbied in behalf of immigration reform, said: "Kennedy and McCain owned the process. They were on the front lines, they owned the bill." When the temperamental McCain learned that Mel had been meeting with Hagel to rework his bill on the issue of undocumented workers, he confronted the younger senator, asking him heatedly what was going on. In Jacoby's view, Mel had the guts to tell the senior senator that his bill was deficient on that issue. Eventually McCain agreed.[16]

With President Bush's support, the three-tier approach championed by Hagel and Martinez was incorporated into the Kennedy-McCain bill. It was also supported by two key GOP senators, majority leader Bill Frist and Judiciary Committee chairman Arlen Specter. Using Senate Rule 14, the Kennedy-McCain bill was sent back to committee and reported back out the same day with the Hagel-Martinez provision attached. Afterwards, as Brian Walsh related, some lobbyists began referring to the amended bill as "Hagel-Martinez," although technically it was not.

The bipartisan group of Senate supporters who had been working on the bill agreed to oppose amendments from the left and right that would undo the compromise they had already struck. They succeeded in the GOP-controlled Senate, and on May 25 the bill passed, 62–36, with Frist and his Democratic counterpart Harry Reid both voting yes. The bill would create a pathway for undocumented workers to become citizens, in addition to creating a new temporary-worker program that would provide U.S. legal status for as much as six years.

The problem lay in the House, where the legislative focus was on border security. In the lead-up to the 2006 congressional elections, the House passed a bill that dealt only with tighter border controls and deportation standards, along with tougher enforcement of employment rules. Most notably, it called for a 700-mile fence along the Mexican-U.S. border. These different bills set the stage for a dueling set of committee hearings in the summer of 2006, as the judiciary committees from both chambers sought to influence public opinion in support of their approach to immigration reform. Each wanted to gain leverage in the House-Senate conference committee that would resolve differences before either approach became law.

Interestingly, the tandem hearings were not a partisan duel. The debate was essentially between House and Senate Republicans, with President Bush favoring the Senate side but unwilling or unable to force a resolution. As the *Washington Post* reported on July 5, 2006, "House and Senate Republicans sparred over immigration in hearings on opposite coasts Wednesday, holding firmly to their starkly different viewpoints on what has become one of the most intractable and divisive issues to confront the GOP in years." The article said some advocates for the Senate approach were disappointed that Mr. Bush had not moved more decisively to weaken House Republicans' opposition to a pathway for citizenship and a guest-worker program. Senate Judiciary Committee chairman Arlen Specter called on the president to "provide the leadership to bring the House and Senate together" as well as to engage in the "nuts and bolts" of consensus building between the warring GOP factions. The intraparty debate had intensified, the *Post* noted, as the midterm elections neared and conservatives supported by House Republicans tried to rally their voting base.[17]

The Senate hearings in Philadelphia, Miami, and Washington, D.C., heard testimony on immigrants triumphing over adversity in pursuit of the American Dream. The House hearings, engineered to win points for border security, elicited testimony in such places as San Diego, Laredo, and Yuma on the perils of immigration. The titles for the hearings indicated the difference in orientation. In Philadelphia the Senate used the title "Comprehensive Immigration Reform: Examining the Need for a Guest Worker Program"; in Miami the title was "Contributions of Immigrants to the U.S. Armed Forces." In contrast, the House hearings in San Diego were titled "Border Vulnerabilities to Terrorist Threats." In Yuma, the House Judiciary Committee addressed "Costs to Federal, State, and Local Government of an Unsecured Border."

Tamar Jacoby, who lobbied for compromise legislation, said: "The House hearings were by the fringe and for the fringe," as the House leaders were responding to the hysteria whipped up by right-wing radio hosts, especially in the states along the U.S.-Mexican border. They were also responding, in part, to the May Day rallies that occurred in major cities across the country, including Orlando. Heavily promoted by Spanish-language radio stations, these rallies sought to demonstrate Hispanic support for immigration reform. The demonstrators' signs—those the author saw—were variations on the theme of "We work for you. Let us be citizens."

But the rallies also had a reverse effect. The sheer number of participants reminded Anglos—who were already amply reminded by right-wing media—of the growing Hispanic population, which is projected to outnumber the Anglo population by 2050, based upon current immigration, legal and illegal, and upon the differential birth rates of Anglos and Hispanics. There were also complaints in the media about immigrants carrying flags from their home countries—Mexico, Ecuador, Venezuela—rather than the Stars and Stripes.

More fundamentally, the House GOP leadership employed a different political calculus than their Senate counterparts on what was good for their party. This difference was partly institutional: House members run for reelection every two years, senators every six. As widely reported, Speaker Dennis Hastert believed the key to retaining Republican control of the House (and keeping his Speaker role) was to appease the GOP base on the issue of border security. Anything sounding like amnesty for undocumented workers was anathema to House Republican leaders. The difference in language was instructive. Martinez and other supporters of the Senate bill talked about "undocumented workers" and "bringing them out of the shadows" and "creating a pathway to citizenship," while their House counterparts referred to "illegals" and the danger of granting "amnesty"—varying descriptions, with sharply different connotations, of the same legislative provisions.

White House political strategist Karl Rove saw a different need than House GOP leaders did. They wanted to appeal to the base of the party on immigration reform, emphasizing border security at the risk of offending Hispanic voters. Rove and his client, President Bush, were responding to the longer-term need of the party, recognizing that Hispanics were swing voters with the potential to swing Republican, helping to make the GOP a permanent majority party. Getting there required building bridges to Hispanics and trying, at all costs, not to offend them.

That was why the president favored an approach to immigration reform that would grant undocumented workers a pathway to citizenship, which opponents called amnesty. What the White House political operation knew was that Hispanics are plausible converts to the GOP. They have low rates of participation in welfare programs and low rates of union membership, combined with high rates of homeownership, business formation, and military service—all Republican attributes. They are also overwhelmingly Catholic, with corresponding views on gays and abortion, making them susceptible to the Republican social agenda.

In all these respects, Hispanics are different from African Americans, the Democrats' major minority group. On immigration, moreover, blacks and Hispanics were potential adversaries. In the popular perception, immigrants took jobs away from African Americans and suppressed wage gains. More immigration, both legal and illegal, also threatened one of the Democrats' key interest groups: organized labor. By creating a ready supply of workers willing to toil at low wages, immigration weakened labor unions' ability to organize and bargain collectively in behalf of their members. Hence immigration reform was a potential wedge issue dividing Democrats, separating Hispanics from blacks and organized labor.

House Republicans' stance on immigration was wildly unpopular, and it backfired on a number of candidates in the 2006 midterm elections, ceding an advantage to Democrats with the fast-growing Latino electorate. As Fred Barnes, writing in the conservative *Weekly Standard*, wryly observed, the GOP defeat in 2006 was "short of devastating—but only a little short." The party lost seats not only in New York, Connecticut, and Pennsylvania, strengthening Democratic dominance there, but also in the West, most notably in Colorado and Arizona, and in the key border state of Virginia, raising concern over which way these states would fall in the 2008 presidential race. About the immigration issue, Barnes wrote: "Already the wail of the immigration restrictionists is rising, insisting Republicans lost because they were not tough on keeping illegal border-crossers out. Not true. The test was in Arizona, where two of the noisiest border hawks, Representatives J. D. Hayworth and Randy Graf, lost House seats." Barnes, a conservative who supports granting undocumented workers a path to citizenship, labeled immigration reform one of the party's biggest failures under President Bush.[18]

Anti-immigrant invective was not limited to Republican House members. Pennsylvania Republican senator Santorum, a friend of Mel's, found himself in a close reelection race. An archconservative who won office as a devout abortion foe, Santorum ranked third in the Senate leadership, yet voted against the administration-backed immigration bill, the highest-ranking Republican to do so. Back home he sought to use the issue against his Democratic opponent, state treasurer Bob Casey Jr., who said he would have voted in favor. Santorum opposed the bill even though Pennsylvania has, in his own words, "remarkably little immigration of any kind."[19] The struggling senator ran attack ads bemoaning the bill's amnesty provisions, calling them a "slap in the face of hardworking Americans."[20] He lost.

Mel was disenchanted. In an interview, he told of meeting with a Hispanic religious leader in Pennsylvania who said his church group had supported Santorum in his initial run for the Senate. "We just can't support him anymore," this leader said to Martinez. "We don't know why he's talking the way he is on this immigration issue." Mel shook his head in telling the story.[21]

There were other senators besides Santorum who disappointed him. Jim DeMint (R-S.C.) was one. DeMint, who along with Jeff Sessions (R-Ala.) led the opposition, claimed at one point during the debate that the bill's backers had "declared war on the American people," which Mel found personally offensive.[22] "I will never forgive him for those remarks," he said.

The impact of this rhetoric on the GOP's appeal to Hispanic voters was significant. Two years earlier, such voters had gravitated toward President Bush in numbers larger than ever. But GOP rhetoric surrounding immigration reform changed all that, as the border hawks within the party drowned out Martinez and other advocates for comprehensive reform, including the president himself. "Pollsters generally agree that the same voters abandoned the president's party in droves" during the 2006 election, wrote Darryl Fears in the Washington Post, "with Latinos giving the GOP only 30 percent of their vote as strident House immigration legislation inspired by Republicans and tough-talking campaign ads by conservative candidates roiled the community. It was a 10-point drop from the lowest estimated Latino vote percentage two years ago, and a 14-point drop from the highest."[23]

Fears summed up the GOP problem with a quote from the Reverend Luis Cortés Jr., founder of Esperanza USA, a network of Latino Christian groups. Offering what Fears called "a velvet slap, mixing praise with criticism," Cortés said: "A lot of the Republican candidates chose immigration as the wedge issue, and polls seem to bear out that it was an error for them to do that. And I think Mel Martinez, because of his life story, is a perfect person to help them find their way back from that era." Cortés was alluding to the next step in Martinez's career path.

⟷

In the hectic week before the 2006 election, Karl Rove left several messages for Martinez. Mel, busy speaking in behalf of Senate colleagues, had been too busy to return the calls. Then at a campaign appearance, Rove buttonholed him to say he had something important to talk about. In a subsequent phone conversation Rove told Mel the president wanted him to take the reins of the Republican National Committee.

Mel met with Rove and the president in the Oval Office, the president in a wing chair and Mel to his right, accompanied by Mike Duncan, the second in command at RNC; Ken Mehlman, the White House political director; and Beverly Davis, president of the National Federation of Republican Women. "What we need is a new face for the party," the president told Mel. Mel voiced his reservations. "I told the president that I was worried about the conflict with my Senate role. I said I would not be an attack dog for the party." The president said this was not a concern. "You'll be the spokesman. You don't need to be the attack dog. Besides, you don't need to do it for long. Just show the right face for the party and raise some money."

Mel remained noncommittal.

Then came a follow-up call from the president. The senator was leaving his home in Orlando, heading to the airport for a return flight to Washington, part of his Tuesday morning ritual. As he tells the story: "I had just told Kitty not to worry, I'm not going to take the RNC job. Then, in the car on the way to the airport, I got a call from the president. It was like an out-of-body experience. I was listening to myself say yes when I had intended to say no."

He would later say, "It was a big mistake, one of the worst I've ever made. But when the president calls, it's hard to say no." It was especially hard for someone who owed his career in national politics, from his cabinet appointment to his Senate election, to the support of one man: George W. Bush.

The president, after imploring him to do it for the sake of the party and because he was the right man for the job, clinched the deal by citing

Mel's passion. He reminded Mel of a story he had told about helping an Orlando woman, Liz McCausland, win her mother's release from Vietnam. Authorities there were holding the mother in detention, accusing her of treason for publicly criticizing the regime's human rights record. Martinez was moved by the daughter's struggle because it reminded him of his own efforts to reunite with his parents. It was not just Mel's success in securing the mother's release that Bush cited; it was his passion. Mel had told the president that when McCausland called to thank him for helping her mother, the conversation brought tears to his eyes. Using the story for leverage, Bush told him: "That's the kind of person I want in the RNC job."

The choice of Martinez was not unprecedented. It continued a tradition of members of Congress taking over political parties that had just suffered serious midterm election defeats. After the 1994 midterm, in which the Democrats lost control of Congress, President Clinton talked Senator Christopher Dodd of Connecticut into spending the next four years as chairman of the Democratic National Committee. And after the GOP's setbacks in the 1982 midterm, President Ronald Reagan asked Senator Paul Laxalt of Nevada to chair the RNC during his final four years in office. In announcing the choice, Mr. Bush said of Martinez: "He'll be a person who'll be able to carry our message as we go into an important year in 2008."[24]

To accommodate the selection of a sitting senator as party chair, an organizational change was made. The party's chair was then Ken Mehlman, a protégé of Karl Rove, who managed the RNC on a day-to-day basis. Under the new arrangement, the chairman's job was split in two. Martinez would be the party's General Chairman in charge of fund-raising and message, and Mike Duncan, who had been the party's general counsel, would be the chairman responsible for daily operations.

Some members of the RNC opposed making Mel chairman. When the 165-member body voted, five gave a thumbs-down. "If they hadn't been pressured, maybe twenty would have voted no," said Mel. While he minimized the opposition vote, it was a significant protest against the president's choice for the job, all the more so because the opposition was spawned by his position on immigration reform, which was unpopular with the party's grass roots even though it was the position of the White House.

In a postelection interview with the *St. Petersburg Times*, Senator Martinez sought to defuse accusations from his opponents. He stated:

My role is going to be limited . . . to issues relating to conveying a message for our party to the American people. It is not going to be about solving the problems that may exist with the party structure in Iowa or Nebraska or Florida or anywhere else. . . . When I discussed this with the president I made it very clear to him that I needed to be and intended to be a full-time senator for the state of Florida, and so the job we crafted was very limited in that sense. . . . I would dare say that there may be days at a time when I don't have any day-to-day responsibilities as RNC chair.[25]

He added that the Republican Party would remain neutral in the coming race for the GOP presidential nomination.

He also took several conciliatory steps. On the amnesty issue, *Congressional Quarterly* reported that a Martinez opponent, Randy Pullen of Arizona, met with the senator in the week before the RNC vote and secured a pledge from him to support a resolution adopted the previous year to use "all means available" to secure the nation's border and enforce existing immigration laws.[26] In an interview with the conservative *Washington Times*, Martinez was quoted as saying, "I do not support amnesty for illegal aliens. I do support strong border enforcement, and absolutely I support the rule of law [in regard to] illegal aliens here."[27]

In his acceptance speech to party delegates, Martinez emphasized what he could bring to the party. On one hand, he hoped to broaden the party base by making it more inclusive, reaching out to "those who sometimes have not felt like our party has left the door open to them." He mentioned Hispanics and African Americans in particular. On the other hand, he hoped to unite the party by using his personal story to convey a message of "hope and optimism."

He would not sacrifice immigration reform, however. His conciliatory statements about supporting border enforcement and not supporting amnesty were mostly semantics. He had always supported border enforcement—as part of a larger reform package that included a "pathway toward citizenship," which in his mind differed from "amnesty" because the path to citizenship would be procedurally circumscribed and available only to longtime U.S. residents.

Put differently, he saw no conflict between his senator role and his party leadership role when it came to the immigration issue. Immigration reform was good for the nation and good for the GOP, because the party desperately needed Hispanic support after its disastrous showing in the 2006 midterms. Looking to 2008 and beyond, Republicans could not hope to win elections without at least half of the Latino vote. When asked about immigration reform right after the RNC vote, he told a reporter from *Congressional Quarterly*: "I really hope today is not about that issue. But we didn't get it done, we didn't pass a bill out of the Congress. That's what we need to do. I think that's part of what the voters were dissatisfied with. We as the party in charge could not come together on an issue that was that important. I think now what we need to do is to get something done, pass a bill, when the time comes and the Democrat leadership puts it on the agenda."[28]

His efforts would continue.

10

RETREAT

"We had a breakthrough," said Mel.[1]

For five months, he and a bipartisan coalition of senators had worked to revive immigration reform in the new Congress. The Bush administration supported their efforts by sending cabinet secretaries Carlos Gutierrez of Commerce and Michael Chertoff of Homeland Security to meet with them for weeks on end. The chief White House lobbyist, Condi Wolff, had worked the phones for them, drumming up Republican support for a compromise measure. Now, in the summer of 2007, the Senate logjam seemed to have broken.

Martinez had returned to Congress prepared to try again. The defeat of immigration reform in the previous session had deeply disappointed him. But it also gave him an education. He was learning the ways of the Senate—learning that good ideas do not triumph of their own accord, that winning is about getting the votes, making necessary concessions but avoiding those that lose support, all done cautiously, painstakingly, one step at a time. And that required working with the other side, the Democrats. Not exclusively, of course. In the new Congress, the Democrats ruled the Senate by one vote, making Republican support practically essential for winning passage.

Mel therefore wanted a bill that a modicum of GOP senators would support. They did not need a majority of Republicans, just enough for a bipartisan majority strong enough to defeat weakening attempts in the "other body," the House of Representatives. There, especially there, in the more ideological of the two chambers of Congress, many Republicans and some Democrats opposed making concessions to the estimated twelve million illegal immigrants in the United States. In Mel's view, most of these were hard-working, law-abiding people who were trying to support their families and capture a piece of the American Dream; most had overstayed legitimate visas rather than crossing the border illegally.

"The key was Kyl," Mel said, referring to Republican senator Jon Kyl of Arizona, newly reelected to his third Senate term. Kyl had voted against the previous immigration bill. "I knew if we could get him on board, others would follow. So I came back ready to work with Kyl." He called, went to see him, said let's work together, and asked what the Arizona senator needed to get on board. Kyl was receptive, said Mel. "He had a dustup in his 2006 reelection campaign and came back to the Senate determined to work on immigration reform."

Mel's legislative staff played a key role. He had assembled his staff in fits and starts, sometimes making mistakes, but by 2007 he had a seasoned group of Hill veterans, people with substantive expertise and procedural know-how, not just Young Republican newbies driven by partisan angst. "My staff said stay with Kyl, don't get to the left of Kyl, don't get to the right of Kyl, just stay with him," Mel recounted. "Which I did. Except that Kyl wasn't always right. Sometimes he needed a push or two."

He and Kyl worked together and got other GOP senators to come along. All agreed to support a bill that created a guest-worker program and addressed the problem of undocumenteds, as long as border security was ensured first. The two then approached the other side, knowing they had the key Republican senators that needed to be "on the bill" before negotiating differences with the Democrats. Here Mel was key. Like their GOP counterparts, Senate Democrats genuflected to Mel on this issue, recognized his moral authority, and wanted him on board. He became a natural bridge between the parties, a go-between who could hammer out interparty compromises acceptable to both sides.

The Democrats' point person was the late Ted Kennedy, the lion of the Senate, the iconic liberal whom Republican colleagues loved to mock during campaign season. They mocked him then, but returned to work with him, admiringly and respectfully, during the governing season. Mel was no different. While running for the Senate in 2004, he told voters in The Villages, a vast retirement community southwest of Orlando, "Send me to Washington so I can go toe-to-toe with Ted Kennedy."[2] And he meant it then. Only two years removed from his Orange County chairmanship, three years from practicing personal injury law, he knew little about the Senate. It was easy to beard the lion while running for office; now Mel had to work with him.

Kennedy was the lion especially on immigration. He had the best staff on the issue. Some Republicans thought his staff made him look good, but Mel knew better. Kennedy worked hard, knew the ropes of the Senate, knew how to pass legislation, and knew how to keep bills stuck in committee when he opposed them. And he cared passionately about this issue. Mel the immigrant respected that.

Kennedy cared so much that he bucked his Democratic colleagues when they sought to sideline the issue. Harry Reid, the Senate majority leader, had advised his caucus to proceed slowly on immigration, mindful of the politics. The politics favored the Democrats on this issue. Since the White House and House Republicans were divided on immigration policy, Democrats could benefit whether a bill passed or not. If the legislation failed, they could blame House Republicans for opposing it and President Bush for being too weak or too uncommitted to deliver GOP votes. If it succeeded, they could take credit, saying Democrats won the victory over House Republican opposition.

Given these scenarios, Reid might want a bill to fail, enabling Democratic candidates in the 2008 presidential campaign to use the issue against the Republicans. Or, slightly different, he might prefer a "jump ball" on immigration reform, leaving it to the party's presidential candidate to build consensus on this controversial issue. That was what Senate Republicans thought, according to Mel: Reid did not want a bill.

But Kennedy had bucked the leadership, pushing Reid to work for a bill and, when all hope seemed lost, to allow more time for debate.[3] So Mel needed to work with Kennedy.

His staff encouraged these efforts while also cautioning him. They reminded him that immigration reform had failed in the last Congress because Democrats got too much in the bill. "It was a Kennedy-McCain bill," Mel said in an interview. "But there was more Kennedy than McCain in it."

"Just don't get your picture taken with Kennedy," his staff warned. Wisely, because pictures have a life of their own. The sight of Mel with Kennedy, working together on immigration reform, would send the wrong message to the Republican fold, many of whom opposed giving immigrants a break. It would suggest a repeat of the Kennedy-McCain affair.

To Mel's surprise, Kennedy and the Democrats were receptive to the Kyl-Martinez draft bill, wanting only minor changes. "We felt we had won on this already," Mel said. Thinking that, they rushed to make an announcement, hoping to create a tidal wave of support for their bill. So a press conference was hastily called, held in the newly remodeled Senate press briefing room.

They all stood on the blue-carpeted stage—Kennedy in the center, his Democratic cosponsors to the left and Republicans on the right. Farthest to the right, next to the double columns at the stage's edge, stood Mel, the only freshman senator there. "We all let Kennedy speak first," said Mel. "I wasn't in a hurry to speak. Besides, others had more seniority." He was respecting the power structure, pleased to be included but not wanting to overstep. And so Kennedy the lion approached the microphone first, as a scrum of reporters waited to hear about the breakthrough on immigration reform. The advocates' 380-page plan had arrived just as the Senate began debate on the issue.

"The plan isn't perfect, but only a bipartisan bill will become law," said Kennedy.

After he spoke, the Massachusetts senator walked offstage in Mel's direction. Rather than exiting, he walked directly to Mel and put his arm around him, turning him toward the obliging cameras. He shook his junior colleague's hand, smiling broadly as he did. "The cameras went click, click, click," said Mel, chuckling as he told the story. As the photographers memorialized the moment, the lion whispered in his ear, "I thought your Republican friends might like this picture."

Mel knew that Kennedy had scored in the friendly game of gotcha, but he didn't foresee all the repercussions—not then, at least. He didn't foresee the manifold consequences, how it would send the wrong message to a GOP constituency that was already dubious of immigration reform, as he and other Republican senators were working with the opposition to craft a bill that would, regardless of how they described it, grant amnesty to some illegal immigrants. It would also complicate his service as RNC chair, vastly so.

When the picture of him standing arm in arm with Ted Kennedy appeared in the *Orlando Sentinel* the next day,[4] the bill's passage was probably doomed.

⟻⟶

The agreement would have granted temporary legal status to virtually all illegal immigrants, allowing them to apply for residence visas and citizenship through a lengthy process. They would have to wait eight years before applying for permanent residence status and pay fines of up to $5,000. In addition, heads of household would be forced to leave the country and re-enter legally. First, though, the tough border crackdown would take effect. The Senate bill called for deploying 18,000 new Border Patrol agents and constructing new physical barriers, including 200 miles of vehicle barriers, 370 miles of fencing, and 70 ground-based camera and radar towers. In addition, funding would be provided for the detention of 27,500 illegal immigrants, and new identification tools would be developed to identify illegal job applicants. The granting of permanent resident status to illegal aliens and establishing a new guest-worker program would not begin until these border-crackdown measures took effect.

Achieving bipartisan consensus proved daunting, however. Even with White House endorsement of the compromise, the Republicans could not get support from their caucus leader, Kentucky senator Mitch McConnell. The caucus voted just short of a majority in favor of the bill. Once it became apparent that backers of the bill could not win this initial vote, caucus members were released from their obligations to support the White House, further eroding GOP support.

Under a complicated and rare procedure, the bill could pass only if any amendments offered were defeated through tabling. Backers of the bill allowed votes on amendments they felt confident they could defeat, thereby keeping intact their carefully balanced bipartisan compromise. On June 28 the Senate voted 45–52 against tabling one of the twenty-seven amendments approved for debate. After the tabling vote was defeated, Majority Leader Reid was heard saying into a microphone that he and other supporters of the bill were now "stuck." Senate Bill 1348—the Secure Borders, Economic Opportunity and Immigration Reform Act of 2007—would not pass.

Two days earlier, the Senate had voted 64–35 to consider the bill. This was four votes more than the sixty votes needed to keep the legislation alive, but if five Republicans were lost because of the unsuccessful effort to table that one amendment, the carefully constructed bipartisan compromise would fail. Which it did.

For the ailing Kennedy, the passage of immigration reform was supposed to be a victory lap. As he sat resignedly at his desk after the vote, Martinez walked over to him and extended his hand. Kennedy shook the junior senator's hand and said: "Thank you, my friend." Despite his disappointment, the Massachusetts senator vowed to soldier on, noting that legislation on emotionally charged issues—such as civil rights and proposals for ending discrimination in housing—lingered in the Senate for many years before earning final passage.[5]

New Mexico senator Pete Domenici, a onetime supporter of the bill who was facing an uphill reelection battle, complained during floor debate that Republicans were "getting hammered here and at home, and for what? Something that doesn't even have a chance of becoming law? No. This bill is going down."

Even if the Senate had passed the bill, its prospects in the House were dim. Despite the change in partisan control of Congress, there was still less sentiment in the House than in the Senate for any bill perceived as favorable to illegal aliens. The White House needed to produce sixty or more Republican votes in the House to pass an immigration bill similar to the Senate proposal, which would have been tough to get. "This proposal would do lasting damage to the country, American workers and the rule of law," said Lamar Smith of Texas, ranking Republican on the House Judiciary Committee. "Just because somebody is in the country illegally doesn't mean we have to give them citizenship."[6]

In the end, the House failed to vote on comprehensive immigration legislation in 2007, thus killing the measure. The breakthrough trumpeted by Mel and Ted Kennedy, among others, came to naught.

All this occurred against a backdrop of bitter complaints on talk-radio programs and CNN's *Lou Dobbs Tonight* about illegal immigrants breaking the law and draining public resources. Some in the party wanted to use immigration to energize the Republican base and divide Democrats by exploiting anti-immigrant prejudices. Martinez used the example of Republican congressman Tom Feeney, who represented a district east of Orlando with a growing number of Democratic and Independent voters. Feeney told Mel that he had found a great issue for the party. "Basically, he wanted to use the immigration issue as a wedge issue," Mel said in an interview. "No, I don't think so," the senator said, shaking his head.[7]

After immigration reform's defeat, Mel had an opportunity to speak to a meeting of the National Association of Latino Elected Officials (NALEO), held in his hometown of Orlando. In his remarks he expressed his "deep disappointment" over the bill's defeat, saying both parties were responsible. Now it was up to the critics, he said. "To those who have only nitpicked from both sides of the aisle . . . the burden has now shifted. What will they do? How will they continue to grow our economy? How will they bring people out of the shadows for our national security and for the sake of being a country that is just?"[8]

"The status quo was neither practical for meeting the workforce needs of the twenty-first century nor fair," he added. There would be no tamper-proof ID cards for undocumented workers, so that all who worked in this country could work legally within an established guest-worker program to provide a continuing flow of needed workers and to protect workers' rights. Nor was it just to carry out enforcement actions that would rip families apart by deporting fathers while allowing children born in the United States to remain. Invoking his own biography, he reminded the audience, "I understand what it means to be apart from one's family at a tender age."

In an interview conducted soon after the NALEO speech, he expressed particular bitterness toward his fellow Republican, New Mexico senator Pete Domenici, who had first agreed to support the Senate bill and then turned against it.[9] Fearful of losing reelection—he would later retire rather than seek another term—Domenici decided to side with anti-immigrant forces in New Mexico, a miscalculation in a state with a large Mexican American population, Mel believed. But it was more than that. Mel did not understand how someone like Domenici, the child of Italian immigrants, could turn his back on later immigrants. "His immigrant mother scrubbed floors in the capitol building to support his family, for God's sake," said Mel. For him, deserting your own as Domenici did was unimaginable.

The fight over immigration reform marked a change in Martinez. Building upon his socialization process in Orlando, his Washington experience had developed in him a pan-Hispanic consciousness. This was why he found Domenici's turncoat behavior so hard to fathom.

Martinez's devotion to immigration reform was not driven by electoral considerations. Although Florida employer groups in the tourism and agricultural industry favor a guest-worker program for obvious reasons, that does not translate into support for granting amnesty to undocumented workers. The state's Hispanic population consists primarily of Cubans and Puerto Ricans, and neither group has an immigration problem. Moreover, the base of the Republican Party in Florida and elsewhere was hostile to anything that sounded like amnesty for illegal aliens. But Mel's time in Washington had developed in him a stronger ethnic bond, one that embraced not just fellow Cuban Americans but Mexican Americans, Puerto Ricans, and other Spanish-speaking nationality groups.

When interviewed in 2005, he proclaimed passion for only two issues: abortion and Cuba. Two years later he added a third passion: immigration reform. As he explained, his commitment on that issue came from his experience in the cabinet, where he served as the Bush administration's troubadour to Latino groups, the Hispanic face of the Republican Party. Of that experience he said: "You just can't go speak to Hispanic groups and not be changed by the experience. You go and do that, and you learn from people. They admire you because they see you as a role model. But the process works in reverse too. You begin to see yourself as their representative."

Martinez was describing how he became "pan-Hispanic," recognizing that "Hispanic" is a term used mostly by Anglos. According to polls, however, most "Hispanics" in the United States prefer to be identified by their provenance—as Cubans, Puerto Ricans, Mexicans, Nicaraguans, Colombians, and so forth. By this description Mel was Cuban, a nationality group that many Latinos dislike because of Cuban immigrants' bourgeois background (having fled a communist revolution) and right-wing politics. But Mel had transcended this label, becoming not just a Cuban American leader but in some real sense a representative of all U.S. Hispanics, a status achieved by few other leaders of Hispanic heritage in contemporary America.

Asked about this, Martinez proudly agreed that he had developed a pan-Hispanic consciousness. He added that his socialization experience in Orlando was instrumental in this regard. It mattered, he said, that the Peter Pan program dropped him there rather than in Miami, where most of the Peter Panners were sent. As a Cuban in Orlando, he was part of a minority within a minority, outnumbered by non-Cuban Hispanics. As more Puerto Ricans moved to the area, Cubans like him were an even smaller minority within the Hispanic population. "As a Cuban I was never part of the majority within the Hispanic community," he said of his Orlando experience. "It made me feel like a brother to all Hispanics."

When he became Orange County chairman in 1998, Hispanics were a small part of the electorate. But once he was elected, "the communal pride they felt toward me made me want to represent all of them. The Mexicans, Colombians, and Puerto Ricans all felt I was their guy. Then when I got to the cabinet the same thing happened, magnified on a national level. As I traveled the country, I got to know Hispanic groups from across the country. I got to know their anxieties about the immigration issue, becoming more understanding of it and knowledgeable about it. Cubans and Puerto Ricans don't have an immigration problem, but it is truly a problem for other nationalities. It became a shared problem for me."

Once in the Senate, he began to recognize how the immigration issue could become his calling, a way to set him apart and make a difference. He was not looking for a career in politics, he always said; he was there to make a difference. He credited his friend, fellow senator John McCain, for urging him on. "John talked to me and said you need to get involved in this thing. It's the right issue for you. That's where my bond with John began." It caused Mel to reflect on his special status as the Senate's lone immigrant, one of the few people to serve in that august body in modern times who was born outside the continental United States. "What a unique opportunity [I have] to be a voice for other immigrants," he remarked.

His party affiliation added to that opportunity. He saw a chance to thread the needle politically, uniting those in Congress who wanted border protection and better law enforcement against illegal immigrants with those advocating a pathway to citizenship, a split clearly evident between House and Senate Republicans. Somewhere between these two poles he thought there was a place where reasonable people could come together in support of a comprehensive approach to immigration reform. In his own view, he played "an amazing role in the immigration debate for a brand-new senator." But that achievement came at a price. "It typecast me a little bit" as an advocate for immigrants, especially Hispanic ones, he said. "Now it's hard to break out of that role."

Mel's pan-Hispanic consciousness also grew from his frequent appearances in the Spanish-language news media, he acknowledged. The timing was fortuitous. Telemundo and its TV rival Univision were fairly new to public-affairs reporting from the nation's capital when Mel came to Washington. Telemundo, for example, began national news programming only after 9/11. And there was a natural synergy between Mel and these networks. He gained a forum—an opportunity to create a national following, sending a message that the GOP welcomed Hispanics. Equally important, he gave the networks a Hispanic role model who could speak good Spanish.

His language skill was pivotal in this regard. He spoke excellent Spanish, aided by his experience in Cuba. He had taken three years of high-school

Spanish there, something that distinguished him from his Senate colleagues Ken Salazar of Colorado and Bob Menendez of New Jersey, both Democrats. Salazar is of Mexican descent, Menendez Cuban American, but both grew up in the United States and learned Spanish at home rather than at school. Further, Martinez's Spanish is largely unaccented. Being part of the Cuban minority in Orlando's Spanish-speaking community caused him to abandon the clipped speech, strongly trilled *rr*, and swallowed *s* that characterize Cuban Spanish. It was an asset noted in his first job out of college, when he served as translator for Florida secretary of state Tom Adams.

All these traits made Martinez a star of Spanish-language television. "They know my face," says Mel. "They know my face because I do Spanish TV all the time." As his wife likes to say, Mel is known by "Hispanic busboys all across America." When they first came to Washington, attending fancy parties at embassies with the movers and shakers of the city, the people there did not know their names, "but the [Hispanic] busboys all knew me and came up to me." He was very conscious of how Hispanics of all descriptions knew and identified with him. Buying a pair of shoes in Dallas, he saw how his salesman nodded in his direction to another store employee, both of them Mexican American.

Here he was, the immigrant kid who became a United States senator. He alone among his ninety-nine Senate colleagues could not serve as president or vice president, owing to the requirement in the Constitution that the president (and therefore the vice president) be a natural-born citizen. On immigration reform, however, that prohibition became an opportunity. It gave him instant credibility on the issue, because senators from both parties looked to him for guidance and approval. He might not be the Senate's top expert on immigration—a distinction belonging to Ted Kennedy—but he had more moral authority on the issue than any of his colleagues.

"It seemed like the stars were all lined up for this thing to pass," Mel said. "Some senators wait a lifetime for something like this to happen, and still it doesn't happen."[10] You work in the trenches, laboring on mundane legislation, wanting to make a difference, trying to advance yourself in the Senate hierarchy like Sisyphus pushing a boulder uphill, worried that your plodding efforts will go unheralded when you seek reelection. Then an issue comes along that relates to the core of your being, and you have an opportunity to make a big difference, to resolve your identity conflict in a way that benefits the nation as a whole.

It was like the opportunity handed to President Lyndon Johnson with civil rights legislation. A white southerner, the product of segregation, he used his credibility from working with other white southern Democrats, men like Senator Richard Russell of Mississippi, to end racial segregation of public facilities through passage of the Civil Rights Act of 1964, something the Kennedy brothers (whom Johnson hated) with all their fancy education and sophistication proved incapable of doing.

And now it was Mel's turn. Not just to escape from his role as a freshman senator and exercise real leadership. Not just to demonstrate the bargaining skill he acquired from negotiating the cultural boundaries of Bishop Moore High School, learning to step lightly while living with Anglo foster parents in Orlando, and then later, working as a personal injury attorney, trying to win big settlements for his clients but preferring to bargain out of court. No, it was more than that. It was his opportunity to come full circle, from immigrant kid to immigrant prince, from victim to savior, from beneficiary of others' goodwill to giving back to the country that he had learned to love so passionately. Yes, passionately. Now he could use his passion—the passion that was such a vital part of his being, that came naturally to him from his Cubanness—to serve his adopted country.

He had worked hard for two years on an issue that he cared about passionately, thinking it was his opportunity to shine. But it had come to naught, painfully so, forcing Mel to confront his predicament with sober detachment. He was a very junior member of what was now the Senate's minority party, allied to a weak president who was distracted by the war in Iraq and whose poll numbers were plummeting.

Mel's fortunes had changed.

———

Politically, Mel paid a stiff price for advocating immigration reform. Saying that he got "typecast a bit" was an understatement.

When he and others announced their "breakthrough" on immigration reform, radio talk-show host Rush Limbaugh dubbed it the Comprehensive Destroy the Republican Party Act, and California Republican congressman Brian Bilbray said Martinez was "operating off an illusion and that is that somehow the Republican Party can flourish off of rewarding illegal behavior."[11] An organization called English First created a "Martinez Watch" blog dedicated to "keeping a wary eye on the Martinez record on immigration and multiculturalism." Postings to this and other conservative blogs referred to him as "Amnesty Mel" and "Sell-out Mel." A typical posting from a *Washington Times* blog said, "Martinez was hand-picked only to shove Bush's immigration bill down Congress's and the Republican faithfuls' throat."

By almost any standard, Mel's service at the RNC was a failure. His job, he said, was to raise money and project an image of "hope and optimism" for the party, but fund-raising declined on his watch, and the furor over immigration reform relegated him to a nominal role as party leader.

The Federal Elections Commission reported in August 2007 that GOP fund-raising experienced a 24 percent decline when compared to the previous year. Worrisome for party leaders, the Democrats increased their fund-raising by 29 percent over the same period.[12] A September 11, 2007, article in the conservative *Washington Times* newspaper attributed these problems to Martinez's immigration stance. It said this made him such a divisive figure within the party that they seldom used his name in e-mails and fund-raising appeals to the Republican constituency. The article added that Martinez had attacked the party's top two presidential candidates, Rudy Giuliani and Mitt Romney, for opposing and mischaracterizing the Senate immigration bill. Only two weeks earlier the RNC had voted to embrace an enforcement-first strategy for handling illegal immigration. Embarrassing for Martinez and President Bush, that policy was closer to Giuliani's and Romney's position on immigration reform than to Bush's and Martinez's.[13]

As evidence of his nominal role as party chair, in his first two and a half months in the job there were no press releases, only a handful of fund-raising calls, and few meetings with supporters. He took his first out-of-state trip for the RNC in early April 2007, introducing President Bush at a Los Angeles fund-raiser that brought in $2.3 million. In an interview, Martinez acknowledged that he had not reached out to mend fences with his immigration critics, a group he discounted as a "couple of handfuls of people. I don't see a huge party division that requires fixing a rift."[14] Tina Benkiser, the Republican Party chairwoman in Texas who opposed his election as party chair, continued to complain about him, saying she had not heard a word from him since his election in January. "At this time

Republicans need someone talking about who Republicans are as a party, our core values. We need to be making our case, and we've seen very little of our Republican general chair," she said.

Martinez defended himself by saying that he was not comfortable being out front. "Everything I do has to be comfortable with my style." The RNC defended him with statistics noting that in his first three months in office he had given more than fifty interviews and ramped up the party's Hispanic outreach. The latter, of course, was why Bush and Rove selected him for the post. The Florida senator acknowledged the "tremendous angst" in the Hispanic community over immigration, suggesting that even if the party could not forge a compromise on the issue, he could talk to voters about its content. "I can speak with a voice that lets people know that the Republican Party doesn't stand for bigotry and meanness," he told the *Miami Herald*. "It's a party that is trying to find a way to solve the problem. We're working on it. We're working on it from good faith, in the spirit of trying to get something done."

That message was all but drowned out by other voices in the party. One, former House Speaker Newt Gingrich, gave a high-profile speech in August 2007 ranting about two suspects in a triple murder in New Jersey who turned out to be illegal immigrants. He argued that President Bush should call Congress into special session to address the matter, calling himself "sickened" by Congress being in recess "while young Americans are being massacred by people who shouldn't be here." The onetime Republican leader said Bush should be more serious about "winning the war here at home, which is more violent and more dangerous to Americans than Iraq or Iran."[15]

Amid this hostile environment, Martinez went to see the president and told him that he wanted to resign from the party post. He was uneasy doing so, feeling he was letting the president down. But Bush was understanding, Mel reported. The president told him, "Don't worry. You only needed to stay in that position for a little while. It's not something you want to do, then don't do it."[16]

Bush would have been aware of Mel's lackluster fund-raising performance, making it easy to accept the senator's resignation. In truth, Mel never spent much time on the party job. Recognizing his figurehead status, he had not taken the largest office in the Republican headquarters executive suite, leaving that for Mike Duncan, the party's vice chair responsible for day-to-day operations. For himself Mel took a significantly smaller corner office. He spent approximately one day a month there, according to aide Matthew Hunter, though he was active in the job in other ways, making phone calls to raise money and attending showcase events.[17] True, he seldom appeared on the Sunday morning talk shows, as previous party chairs had done, but that was because he was not invited. The media were more interested in the Republican presidential hopefuls than in a party chair who was pretty obviously not in charge.

⟵⟶

Mel left the GOP post as the 2008 presidential election campaign was getting under way. On the Democrats' side, the other minority in his Senate class was attracting all the attention. Barack Obama was someone with whom Mel had worked on immigration reform, someone whom he admired. In a way both were immigrants to America. Obama was born in the nation's most ethnically diverse and geographically distant state, Hawaii, and spent part of his boyhood in another country, Indonesia. They both entered the continental United States in their teen years, Martinez at fifteen and Obama at eighteen. The key difference was that Obama entered as a citizen and Mel as an immigrant kid. In most respects that difference was inconsequential, because Mel had quickly earned citizenship, entitling him to full legal rights save for one thing: he can never be president. As a result, the swirl of speculation about who might be a running mate for the candidate of his party never turned to Mel, despite his being personally close to John McCain and representing electorally important Florida.

Mel had initially stayed neutral in the race for the Republican presidential nomination, though his sympathies lay with McCain. The two men had been strong allies on immigration reform, even though Mel's stepping outside the GOP caucus in 2006 to create a bridge to Democratic senators led by Ted Kennedy had initially angered the mercurial McCain. Still, Mel had brought McCain to Florida numerous times for joint appearances and fund-raisers. At one appearance Martinez introduced me to McCain, saying I was writing a book on him. The Arizona senator responded that his colleague was "a good man who deserved a good book."

During his presidential run McCain modified his stance on immigration, attesting to the anti-immigrant ardor of the Republican base. Since the reforms he supported, granting some illegal immigrants a pathway to citizenship, were called amnesty by critics, McCain as a presidential candidate talked about immigration reform exclusively in terms of border security and enforcement measures aimed at identifying and exporting undocumented workers. During the GOP primaries, immigration was a major issue, and the other candidates pummeled McCain for his stance, in 2006 and again in 2007, in favor of a comprehensive reform bill that included a pathway to citizenship.

McCain got the message and worked to shore up support from the party base. According to the *Boston Globe*, he told congressional Republicans in a closed-door meeting in early February 2008 that he had been "badly bruised" by his push for immigration reform and had "learned the hard way" that sealing the borders should be his priority.[18]

Martinez equivocated on whether his friend erred in talking about immigration differently. "He packaged it in a way that was okay with me," the senator said. "At least he didn't say it was a mistake to do what we were doing," which was to press for comprehensive reform that included amnesty as well as border protection and increased enforcement of existing law. Still, Martinez thought McCain miscalculated in trying to parse the immigration issue. "You're not going to gain the support of people who don't like you because you [previously] favored a pathway to citizenship." It would have been better to stand up for what he believed in; then voters would have respected him, even if they disagreed with him on this particular issue, the senator thought. "But when you begin to start saying I'm for immigration but maybe not as much as I used to be, then you begin to lose the people who are for immigration without necessarily gaining the support of people who hate you."[19]

During McCain's campaign appearances in Florida, Mel stood beside him on stage on every visit to the electorally important state, except when the Senate was in session. He also appeared with GOP vice-presidential candidate Sarah Palin on one of her Florida visits. Nonetheless, he thought McCain's selecting Palin was a huge mistake. "They were trying to reassure the base of the party when they should have been reaching out to Independents in the middle," he said.

Mel publicly said so following the election. The producers of *Meet the Press* told him that his appearance, as their lead guest in the week following the 2008 election, received more positive response from viewers than any program in recent memory. His hometown paper, the *Orlando Sentinel*, captured his remarks with the headline: "Mel: I Told You So."[20] Asked whether that was a fair characterization of his message, Martinez said it was.

Here are his remarks:

BROKAW: Senator Martinez, as you know, politics is about keeping score. I know this is tough for you to hear, probably, but you were 0-for-3 last Tuesday. You're a Republican; you are from Florida, that went to the Democrats; and you're Hispanic, or Latino in some parts of this country, and the Hispanics went overwhelmingly for the Democrats this time. Jill Lawrence wrote in *USA Today*: "If the Republicans don't make their peace with Hispanic voters, they're not going to win presidential elections anymore. The math just isn't there." That's according to Simon Rosenberg, head of the NDN, a Democratic group that studies Hispanic voters. How do you get back the Hispanics?

MARTINEZ: Governor Jeb Bush—former governor Jeb Bush—last week made a comment that, if Republicans don't figure it out and do the math, that we're going to be relegated to minority status. I've been preaching this for a long time to my colleagues within my party. I think that the very divisive rhetoric of the immigration debate set a very bad tone for our brand as Republicans. . . . I think in Florida there was not a great ideological shift, but I think there was plenty of room for improvement in how that state was looked upon.

The fact of the matter is that Hispanics are going to be a more and more vibrant part of the electorate, and the Republican Party had better figure out how to talk to them. We had a very dramatic shift between what President Bush was able to do with Hispanic voters, where he won 44 percent of them, and what happened to Senator McCain. Senator McCain did not deserve what he got. He was one of those that valiantly fought, fought for immigration reform, but there were voices within our party, frankly, which if they continue with that kind of rhetoric, anti-Hispanic rhetoric, that so much of it was heard, we're going to be relegated to minority status.[21]

After the GOP nominee's defeat, rumors began swirling that Martinez would not seek reelection in 2010. At a hastily called press conference in Orlando on December 2, 2008, he confirmed the rumors. With Kitty standing at his side before a scrum of local reporters, he said, "The call to public service is strong, but the call to home, family, and lifelong friends is even stronger." He refused to say he was in trouble politically. "Some will say a reelection campaign would have been too difficult, but I've faced much tougher odds in political campaigning and in life," he declared, his voice catching at several points. He continued by noting the demands of representing a large and complex state. "When you represent . . . a small state, you go home and you go to one or two cities and you've covered the state. When you represent a state as big as Florida, you never catch up, in addition to going back and forth [to Washington]. It is very, very demanding." To which he added, "No regrets or any complaining or anything," but "I am equally pleased to just bow and move on."[22]

As he left the podium, a newspaper columnist asked him: "Was that hard?" Mel's eyes filled with emotion. "Damn hard," he responded.[23]

To most close observers, his explanation for retiring was honest. Uppermost in importance was being a good father to fifteen-year-old Andrew. He and Kitty had begun talking seriously about his political future while vacationing the previous summer. His advisers were urging him to begin his reelection effort and ramp up his fund-raising. But Mel was dragging his heels, concerned about spending so much time away from friends and family in Orlando. He and Kitty were okay with his being in Washington three days a week. She came up for social events, so they were together publicly. Mel was troubled, though, about being away from Andrew so much. He remembered too well his Peter Pan experience, playing baseball and basketball at Bishop Moore and not having parents in the stands as the other boys did, because his parents were still in Cuba. It was not something he wanted for Andrew.

He was also deciding what to do with the rest of his life. He was then sixty-two. If he spent two years campaigning and won reelection, he would finish at age seventy. "Basically that would mean all I'm going to do for the rest of my productive life is be a senator." He had not foreseen that, back when he ran for county chairman in 1998, before a whirlwind tossed him into national politics courtesy of George Bush and Karl Rove and the GOP's need for Hispanic faces. As former Republican Senate leader Trent Lott had told him, "These are six-year decisions. When you get to be a certain age, six-year chunks of your life matter. Before I run again I'd give it a helluva lot of thought."[24] Lott had not followed his own advice, resigning one year into his final term. Mel wanted to be different.

Economic factors also weighed in his decision. "Financially, shouldn't I go back to work and secure my retirement a little bit better?" he asked himself. As a senator, he made $180,000 per year with abundant benefits. As a personal injury attorney before 1998, he was making seven figures. He could do that again as a retired senator—serving on corporate boards, introducing corporate clients to government officials, and giving speeches for big honoraria.

More, he was disenchanted with Washington politics. It was far different from being county chairman, where he could escape to private life. "When you're in Washington, you lose your sense of normalcy. You lose touch with your friends and family. People treat you differently." At his fortieth high school reunion there was an event honoring him, but Mel missed it. Senate majority leader Harry Reid had kept the chamber in session for an unusual Friday night vote, delaying Mel's return home until Saturday. When he arrived at the reunion, an old baseball friend said to him teasingly, "What kind of job is this that you don't have Saturdays off?"

The experience grated on Mel, a consultant friend said. He added that Reid, who returned as majority leader when the Democrats retook control of the Senate in 2006, had made Mel's life more difficult. Under Republican control, the Senate had a three-day work week, Tuesday to Thursday, but Reid and the Democrats put the chamber on a four- and sometimes five-day schedule.

It was not so much Democrats taking control of the Senate and White House that bothered him; it was his place in the Senate seniority system. That system was stifling under any circumstances, he said, but especially for someone with executive experience as a mayor or governor or in business, as opposed to someone with legislative experience. His age was also a factor. It normally takes three terms to achieve a leadership position—imaginable for someone who comes to the Senate in his thirties or forties, but more difficult for someone arriving in his late fifties, as Mel did. "It takes a couple of six-year cycles before you have time to be in a significant legislative position. In a big state like Florida, where the demands are so great, it's hard to [speed up the process] by being up there playing leadership games," he said.

To make things worse, Mel occupied the lowest rung in his Senate class. He belonged to a seven-member GOP class, but the other six had served in the House and ranked ahead of him by Senate rules, despite his having served in the cabinet as HUD secretary. In addition, he joined the Senate at the Republicans' high-water mark, when they controlled 55 seats. Mel then ranked 55 out of 55. But instead of growing their majority, the GOP lost ground, as the Democrats increased their presence to 51 in 2006 and 59 in 2008. What affected Mel more, though, was his low ranking in the Republican caucus, meaning he could advance only at a snail's pace. His chance of becoming a ranking minority member on a committee, his only way as a Republican to exercise real influence, was essentially nil. "I would pretty much end up sitting at the end of the table for a very long time," he said.

Adding to his woes, on October 10, 2008, his 2004 Senate campaign organization, Martinez for Senate, was fined $99,000 by the Federal Elections Commission for fund-raising errors. The FEC's audit on April 17, 2007, of the campaign's financial reporting revealed that Martinez for Senate had failed to comply with federal reporting regulations despite three written warnings from the FEC during the ten-month campaign.

The FEC's Audit Division found that Martinez for Senate violated several statutes by failing to disclose occupation and employer information for 46 percent of the individuals who contributed to the campaign, and by failing to provide any contributor identification information at all for approximately $320,000 in contributions. It also found that Martinez for Senate accepted $313,325 in excessive contributions. Additionally, in the last twenty days before the 2004 general election, the campaign received but failed to disclose $140,514 in contributions. An organization known as Citizens for Responsibility and Ethics in Washington (CREW), which filed an FEC complaint against Senator Martinez based on the FEC's earlier audit, summed up the matter this way: "Basically, Mel Martinez broke the law in order to win an election."[25]

Though Mel gave personal reasons for retiring, the Florida press saw his announcement largely in political terms, colored by his relationship with a disgraced president, his unpopular immigration stance, his low poll numbers, and his potentially uphill reelection battle. The *Miami Herald* emphasized his "slumping poll numbers and lackluster reelection fund-raising."[26] An *Orlando Sentinel* columnist attributed his retirement to the firestorm of criticism, in his own party, ignited by his stance on immigration reform. "Ironically," after throwing himself into GOP politics, "it was a profile in courage—a willingness to look for a compassionate compromise in the charged immigration debate—that ultimately did Martinez the most damage," wrote *Sentinel* columnist Scott Maxwell.[27] A *Sentinel* editorial appearing the same day said he was too connected to the president. "For all his bipartisan middle ground, Mr. Martinez is tethered to the unpopular Mr. Bush and many of his policies," it said.

Still, all the stories spoke kindly of Mel personally. "For a big-name politician, Mel Martinez is an easy-going guy" was a typical comment.[28] "He's been a watchful steward for this region, and the state," said the Orlando paper.[29] The *Tampa Tribune* said he had "cause to be proud of his tenure."[30]

Despite the plaudits, Mel resented some of the criticism. Most of the commentary cited his stint as RNC chairman unfavorably. While he agreed in retrospect that it had been a mistake, he also minimized its importance, saying it mattered only to a small number of politically attuned voters, most of them Democrats, who would not vote for him anyway. "Average voters don't know what the RNC is," he said in an interview.

Against the claim that he was tethered to President Bush, he cited his disagreements with the president. When he took the RNC position, he said he would be Florida's senator first and the GOP head second. At the time he said he disagreed with the administration's efforts to allow oil drilling off the coast of Florida. In June 2008 he directly challenged statements that Vice President Cheney, the former CEO of the oil services company Halliburton, made. At a speech before the Chamber of Commerce, Cheney claimed that China was pumping oil sixty miles off the coast of Florida in cooperation with the Cuban government. "Even the communists" understand the need for more drilling, declared the vice president. Armed with maps and reports, Martinez took to the Senate floor to rebut Cheney's claim. "China is not drilling off the coast of Cuba," he said. "Reports to the contrary are simply false . . . so any talk of using some fabricated China-Cuba connection as an argument to change U.S. policy, in my view, has no merit."

Earlier, Senator Martinez criticized the administration for not mentioning Cuba in a State of the Union address. On February 8, 2006, he wrote to Secretary of State Condoleezza Rice and Assistant to the President for National Security Affairs Stephen Hadley complaining about the speech. The president had cited several countries that, he said, should not be forgotten in their search for freedom. "As the President discussed areas of the world that must not be forgotten in their quest for freedom—Syria, Zimbabwe, North Korea, and Iran—I must confess my profound disappointment that the longest lasting tyranny remaining in the world, communist Cuba, was overlooked," the senator wrote.[31]

The implication in news articles that he could not win reelection gave Martinez particular heartburn. True, his poll numbers were down and never exceeded 50 percent. His positive-to-negative ratings were 37–39, compared to Florida Democratic senator Bill Nelson's 47–28 in August 2009.[32] But his support was the same as Nelson's had been three years before the former House member ran against the GOP's Katherine Harris to win his Senate seat. The only difference was that Martinez's negatives stood at 39, compared with Nelson's 34 percent at the same stage. And if his fund-raising totals were modest, that was because he had dragged his heels on running again. He had about the same totals Nelson did three years before his Senate run, though he could not expect an opponent as weak and loopy as Ms. Harris.

His better argument was that no strong Democrat wanted to run against him. Only one day before Mel's retirement announcement, the Democrats' best contender, Alex Sink, the state's chief financial officer, had declared she would not run for the Senate. Afterwards she said she would reconsider, then affirmed her original decision. "What does that tell you that Sink was not willing to run against me? After her, what other Democrat would be so formidable?" said Mel, cackling.

He saw the underlying factor as ethnicity—his. His poll numbers were low because Republicans disapproved of his immigration stance. Granted, his stance on granting amnesty was the same as McCain's and Bush's. That was where ethnicity mattered. His weakness lay with right-wing Republicans in the Panhandle, he believed. It was the same deficiency he experienced during his Senate run against Betty Castor. Until he corrected it, she was running ahead of him.

"It was a strange thing," he said, frowning. "My views were the same as George Bush's, yet Bush was running at sixty-four percent in the Panhandle, I'm running at fifty-five percent, and I'm losing statewide to Betty Castor by four, five points." In the end, Bush won the Panhandle with 65 percent support and Mel with 61 percent, a strong enough performance to win statewide. In his view, he was slow to win support in this Old South region of the state either because he was less well known there or because his ethnicity made him a hard sell.

He also disagreed that his long support for President Bush hurt him politically. His poll numbers were low because he was winning only 70 percent support from Republicans instead of the 90 percent that was normal. The reason, he thought, was immigration. "They ask Republican voters:

Are you satisfied with Mel Martinez? They say, 'Hell, no. He was the guy for immigration,'" Mel declaimed. But he still could have won reelection, because no strong Republican would challenge him in a primary, and disaffected GOP voters would choose him over a Democrat.

His analysis underscored John McCain's strategic blunder. Running against a Democratic opponent with Democratic views, Martinez would have won solid support from the party's right wing, including Panhandle Republicans skittish about voting for a Hispanic, the senator reasoned. It was the same in presidential politics. The party didn't need Mitt Romney as a candidate to turn out conservative Republicans. "At the end of the day, John McCain had the support of the right-wing base. He lost the Independents, he lost the middle. The same would have been true for me," said Martinez.

Analysts in the media who downplayed his reelection prospects also failed to appreciate the Hispanic vote. Martinez believed that pollsters routinely underpolled Hispanic voters, which was too easy to do. "Do they poll with bilingual callers? Hell, no." Bolstering this view was his experience. In every election, whether for county chairman or U.S. Senate, in both the primary and general election phases, he had performed better than preelection surveys predicted. It bears repeating: the explanation, he believed, was his strong support and high turnout from Hispanic voters. "I won Dade County. Jeb never won Dade. McCain never won Dade. You only win Dade by winning the Hispanic vote by an overwhelming margin and getting a disproportionate turnout from Hispanics."

It was a lesson that national Republicans needed to learn, Mel believed. The race was for the middle, not the right-wing base, and the Hispanic vote was hugely important. As a voting bloc they were potentially more important than African Americans. There were already more Hispanics than blacks in the United States, though more blacks were registered voters and blacks voted in larger numbers. If the GOP showed the right face to Hispanics—if the party avoided the kind of mistake that former California governor Pete Wilson made when he promoted a referendum, Proposition 187, to deny publicly funded social services to undocumented immigrants—the party could win enough votes from Hispanics to prevail in national elections.

The GOP did not need the same 80 percent support from Hispanics that Democrats received from African Americans. Winning 55 percent from

Latino voters was enough for Republicans to prevail. And these two objectives—winning the middle and winning majority Hispanic support—were compatible. The alternative strategy of reassuring the base, of appealing to the party's right wing, as McCain sought to do in selecting Sarah Palin as the GOP vice-presidential candidate and unleashing her to campaign among what she called "real Americans," lost the middle and alienated Hispanics at the same time. It was a losing strategy.

What Martinez tried to do—promoting immigration reform to attract Hispanic support—fit the party's enlightened best interest. As a Hispanic and a steadfast Republican, he wanted to expand the GOP tent to include more Latino voters. The problem was those already in the tent—the angry white people who disdained those who looked and sounded different from them. Thus Mel had not failed the party in failing to pass immigration reform. Rather, the party had failed him.

On August 7, 2009, Senator Martinez made a surprise announcement that he would resign before his term ended. He would resign just as soon as Florida governor Charlie Crist named a replacement for him. Since his announcement that he would not seek reelection, his mother had fallen and broken her hip, and he knew her time was limited at the time he resigned. A month after her fall, an unmarried cousin in Miami who was a federal judge was diagnosed with terminal brain cancer. Her name was Margarita, just like his sister who had died from brain tumors. He was very close to his cousin and had become her custodian. These were all reasons for retiring early.

Mitch McConnell, the Senate minority leader, understood when Mel explained his decision. "Most of the time when people say they're resigning for personal reasons, it's BS," McConnell told him. "In your case it happens to be true."[33] A mother's passing is traumatic for anyone, but especially for a Peter Panner who suffered a heartrending separation from his mother at a tender age. Likewise, attending his son's high school baseball games assumed special importance because of his refugee experience. Andrew was four when Mel was elected county chairman; he had been a political child virtually his whole life, and he had only three more years at home before going off to college. All the more reason to retire early.

There was also a political backstory, of course. The senator did not think he would be missing much by retiring a year early. By August, Congress would descend into partisan rancor. The debate would be nominally about issues like health care but really about positioning for the 2010 election. "The real issue will be who is going to govern next," he said. More, the GOP's mishandling of "the whole Hispanic thing" troubled him.

It was astonishing how they had misplayed President Obama's nomination of Federal Appeals Court judge Sonia Sotomayor to the U.S. Supreme Court. Supporting her was a no-brainer, Mel thought. Her views were within the mainstream of judicial opinion. And she was guaranteed to win confirmation, given the Democrats' 59-vote Senate majority. Why play to the base of the party in deriding her, as leading GOP senators sought to do? Why not embrace her instead? "It could have been a great pro-Hispanic moment for us," he said. Judge Sotomayor was approved 68–31, with all Democrats and only nine Republicans voting in her favor. Significantly, the Senate's lone immigrant cast his last vote for the nation's Hispanic Supreme Court justice.

But the damage was done. The Pete Wilson tragedy in California had repeated itself at the national level. Before the immigration debate, before the Sotomayor nomination, another political outcome was possible. But the voices of xenophobia had drowned out the advocates of change. Mel singled out Jim DeMint, an archfoe of immigration reform and a proponent of the Tea Party Movement (Taxed Enough Already) that emerged in 2009. "They want the GOP to be a party of dyed-in-the-wool conservatives, but it's a narrow band, about the same size as the pacifist wing of the Democratic Party," he said of these activists. For the first Hispanic RNC head, the question was how to "get back to that moment"—before the immigration reform struggle, before loud voices alienated so many Hispanic voters—"when something different was possible."

11

⬦

CONCLUSION

Who is Mel Martinez?

The answer is complicated because his genius lies in his mastery of men. He possesses a chameleonlike ability, arising from his immigrant experience, to be what people want him to be. Unlike the Cubans who settled in Miami, Mel was sent to Orlando, where no support group existed to aid his assimilation into American culture save for the other eleven Peter Panners who entered Bishop Moore Catholic High School with him. Significantly, the twelve boys were advised against speaking Spanish in public by their Anglo foster parents. In essence, his assimilation experience amounted to being thrown into the water and told to swim.

Support systems can sometimes exercise a negative influence, however. The Cuban émigrés who came to Miami, initially as refugees intending to return to Cuba, generally became successful economically, creating an "enclave economy" that encouraged Spanish-language maintenance and provided jobs for a steady succession of fellow immigrants.[1] The enclave they created in Miami's Little Havana, in Hialeah, and in other sections of the Miami metropolitan area has delayed their assimilation into the American mainstream and left them with a Cold War mentality against which many younger Cuban Americans today rebel.

For Mel, not finding an ethnic support group in Orlando ultimately exercised a positive influence. It gave him a burning desire to fit in, to be liked, to win approval and esteem—as well he did. This immigrant experience fostered his oft-recognized good qualities: his optimism, kindness, genial nature, and moderation of temperament.

These qualities were strengthened by his teenage friends in Orlando, who came uniformly from the same lower-middle-class milieu as Mel's first foster parents; by his experience playing sports, where he showed humility and self-restraint; by his law school experience, where he demonstrated a high quotient of emotional intelligence and the capacity for understanding the motives of others; by his work as a personal injury attorney, where he represented the "little guy" against corporate interests; by his experiences at the Orlando Housing Authority and the Orlando Utilities Commission, where he learned the value of pacing and how to bring others along; and by his experience in 2006, in the first round of the immigration debate, where he learned again that good ideas do not succeed on their own merits but require careful coalition building.

His immigrant experience also gave him a desire to give back, facilitating his passage from *homo civicus* to *homo politicus*, from private citizen to member of the politically active stratum. His story thus provides one answer to the question posed in the opening pages: Where do politicians originate? In a word, Mel Martinez became a politician out of gratitude. Not an ego-driven desire to exercise power and capture attention, but a morally driven desire to return the favor for all that he and his family received from their adopted country. His memoir covering the early years of his life, *A Sense of Belonging*, is aptly titled. From his immigrant experience he gained a sense that he belonged to more than himself and his family, to more than his Cuban ethnic group and his church. He also belonged to his community, Orlando, as well as his state and nation. As reflected in his resignation, he did not owe them everything, but he did owe them something—in his case, a eleven-year chunk of his life—for all that he received.

Perhaps there are two kinds of politicians: those motivated by gratitude and those motivated by grievance. The former see politics as a means of fulfillment, the latter as a means of redress. Those motivated by grievance have an us-versus-them mentality, stimulating the kind of unbridled passion that, sociologist Max Weber feared, would lead to demagoguery. Mel largely escaped such thinking, keeping his passions in check except on issues concerning Cuba and abortion. Even on those issues, he is more moderate in temperament than many advocates for these causes, owing to the temporizing effect of his immigrant experience.

His immigrant experience also makes him an enigma. Though comfortable in his own skin, he seems compartmentalized ethnically. He appears to exhibit a stronger core personality among his Cuban friends than he does among Anglos. His aides say you don't really know him until you see him campaign in Miami. There, culturally, he goes native. There, in his guayabera shirt, smoking a cigar, speaking Spanish rapidly, trilling the *rr* Cuban style, enjoying the adoration of the crowd, one glimpses the Mel he might have become. That is, if Fidel had failed and Mel remained in Cuba, or if the Peter Pan program had dropped him in Miami with so many other Cuban refugees. But that is the point: none of this happened. The Cuban Revolution did occur, and Peter Pan deposited him in Orlando rather than Miami. These experiences changed him, making him a boundary crosser and a bridge builder—qualities that served him well in the Senate and in his former career as a personal injury attorney who preferred negotiating out of court.

Occasionally his Cubanness boils over, not always for the better. In revolutionary Cuba, the political stakes were high: people lost their lives, their parents, their homes. This historical backdrop helps to explain Mel's passions and his occasional ruthlessness. His list of passions has been short, checked by his desire to fit in. He has allowed himself to be passionate only about Cuba, abortion, and more recently immigration. Accordingly, one should not overgeneralize about his passions. In chapter 1, I asked whether he was an absolutist or a pragmatist, citing evidence for both qualities. The answer is, he is both—most of the time pragmatic, not wanting to offend, and other times passionate, reflecting his Cubanness, on issues close to his heart.

Mel's ruthlessness was evident in his campaign's accusation that his Senate primary opponent, archconservative Bill McCollum, was the darling of "homosexual extremists." It was evident as well in his accusation that Betty Castor, his Democratic opponent in the Senate race, was soft on terrorism for not firing the Palestinian faculty member Dr. Sami Al-Arian when she was president of the University of South Florida. It was likewise evident in the Terri Schiavo affair, when he inadvertently revealed a memo written by a staff member urging Republicans to exploit the end-of-life controversy surrounding Ms. Schiavo.

This ruthlessness derives from Mel's Cuban political experience. For first-generation Cuban Americans like Mel, politics takes on a special meaning. They have seen how things can spin out of control, how people can lose it all, how popular movements can go awry. These experiences grant them authorization in their own minds to cut ethical corners, knowing or thinking they know all that's at stake. Mel's lapses into such thinking on issues that stoke his passions derive from his political socialization in the context of the Cuban Revolution, a revolution that he did not have the luxury of reading about in a newspaper, but rather one that he experienced personally, at a tender age, leaving parents without knowing whether he would see them again. That experience is the wellspring of his Cubanness, for better and for worse.

It was Mel's passions that first drew him to politics. These passions arose from his historical experience; without them he would still be a private citizen. They gave him the fire in the belly that made political life morally and psychologically rewarding, worth the personal sacrifice of lost income and lost time with his family—for a while.

In the language of Max Weber, cited in the opening pages of this book, his "passionate commitment to a realistic cause" transformed Mel from citizen to politician. It likewise created a bond between him and his followers on the issues that mattered to him—Cuba, abortion, and immigration.

Weber counsels that politicians, to be successful, also need reason. It checks the passion, explaining the phrase "passionate commitment to a *realistic* cause." The challenge, he says, is to combine "hot passion and cool judgment in the same personality." As we have seen, Mel acquired this reason from his immigrant experience, from his need to fit in and be accepted—in his foster home, among his high school classmates in Orlando, and in mainstream America more broadly. His Senate experience also contributed to this realism, explaining his grudging admiration for Ted Kennedy, whom he regarded as a master of parliamentary procedure. In the end, his Senate experience also told him when to quit. Realistically, the seniority system, the challenges of fund-raising, and the dynamics of party politics prevented him from making a difference in the Senate. The rewards from pursuing his passion no longer sufficed to cover the cost of lost income and lost time away from family and friends for Mel at age sixty-two.

He might have stayed in the Senate longer if his desire to participate in politics had arisen from a sense of grievance rather than gratitude. The former is inexhaustible—new grievances can always be found—the latter more bounded. Paraphrasing Thoreau's famous injunction in *On Civil Disobedience*, a person who feels morally compelled to do something is not obliged to do everything.

———

How did Mel get where he did?

Luck was part of it. As his brother, Ralph, lovingly said of him, "Mel is the luckiest son of a gun I know. First he was there when Bush came to town to promote his education program, and Mel rode in the limousine with him. Then Bush and Karl Rove picked him because they needed a Hispanic in the cabinet. And then, Bush and Rove chose him to step into the Senate race."

In the cliché, Mel was in the right place at the right time. He said it best himself. "I was Hispanic when Hispanic was in"—meaning, in with Republicans. That realization began to form while watching the 2000 Republican nominating convention. Orchestrated by Karl Rove, the convention presented an altered image of the GOP. Belying its status as the party of white people, a parade of minorities appeared on stage. Mel was then Orange County chairman, two years into his first elective office, serving in a nonpartisan position while actively playing partisan politics behind the scenes. He was hungry for advancement and saw Republican politics as the ramp. A friend standing with him at the 2000 convention urged him to take note of the many minorities on stage, saying, "Mel, you should get involved in this. The time is right."

Mel did take note. In his 2008 memoir he writes that political involvement "sneaked up and tapped me softly on the shoulder."[2] The metaphor is nice but the characterization imprecise, because Mel seized the opportunity to enter politics as much as the opportunity seized him. He was not only a Hispanic when GOP strategists wanted more Hispanic faces on stage. He was a Hispanic with innate political skill, fire in the belly, and the right story. His story affirmed the Republican view of America as a place where talented people can rise to the top through personal effort, private charity, and faith-based assistance (like the Peter Pan program administered by the Catholic Church).

He caught a wave and rode it until it crashed. When it did crash—when his diaspora story became window dressing for a political party that was basically inhospitable to minorities—he withdrew. Not so much in anger as in resignation and frustration. His experience demonstrated that the GOP was open to diversity at the top—in 2009 the party chair went to an African American, Michael Steele—but not to accepting minorities on their own terms at the base of the party.

More than being in the right place at the right time, he had the right stuff. He served the GOP so well because of what he so convincingly represented. Where others make calculated use of the Republican mantra of faith, family, and country, endeavoring to divide and conquer Democrats, Mel genuinely believed in that agenda. Where others profess belief in self-help, faith-based initiatives, entrepreneurship, and the private sector, he embodied those values, making him an exemplar not only of Republican thinking but of the whole GOP narrative. He recognized this about himself when he became RNC chair, saying he would quell internal division and advance the party's cause by telling his personal story, calling it a story of "hope and optimism."

Martinez's story attests to the continuing power of the American Dream saga. In their joint appearances, President Bush routinely called Mel a "living proof of the American Dream." His story resonates with audiences, whether in the Senate cloakroom or on the public stage, because it reaffirms the idea of America as the shining City on a Hill where the talented succeed by dint of pluck and effort. That's why Mel's story was such a godsend for the GOP. The story and Mel's presence on stage as a Republican officeholder, combined with his Spanish-language ability and personal charm, worked as magnets for attracting Hispanic voters to the party.

Initially he felt uneasy about making political use of his American Dream saga. For good reason, because his publicists in the county chairman campaign, at HUD, and especially during his Senate campaign repeated the story so incessantly that it became stale and platitudinous. Still, the story worked for him up to a point. It aided him in attracting support from other diaspora people, whether Nicaraguan, Mexican, or Jewish. It failed, though, to paper over cracks in the GOP base. When he sought to "use his story to unite the party," the voices of reaction triumphed over the voices of hope and inclusion, and he was sent packing.

At HUD his American Dream story produced mixed results at best. There the American Dream ideal was tied to minority homeownership, which did increase on his watch. It was with the new secretary in mind that the department created the Blueprint for the American Dream Partnership to encourage minority homeownership, and promoted the initiative across the country using a large bus with "American Dream Express" emblazoned on its side. Yet the gains made in homeownership by African Americans and native-born Latinos fell more sharply in the economic downturn than those of whites. As the Pew Hispanic Center reported in 2009, blacks and Hispanics were more than twice as likely to have subprime mortgages as white homeowners, even among borrowers with comparable incomes and credit scores.[3]

In the course of his rise he resolved his identity conflict between the two worlds he inhabited, one Cuban and the other Anglo, in ways that fostered his political progress. It started with the Elián González affair when he came out strongly Cuban, casting aside his Anglo identity in a way that seemed reckless for Orange County's elected executive. Indeed, few of his Anglo friends and supporters agreed with him on this issue. But his passionate stance in favor of keeping Elián in the United States, driven by his strong identification with the Cuban boy, put Mel on *Larry King Live* and earned him national attention.

If coming out Cuban in the Elián affair catapulted him into national politics, his involvement in the immigration debate broadened his ethnic identity, from Cuban American to pan-Hispanic. His push for comprehensive immigration reform was not electorally driven, as we have seen. Puerto Ricans and Cubans, the two largest Hispanic nationality groups in Florida, do not have an immigration problem, and the Mexican Americans who do are a small, and overwhelmingly Democratic, constituency. Rather, his commitment to immigration reform arose from his identification with Hispanics of every provenance. This is the meaningful sense in which he did change in Washington. He developed pan-Hispanic identity. It was shortly after his tenure at HUD that he said, "You just can't go speak to Hispanic groups and not be changed by the experience. You go and do that, and you learn from people. They admire you because they see you as a role model. But the process works in reverse too. You begin to see yourself as their representative."

Of course, Mel also had a strong sense of identification with the GOP. That was another change that occurred during his Washington tenure: the former Democrat and trial lawyers' president of pre-Washington days developed a stronger partisan identification. That Republican identity comported with his Hispanic identity. At least, it did until the defeat of immigration reform and the unleashing of anti-immigrant invective from the party's base. Before that, the two were compatible, because the GOP needed Hispanic voters. Likewise, the pro-business wing of the party that was more ascendant in the Senate than in the House favored a steady flow of immigrant workers, legal or illegal. What was good for Hispanic immigrants was largely good for these business groups. In practice, though, the right-wing base of the party was too driven by the politics of resentment to accept what was good for the party: more Hispanics, including some who had arrived in the United States illegally.

In seizing the moment, Mel threw caution to the wind. The wise thing for a freshman senator, party leaders counseled him, was to keep his head down, avoid controversy, and focus on constituent service. But that assumed he was there for the job, which he was not. Having started his political trajectory fairly late in life, at fifty-one, arriving in the Senate at fifty-eight, he was not there to put "points on the board," as he said in an interview. He was there to make a difference. Otherwise he would have taken a pass on immigration, kept his head down as Florida Democratic senator Bill Nelson does, and focus on reelection.

◁══▷

What does Mel's remarkable political odyssey mean?

The preceding chapters show how Mel's political career arose from the confluence of good fortune, a remarkable personal story, and a series of favorable trends and events. Three sets of trends have been addressed: the rise of Hispanic politics, the growing role of religion in politics, and the post-9/11 focus on security concerns. Martinez's odyssey gives meaning to these trends, and they help explain his political rise and subsequent retreat.

The Rise of Hispanic Politics

Black-white differences no longer represent the central group dynamic of American politics. As the election of President Barack Obama symbolized, these differences have receded in importance, at least politically. African Americans are now a stable part of the Democratic constituency, and the South was solidly Republican until 2008, when Barack Obama narrowly won Virginia and North Carolina. In their 2002 book *The Rise of Southern Republicans*, brothers Earl and Merle Black argued that the "partisan transformation of southern conservatism" from Democrat to Republican was mostly about race—that is, about black-white racial differences. What was once true is no longer: American politics is no longer centrally about black-white differences.

In 2000, Hispanics became the nation's largest minority; they are now 14 percent of the national population and African Americans 12 percent. In the South, the Hispanic population is growing faster than anywhere else. Virginia, North Carolina, Georgia, and Florida have all registered a tripling of their Hispanic population, experiencing population growth rates upwards of 200,000. Within this region, Latinos are still a sleeping giant—because so many lack citizenship and because only 58 percent of those with citizenship are registered to vote, compared with registration rates of 75 percent for whites and 69 percent for blacks.

As a result, the two parties are locked in a war of epic proportions. If the Democrats succeed in this war, they will dominate American politics for the foreseeable future; if not, their conquest of national politics will remain incomplete. Before 2008, Latinos looked very much like swing voters. In 2004, President Bush improved his share of their vote by 5 percent over his 2000 performance, winning 40 percent of this demographic. He did so by sending tailored messages to different nationality groups among Hispanics, paying attention to differences of idiom and pronunciation in recorded phone messages (something the John Kerry campaign failed to do); by appearing on stage frequently with Republican officeholders who were Hispanic (which Kerry likewise failed to do); and by repeating the GOP mantra of faith, family, and country.

Regarding faith and family, his campaign pushed social issues that resonated with Hispanics' Roman Catholic and evangelical Protestant faiths—namely, gay marriage and abortion. Regarding appeals to country, his campaign took advantage of Hispanics' high rates of participation in the military, making them susceptible to patriotic appeals in the context of the war in Iraq and concerns over terrorism. Since Hispanics rank high not only in military participation but in homeownership and self-employment, while ranking low in both trade union participation and welfare dependency—all Republican voter attributes—it is unsurprising that the immigration issue is so important to the partisan contest for the Hispanic vote. The steady stream of South American immigrants into low-paying jobs in the United States provides a flow of recruits into the Democratic Party. Without that stream of recruits, the Latino population might become predominantly Republican as more established Latino voters join the middle class, a pattern that occurred among second- and third-generation Italians.

Prior to the immigration debates in 2006 and 2007, the political question was whether the cultural appeal of the GOP mantra, emphasizing issues like abortion and gay marriage, would trump Democratic appeals to Latino voters based on antidiscrimination measures, extending Medicaid, and raising the minimum wage. But the immigration debates changed that, giving Hispanics of all classes reason to vote Democratic. It was Mel Martinez's worst fear: that the national Republican Party would alienate Hispanic voters in the same way that California governor Pete Wilson did in 1994 when he pushed hard for Proposition 187, designed to block illegal immigrants from receiving most public services. The proposition passed, and Wilson won reelection, but it turned Californian Hispanics against the GOP, helping push the state into the Democratic column in national elections.

Having been recruited to bring Hispanics to the party, Martinez saw more acutely than his sponsors the importance of expanding the party's tent to include Latinos. If they could not win more than half of this demographic, they were doomed to lose future presidential races. The problem, as Martinez discovered in the immigration debate, was the others in the GOP tent. The politics of resentment that came to dominate the party in the aftermath of the political transformation of southern conservatism, dating back to Richard Nixon's racially coded law-and-order messages in his 1968 presidential campaign, worked against opening the party's door to persons of Hispanic heritage.

The underlying problem is the contradiction within the soul of the party. On one hand, it is the party of angry white men, in thrall to the likes of Sean Hannity and Rush Limbaugh, resentful of people who look and talk differently, especially when they appear to get unfair advantages. On the other hand, in its rhetoric the party professes commitment to entrepreneurship, family, getting ahead, pulling oneself up by the bootstraps, pluck, and personal drive.

Nothing brought this contradiction to the fore more than the debate over immigration reform. Martinez's failure to win passage of the legislation was not a failure of his making. Rather, his efforts exposed the contradiction of the GOP. He was the exemplar of their contradiction. As we have seen, it was the GOP that failed him.

The immigration debate highlighted a long-standing divide in the Republican Party between the elitist Rockefeller business wing and the party's conservative populist base. The business elites are interested in a large supply of cheap labor and support unfettered immigration and open borders. The populist base supports legal immigration but is concerned about lawlessness on our border, national sovereignty, and the real security threat posed by porous borders.

There is nothing new about this. It is a forty-year-old conflict that has its roots in the cultural, economic, regional, and theological differences between the two camps. In the immigration debate, the country club wing of the party (more influential in the Senate) sought to assert its control over the populist wing (more influential in the House). The populist wing won, but in doing so it revealed its blindness to the reality that, with the rise of Hispanic voters, America has changed. Attracting these voters will require something different from the social issues that gave the party dependable majorities in the Reagan era. As Senator Martinez said of Hispanic voters on *Meet the Press*, "The Republican Party had better figure out how to talk to them."

President Bush got it too. When GOP senators balked at supporting the White House's approach to immigration reform, in June 2007, the president went to Capitol Hill and told them, according to *Washington Post* columnist Mark Shields, "Look, you're going to lose and alienate the growing and perhaps most influential new constituency in American politics."[4] To win GOP lawmakers' support, the president offered more funding for a security fence and enforcement—their principal concern. Senator McCain was concerned too, despite having backtracked on immigration reform in order to win the Republican presidential primary. He told ABC reporter George Stephanopoulos that Latino voter registration in the Phoenix area was running 6–1 Democratic. When it came to winning the Hispanic vote, Republicans were their own worst enemy.

The Growing Role of Religion in Politics

Much of the energy fueling religious activism has come from evangelical Christians. While religion has always been woven into the fabric of American politics, the level and type of activism within the churches is something new. Parishioners' shared beliefs have been transformed into a blunt political force by the self-conscious actions of clergy, active laity, and specialized political groups.

This politicizing of religion derives from two contextual factors—the changing role of women in society and Supreme Court decisions regarding school prayer and abortion. On the political side, it can be traced to the presidency of Ronald Reagan and his emphasis upon traditional values and patriotism. In the 1960s, before moral issues like abortion, prayer in school, and homosexuality pushed them to the GOP, white evangelicals voted Democrat by a 2–1 margin.

As the issues of abortion and gay marriage have gained ascendancy, the Catholic Church has likewise played a larger role in politics. As we have seen, Mel Martinez is a devout Catholic whose faith is elemental to his personal identity. He was educated in Catholic schools in Cuba and graduated from a Catholic high school in the United States. His parents removed him from Cuba when government agents harassed him at a high school basketball game with shouts of "Kill the Catholic." When the Church took a strong stand in the Terri Schiavo case, Martinez was there to help, pushing through a bill requiring a federal court review of her husband's attempt to have her feeding tube removed.

For a time, the rise of religious politics and the ascendancy of evangelical Christians within the GOP aided the party in winning majorities. Now the tail has come to wag the dog. The GOP, starting with the election of Ronald Reagan, used social issues as wedge issues to divide the Democratic coalition and attract white, often lower-class, evangelicals to their party. Their success aided them in winning the White House and gaining control of Congress, for a time. The problem now is that, in presidential campaigns at least, this evangelical wing appears to be in control, pushing the party to the right and, on the immigration issue, preventing the business wing of the party from getting its way. The same has applied to the GOP "noise machine," from Limbaugh and Hannity to their smaller-market wannabes, who fanned the flames of xenophobia during the immigration debate. Sarah Palin, her remarks about representing real Americans, and the hostile reaction to her by minorities of all stripes are potentially ruinous for the party—as Mel understood.

Again, Mel's experience with immigration reform exemplifies the contradiction between the GOP's business wing, which regards government intervention warily, and its evangelical wing, which wants to use government to impose its social agenda.

The Post-9/11 Focus on Security Concerns

The party stance on terrorism likewise relates to this conflict between the party's two wings. And Martinez's Cold War mentality, driven by his hatred for Fidel, puts him center stage in that debate.

The 9/11 terrorist attacks and the War on Terrorism stanched a lot of wounds within the party, helping to unite the elitist Rockefeller business wing and the party's conservative populist base. But as the terror issue subsides, the old fissures reemerge. Historically, the GOP used the "communist threat" arising from the Soviet Union and China as a wedge issue, branding the Democrats "soft on communism." When the Soviet Union fell and China began pursuing a capitalist road, making it an economic rather than a military threat, the GOP lost its principal foreign-policy issue. This culminated in the election of Bill Clinton, the first Democrat to win two terms in office since World War II.

As a refugee from Cuba, the only outpost in the Americas of Soviet-style communism, Martinez is a throwback to the bygone Cold War era. His anticommunist credentials are impeccable. The only problem is, communism has fallen almost everywhere except in Cuba. His challenge as a political figure, like the larger challenge facing the GOP, was to use the fear of terrorism as the party had earlier used the fear of communism, mobilizing voters against global terrorists as the new barbarians at the gate. He succeeded at this in his 2004 Senate race, vilifying his opponent, former university president Betty Castor, in constantly repeated TV commercials for not firing a Palestinian professor with alleged ties to terrorists.

He succeeded in Florida, in part, because of the presence there of so many diaspora people. In the Jewish community, for example, he found receptive ears when he said: "The Yasir Arafats of the world run in the same circles as Fidel Castro and Saddam Hussein. I know the price of tyranny, what it means to be religiously persecuted, and to yearn for freedom." The potential of this message was reflected in Bush's improved performance among Florida's Jewish voters, from 4 percent in 2000 to 22 percent in 2004—an improvement aided by the efforts of the Republican Jewish Coalition, which sent direct mail to Jewish voters asserting that Bush, not Kerry, was the best president to continue the War on Terror.[5] Obviously, the success of this approach depends upon a continued terrorist threat.

With a terrorist threat, the message laid down in the Natan Sharansky book that Mel kept on the coffee table in his Senate office made some sense. That book, *The Case for Democracy*, essentially equates Middle Eastern jihadists with the Nazis and communists who threatened the United States in an earlier era. The commonality between our past and present predicaments is the struggle for freedom. Absent that threat, a foreign policy of continued vigilance against jihadists at great costs in American lives and dollars is politically unviable. That leaves the GOP without an external threat and essentially without a foreign policy. More than that, it leaves the two wings of the party with little to unite them except, of course, lower taxes.

The GOP is likewise divided over U.S. foreign policy toward Cuba. Soon after the inauguration of President Obama, who said that he would meet with Raul Castro without preconditions, a U.S. Senate staff report issued on February 23, 2009, by Richard Lugar, the Indiana Republican who is the ranking member of the Senate Foreign Relations Committee, stated the obvious: our policy of strangling Cuba by imposing a strict trade embargo has failed to produce any significant change in the island's government. Lugar said it was time to review the policy of trying to isolate Cuba economically and deal with it "in a way that enhances the U.S.'s interest."[6]

The Senate report followed on the heels of a declaration, late in 2008, by the heads of thirty-three Latin American and Caribbean nations calling for an end to the U.S. embargo. Mirroring this change of sentiment among leaders to the south, Cuban Americans in the United States are changing their tune, at least younger ones. According to a 2008 poll of Cuban Americans living in Miami-Dade County, 56 percent believe the trade embargo has not worked at all, with younger Cubans and those who immigrated later expressing stronger negative views.[7] Similarly, a preponderance of those surveyed (65 percent) want to end the Bush administration policy adopted in 2003 that makes it more difficult to send money to Cubans, and a similar percentage favor ending the restrictions on travel to Cuba and reestablishing diplomatic relations with the island nation. In each case, Martinez stands opposite to majority opinion in the Cuban-American community.

Younger Cuban Americans and those who immigrated later have different views on these issues, which may explain why pro-Republican sentiment is declining in this demographic. Only 52 percent of Miami-Dade's Cubans are registered Republican. The remainder are Democrats (27 percent) and Independents (21 percent). Since Independent registrants are often transitioning from their party of origin, this may presage further GOP erosion. Once again, support for Democrats is stronger among younger Cubans and those who arrived in the United States later. Of greater relevance, Cubans aged 18–44 actually gave a majority of their vote to Obama, though McCain with Martinez's help won 62 percent of Miami-Dade's Cuban vote overall.

Still, Martinez steadfastly supports the trade embargo. On this issue he was the Senate's most committed cold warrior, a captive of his own history. As Machiavelli wrote about political leadership: "Those princes who are utterly dependent on fortune come to grief when their fortune changes." His recommendation: that the prince "adapt his policy to the times" when the times change.[8] This and much more of Machiavelli's sage advice to would-be leaders is in the copy of *The Prince* that the author gave Martinez many years ago. Guided by the book's advice, Martinez could become a positive force for change in U.S.-Cuba relations, if not in Cuba itself. Coming full circle, this Cuban immigrant could become an Immigrant Prince, a genuine leader who escapes from his own history and shows others the way forward. That next chapter could be his best.

At this writing, Mel is happy making money as JPMorgan Chase's senior executive in Florida and a member of the firm's executive committee. His executive responsibility extends from Florida to Mexico, Central America, and the Caribbean. His charge is to grow the firm's practice in Latin America, making connections for the firm's clients with foreign leaders he met during his public service. From such work he could easily step back into the governmental arena in an advisory role. He closely follows events in Cuba and "looks forward to helping the next generation of leaders in Cuba when a transition occurs there." He acknowledges murmurings in Miami that he could be the next president of Cuba, but routinely discounts such speculation, saying that the next president of Cuba is someone there now. Still, political life is full of surprises, as Mel Martinez knows better than most. Time will tell.

ACKNOWLEDGMENTS

I am indebted to Mel Martinez for granting me access to write this book. He not only gave freely of his time, a precious resource for a U.S. senator; he shared with me his ideas, beliefs, and experiences, some of them quite personal. He also authorized others to speak with me, making possible my interviews with his wife, Kitty, his mother, his brother, Ralph, his sister-in-law Becky, and his friends, associates, and present and former staff. And he did so without any editorial guarantees from me.

When this project began, I had no way of knowing how it would end. At numerous times in my research I reflected on the advantages of writing about a historical figure, someone finished. Maybe Ben Franklin. Then, from the beginning, I would know how the story ended. When I started, I thought this book might be about a Conquering Hero. I thought Mel Martinez might conquer Washington with his honesty and humility, rather than Washington conquering him, as it more or less did. I thought he might become (for Republicans) a Moses-like figure who delivered Hispanic voters to the GOP Promised Land. I did not foresee the tragic element of the story—how Republicans would squander an opportunity that may not come their way again anytime soon.

I am also indebted to Mel's wife, Kitty, and his brother, Ralph. I interviewed both of them twice, in addition to making numerous phone calls to Ralph to check on this or that fact or to solicit his opinion on something Mel was doing. Talking with Ralph, as others have said, is the next best thing to talking with Mel. Their brotherly love is a model for any two brothers. And Kitty is a model political spouse—devoted to her husband, yet very much her own person; the keeper of Mel's flame, but someone who keeps him grounded.

Scores of people opened their homes, offices, and memories to me over this five-year project. I cannot list them all, though I do in the endnotes;

everyone there deserves my thanks. I particularly want to single out Terry Couch, executive assistant to Senator Martinez, who patiently responded to my interview requests with courtesy and aplomb; former Orlando mayor Bill Frederick, who shared valuable insights into the meaning of leadership; John Sowinski, who explained the nitty-gritty of Mel's election campaigns; Dan Murphy, who talked freely about the political machinations behind Mel's transition from local to national politics; Matthew Hunter, who explained Mel's transition from HUD to the Senate; Skip Dalton, who helped me appreciate the significance of Mel's role in the immigration debate; and former U.S. senator Paula Hawkins, now gone, who prepped me on Senate politics.

I was fortunate to have the benefit of an endowed chair, the George and Harriett Cornell Chair in Politics, during this project. It enabled me to take a full year off from teaching to work on *Immigrant Prince*. Yet the teaching was instrumental in the writing. In all, I taught four seminars at Rollins that contributed to the book—one on immigration policy, another on the GOP, and a third and forth on political biographies. My students' comments and questions not only stimulated my thinking about pertinent topics; they also hastened my progress with their polite inquiries: "When's your Martinez book going to be done?"

Numerous friends and colleagues at Rollins contributed to this book. Bob Smither in Psychology read chapters and made helpful editorial suggestions. Bruce Stephenson in Environmental Studies listened politely when we should have been talking about his book. Socky O'Sullivan in English offered good ideas on marketing and placement. Ilan Alon in International Business gave encouragement and support, as did my provost, Roger Casey. And former president Rita Bornstein gave me insights into the psychology of leadership.

At University Press of Florida, Meredith Babb has been unfailingly patient, cheerful, and supportive, even when I missed deadlines. My copyeditor, Ann Marlowe, polished my prose and diligently ferreted out factual errors both large and small; thank you, Ann, for making this book so much better. My reviewer, Gary Mormino, professor of history and Florida studies at the University of South Florida, went beyond the call of duty. Besides helpful comments and suggestions on the manuscript, he has offered a continuing stream of news articles and source materials: I wish I could have used them all. The series coeditor David Colburn at the University of Florida was a wise and patient umpire of the review process. Aubrey

Jewett at the University of Central Florida made encouraging comments on the manuscript. My former intern Lara Bueso unearthed mountains of information on the 2004 Senate campaign. And Austa Weaver provided good cheer, a friendly ear, and helpful reminders—what would I do without her?

Many thanks as well to those who cheered me along the way, especially Judson Starr, Mary Wismar, and Al Moe. This is my first book since the death of my parents, but I feel their spirit with me. My sons, Eric and Chris, continue to make me proud. So does my daughter-in-law Crissy. With their husbands, she and my stepdaughter Suzy have given me the gift of grandchildren—the best therapy a writer can have.

This book is dedicated to Jeri Spriggs, the little flower who blossomed into my life during this project. She served as my sounding board, offered helpful suggestions on framing the story, and endured my absences when I slipped away to write or when I was physically present but mentally absent, crafting sentences in my head. Above all, she made me want to hurry and finish so I could enjoy the blessings of life with her. I promise not to do it again, at least not for a while.

NOTES

Preface

1. Goodwin, *Team of Rivals*, 748.
2. Joe Follick and Lloyd Dunkelberger, "Martinez, Castor Ad War," *Sarasota Tribune*, 21 October 2004.
3. Editorial, "McCollum for GOP," *St. Petersburg Times*, 20 August 2004.
4. Weber, "Politics as a Vocation," 116.

Chapter 1. Lucky

1. Interview with Ralph Martinez, 21 March 2005.
2. Bush, "Remarks at a Bush-Cheney Luncheon."
3. Adam C. Smith, "Party People: 20 Hours of Sketches and Observations from Election Day 2004," *St. Petersburg Times*, 7 November 2004.
4. Martinez, *A Sense of Belonging*, 199.
5. Keith Epstein, "Humble Origins Are Key to Martinez's Persona," *Tampa Tribune*, 10 August 2004.
6. Interview with Mel Martinez, 3 August 2005.
7. Interview with Kitty Martinez, 23 June 2005.
8. Interview with Mel Martinez, 7 March 2005.
9. Machiavelli, *The Prince*, trans. Bull, 131.
10. Black and Black, *The Rise of Southern Republicans*, 34.
11. See, for example, Lublin, *The Republican South*.
12. Kochhar, Suro, and Tafoya, "The New Latino South: The Context and Consequences of Rapid Population Growth."
13. Pew Hispanic Center, "The Hispanic Electorate in 2004."
14. "Latino Power: L.A.'s New Mayor—And How Hispanics Will Change American Politics," *Newsweek*, 30 May 2005, 25–35.
15. "The 25 Most Influential Hispanics in America," *Time*, 22 August 2005, 42–56.
16. Suro, Fry, and Passel, "Hispanics and the 2004 Election."
17. Pew Hispanic Center, "The Hispanic Electorate in 2004."
18. Micklethwait and Wooldridge, *The Right Nation*, 241.
19. *Newsweek*, "Latino Power," 27.
20. Interview with Ralph Martinez, 21 March 2005.

21. Florida International University political scientist Dario Moreno, quoted in *Time*, "The 25 Most Influential Hispanics in America," 47.

22. Kohut et al., *The Diminishing Divide*, 2.

23. Pew Forum, "Religion and Public Life," 26.

24. Kohut et al., *The Diminishing Divide*, 4.

25. Pew Forum, "Religion and Public Life," 31.

26. CNN exit poll, Florida, at www.cnn.com/Election/2004 (accessed 30 June 2005).

27. Crew, Fine, and MacManus, "BCRA," 9.

28. Sharansky, *The Case for Democracy*, xviii–xix.

29. Ignatieff, *The Lesser Evil*, 169.

Chapter 2. Peter Pan

1. Interview with Thomas Aglio, 24 June 2005; all quotation of and information about him comes from that interview.

2. García, *Havana USA*, 24–25.

3. Triay, *Fleeing Castro*, ix.

4. Ibid., 9.

5. Rodríguez, *The Bay of Pigs and the CIA*, 55.

6. Torres, *The Lost Apple*, 63.

7. Ibid., 243.

8. Ibid., 65.

9. Conde, *Operation Pedro Pan*, esp. chap. 12.

10. The official Web site of Operation Pedro Pan reports that 85 percent of the 7,000 unaccompanied Cuban children taken into care by the Catholic Welfare Bureau were between the ages of 12 and 18 upon arrival, and 70 percent were boys over the age of 12. See www.pedropan.org/content/history-operation-pedro-pan. These ratios probably hold true for the 14,000-plus in the Peter Pan program as a whole.

11. García, *Havana USA*, 29.

12. Mormino, *Land of Sunshine, State of Dreams*, 286.

13. Triay, *Fleeing Castro*, 28–29.

14. Interview with Cesar Calvet, 26 January 2005.

15. Interview with Gladys Martinez, 28 June 2005. Mrs. Martinez does not speak English; the interview was conducted and transcribed into English by my student assistant, Lara Bueso.

16. Interview with Ernesto Chaves-Gonzales, 4 February 2005.

17. Interview with Ralph Martinez, 21 March 2005.

18. Interview with Becky Martinez, 4 August 2005.

19. Interview with Mel Martinez, 20 June 2005.

20. Interview with Kitty Martinez, 23 June 2005.

21. Interview with Mel Martinez, 7 March 2005.

22. García, *Havana USA*, 16.

23. Pérez, *On Becoming Cuban*, 359, 388, 385, 410.

24. Ibid., 450–62.

25. Interview with Ernesto Gonzalez-Chavez, 4 February 2005.

26. Interview with Mel Martinez, 20 June 2005.

27. Martinez, *A Sense of Belonging*, 185.

28. García, *Havana USA*, 17.

29. Ibid., 20.

30. Eire, *Waiting for Snow in Havana*, 26, 222.

31. García, *Havana USA*, 5.

Chapter 3. Americano

1. Interview with Cesar Calvet, 5 July 2005.

2. Interview with Mel Martinez, 20 June 2005. Unless otherwise indicated, all quotation of him in this chapter comes from that interview.

3. Interview with Dennis Young, 5 July 2005. Unless otherwise indicated, all quotation of and information about the Young family comes from that interview.

4. Interview with Thomas Aglio, 24 June 2005. Unless otherwise indicated, all quotation of and information about him comes from that interview.

5. Eileen Young, interviewed in Martinez for Senate, *Mel Martinez: An American Story*.

6. Mel Martinez, address to Hispanic Summit organized by Orlando Regional Chamber of Commerce, Orlando, 4 March 2005.

7. Levine and Asís, *Cuban Miami*, 5.

8. García, *Havana USA*, 89.

9. Ibid., 83–84.

10. De La Torre, *La Lucha for Cuba*, 25.

11. Interview with Rick Steinke, 27 June 2005.

12. Interview with Gary Preisser, 22 June 2005.

13. Interview with William Dunn, 16 June 2005.

14. Interview with Ron Edwards, 17 June 2005.

15. Interview with Cesar Prado, 16 June 2005.

16. Interview with Lee Quinby, 16 June 2005.

17. Probably reflecting an increase from the mid-1960s, Orlando in 1970 had 2,085 Spanish-speaking residents, including 448 Cubans, in a city of 98,977 people; see U.S. Bureau of the Census, *1970 Census of Population: General Social and Economic Characteristics, Florida*, tables 260, 263, 335.

18. Interview with Cesar Prado, 16 June 2005.

19. Bacon, *Orlando: A Centennial History*, 2:246–56.

20. Colburn, "Florida Politics," 346.

21. Ibid., 363.

22. The 1970 census reported a black population of 29,156 in a city of 98,977 residents; see U.S. Bureau of the Census, *1970 Census of Population: General Social and Economic Characteristics, Florida*, tables 260, 335.

23. García, *Havana USA*, 44.

24. Colburn, "Florida Politics," 365.

25. García, *Havana USA*, 110.

26. "To Miami, Refugees Spell Prosperity," *Business Week*, 3 November 1962, 92–94.

27. "Cuban Refugees Write a U.S. Success Story," *Business Week*, 11 January 1969, 84–86.

28. Triay, *Fleeing Castro*, 89.

29. Jean Doolittle, "Cuban Family Arrives in Orlando," *Orlando Evening Star*, 31 March 1966.

30. Conde, *Operation Pedro Pan*, chap. 13.

Chapter 4. Kitty

1. Interview with Mel Martinez, 3 August 2005; all quotation of him in this chapter comes from that interview.

2. Interview with Rick Steinke, 27 June 2005; all quotation of him in this chapter comes from that interview.

3. Interview with Richard Gray, 23 June 2005; all quotation of him in this chapter comes from that interview.

4. Graves, *And They Were Wonderful Teachers*, xi, 6.

5. Interview with Ken Connor, 13 June 2005; all quotation of him in this chapter comes from that interview.

6. Interview with Kitty Martinez, 23 June 2005; all quotation of her in this chapter comes from that interview.

7. Interview with Tom Adams, 23 June 2005; all quotation of him in this chapter comes from that interview.

8. Interview with Bill VanDercreek, 21 June 2005; all quotation of him in this chapter comes from that interview.

9. Interview with James Corrigan, 20 June 2005; all quotation of him in this chapter comes from that interview.

10. Interview with John Thrasher, 1 August 2005; all quotation of him in this chapter comes from that interview.

11. The 1970 census revealed 448 Cubans living in Orlando, 109,108 in Miami; see *1970 Census of Population: General Social and Economic Characteristics*, Florida, table 263.

12. Interview with Dan Honeywell, 10 August 2005; all quotation of him in this chapter comes from that interview.

13. Interview with Jerry Billings, 4 August 2005; all quotation of him in this chapter comes from that interview.

14. Interview with Bill Frederick, 1 August 2005; all quotation of him in this chapter comes from that interview.

15. Interview with Skip Dalton, 16 September 2005.

16. Interview with Becky Martinez, 4 August 2005; all quotation of her in this chapter comes from that interview.

17. Interview with Father John McCormick, 21 September 2005; all quotation of him in this chapter comes from that interview.

Chapter 5. Citizen

1. Interview with Bill Frederick, 9 December 2004.

2. Orange County Planning Department, *Orange County Statistical Abstract, 1981*, 10.

3. Interview with Marcos Marchena, 11 March 2005; all quotation of him in this chapter comes from that interview.

4. Interview with Ernesto Gonzalez-Chavez, 4 February 2005; all quotation of him in this chapter comes from that interview.

5. Interview with Dr. Manuel Coto, 8 September 2005; all quotation of him in this chapter comes from that interview.

6. Interview with Bertica Cabrera, 19 September 2005; all quotation of her in this chapter comes from that interview.

7. Interview with James Auffant, 27 September 2005; all quotation of him in this chapter comes from that interview.

8. Interview with Mel Martinez, 3 August 2005; all quotation of him in this chapter comes from that interview.

9. Interview with Bill Frederick, 1 August 2005; all further quotation of him in this chapter comes from that interview.

10. Interview with Bill Warden, 4 August 2005.

11. Interview with Dan Honeywell, 10 August 2005; all quotation of him in this chapter comes from that interview.

12. Interview with Armando Payas, 5 October 2005; all quotation of him in this chapter comes from that interview.

13. "Cuban Crusader Mas Dead at Age 58," *Orlando Sentinel*, 24 November 1997.

14. Interview with John Thrasher, 1 August 2005.

15. Nap Ford, quoted in Myriam Marquez, "Mel Martinez: An Orlando Leader Who Came Up the Hard Way," *Orlando Sentinel*, 16 December 1991.

16. Dan Tracy, "Chicone Halts OUC Hearing," *Orlando Sentinel*, 4 June 1992.

17. Dan Tracy, "Managers Push OUC Spending Changes," *Orlando Sentinel*, 5 June 1992.

18. Dan Tracy, "Investigation Blisters Top OUC Executives," *Orland Sentinel*, 10 June 1992.

19. Interview with Rick Fletcher, 19 September 2005.

20. Interview with Tom Tart, General Counsel for OUC, 26 September 2005.

21. Interview with Kitty Martinez, 23 June 2005; all quotation of her in this chapter comes from that interview.

22. Interview with Becky Martinez, 4 August 2005; all quotation of her in this chapter comes from that interview.

23. 492 U.S. 490 (1989).

24. Interview with Ken Connor, 13 June 2005; all quotation of him in this chapter comes from that interview.

25. Interview with Skip Dalton, 16 September 2005; all quotation of him in this chapter comes from that interview.

26. Interview with Charles Gray, 6 May 2005; all quotation of him in this chapter comes from that interview.

27. Interview with Fred Leonhardt, 13 October 2005; all quotation of him in this chapter comes from that interview.

Chapter 6. Chairman

1. Interview with Dan Murphy, 28 October 2005; all quotation of him in this chapter comes from that interview.

2. Interview with Kitty Martinez, 31 October 2005.

3. Interview with Tre' Evers, 19 April 2005; all quotation of him in this chapter comes from that interview.

4. Interview with John Sowinski, 28 March 2005.

5. Interview with Fran Pignone, 18 January 2005.

6. E-mail from Cheryl Moore, 17 December 2005.

7. Scott Maxwell, "It's a Runoff for Chairman," *Orlando Sentinel*, 2 September 1998.

8. Interview with Ernesto Gonzalez-Chavez, 4 February 2005.

9. Interview with Armando Payas, 5 October 2005.

10. Interview with Evelyn Rivera, 14 October 2005.

11. Interview with James Auffant, 27 September 2005.

12. Interview with Holly Stuart, 20 October 2005.

13. Myriam Marquez, "Hey, Mel: What Would John Wayne Do About Unbridled Growth?" *Orlando Sentinel*, 22 May 1998.

14. Scott Maxwell, "Martinez's Campaign TV Ad Has Ostalkiewicz Fuming," *Orlando Sentinel*, 21 October 1998; Myriam Marquez, "Ostalkiewicz's Record of Distorting the Facts Speaks for Itself," *Orlando Sentinel*, 21 August 1998.

15. Scott Maxwell, "Chairman Race Sets a Record," *Orlando Sentinel*, 3 November 1998.

16. Interview with Evelyn Rivera, 14 October 2005.

17. Scott Maxwell, "New Ads Ratchet Up Nastiness," *Orlando Sentinel*, 21 October 1998.

18. Scott Maxwell, "Astonished Martinez Wallops Ostalkiewicz," *Orlando Sentinel*, 4 November 2005.

19. Interview with Bob Sindler, 20 October 2005; interview with Clarence Hoenstine, 3 November 2005.

20. Scott Maxwell, "Orange Leader Takes Oath," *Orlando Sentinel*, 18 November 1998.

21. Interview with Kitty Martinez, 31 October 2005.

22. Interview with Tom Wilkes, 18 October 2005.

23. Scott Maxwell and Kevin Spear, "Orange Commission Has an Acrimonious Beginning," *Orlando Sentinel*, 1 December 1998.

24. Interview with Agit Lalchandani, 25 October 2005.

25. Interview with Marianne Arneberg, 11 November 2005.

26. See, for example, these *Sentinel* editorials: "Bargain or Boondoggle?" 10 January 1999; "The Clock Is Ticking: The Time Has Come for Central Florida Leaders to Quit Wringing Their Hands Over the Proposed Light-Rail Project," 7 February 1999; "Leadership on Light Rail," 14 April 1999.

27. Editorial, "Positive Reflection," *Orlando Sentinel*, 25 February 1999.

28. Jim Stratton, "Light-Rail Study Puts Costs Higher," *Orlando Sentinel*, 26 January 1999.

29. Interview with Clarence Hoenstine, 3 November 2005.

30. Interview with Skip Dalton, 16 September 2005.

31. Interview with Bob Sindler, 20 October 2005.

32. Editorial, "Floyd Gives Martinez a Voice," *Orlando Sentinel*, 19 September 1999.

33. Interview with Mary Johnson, 10 November 2005.

34. Scott Maxwell and Jim Stratton, "End of the Line for Light Rail," *Orlando Sentinel*, 9 September 1999.

35. Local Government Comprehensive Planning and Land Development Regulation Act; see Chapter 163, Part II, Florida Statutes.

36. Interview with Robert Mandell, 7 November 2005.

37. Interview with Bruce McClendon, 31 October 2005.

38. Editorial, "Floyd Gives Martinez a Voice," *Orlando Sentinel*, 19 September 1999.

39. Interview with Miguel Pagan, 19 October 2005.

40. en.wikipedia.org/wiki/It's_a_Small_World.

41. Kevin Connolly, "Cuban Boy in Custody War Takes Time Out to Be a Kid," *Orlando Sentinel*, 13 December 1999.

42. Scott Maxwell, "Martinez Takes Elián's Case to TV," *Orlando Sentinel*, 11 January 2000.

43. Bill Adair, "Politics, Not Custody, Rules in Elián Hearing," *St. Petersburg Times*, 2 March 2000.

44. Interview with George Rodon, 25 November 2004.

45. Interview with Jacob Stuart, 18 April 2005.

46. Interview with Miguel Pagan, 19 October 2005.

Chapter 7. Secretary

1. Interview with Matthew Hunter, 24 January 2006; all quotation of him in this chapter comes from that interview.

2. Scott Maxwell, "Martinez Caught Bush's Eye Early," *Orlando Sentinel*, 21 December 2000.

3. Interview with Dan Murphy, 27 November 2006; all quotation of him in this chapter comes from that interview.

4. Jodi Enda and Ron Hutcheson, "Bush Names Four Additions to His Cabinet," *Miami Herald*, 21 December 2000.

5. Editorial, "Not His Father's Cabinet," *Washington Post*, 7 January 2001.

6. "Cuba Blasts Naming of Exile to HUD," *Miami Herald*, 21 December 2000.

7. Interview with Sean Smealey, 2 February 2006.

8. Michael Grunwald, "A Slender Record on Housing Issues: Life Story, Politics Led to Martinez Choice," *Washington Post*, 17 January 2001.

9. Senate Banking, Housing, and Urban Affairs Committee, *Nomination of Mel Martinez: Hearings . . .* , 107th Cong., 1st sess., 17 January 2001.

10. Interview with Kitty Martinez, 31 October 2005.

11. Interview with Oscar Anderson, 5 January 2006; all quotation of him in this chapter comes from that interview.

12. Interview with Alphonso Jackson, 7 March 2006; all quotation of him in this chapter comes from that interview.

13. Interview with Phil Musser, 26 January 2006; all quotation of him in this chapter comes from that interview.

14. Ellen Nakashima, "HUD Looks to Its Own Housekeeping," *Washington Post*, 21 February 2001.

15. Interview with Diane Tomb, 27 February 2006; all quotation of her in this chapter comes from that interview.

16. See note 14.

17. Ellen Nakashima, "Homeownership Plan Criticized as 'Mandate,'" *Washington Post*, 13 April 2001.

18. Kochhar, Gonzalez-Barrera, and Dockterman, "Through Boom and Bust: Minorities, Immigrants and Homeownership."

19. He told Congress that when Hope VI was created it was the only means of leveraging private capital to revitalize public housing properties. But that had changed. Public housing authorities were now mortgaging their properties to leverage private capital and cities were committing millions of their own money for this purpose. HUD also had

less costly alternatives to Hope VI. See testimony of Mel Martinez before the Senate Committee on Appropriations, Subcommittee on Veterans Affairs, Housing and Urban Development, and Independent Agencies, 6 March 2003.

20. Kenneth R. Harney, "HUD Chief Seeks Simpler Sale Closings," *Washington Post*, 2 June 2001.

21. Statement before the House Committee on Financial Services, 3 October 2002.

22. Sandra Fleishman, "Fees, Fees, and More Fees: Mortgage Costs Add Up," *Washington Post*, 7 June 2003.

23. Interview with John Weicher, 17 January 2006; all quotation of him in this chapter comes from that interview.

24. Kenneth R. Harney, "HUD Chief Seeks Simpler Sale Closings," *Washington Post*, 2 June 2001.

25. Kenneth R. Harney, "Settlement Industry Opponents Attack Martinez Settlement Reform Proposals," *Realty Times-Real Estate News and Advice*, 28 April 2003.

26. Interview with Frank Jimenez, 23 February 2006; all quotation of him in this chapter comes from that interview.

27. Senate Committee on Banking, Housing, and Urban Affairs, *HUD's Proposed Rule on the Real Estate Settlement Procedures Act: Hearings . . .* , 108th Cong., 1st sess., 20 March and 8 April 2003.

28. Interview with Ron Kaufman, 13 February 2006; all quotation of him in this chapter comes from that interview.

29. Interview with Sean Cassidy, 19 January 2006.

30. Associated Press, "HUD Withdraws Closing Cost Proposal," *Washington Post*, 23 March 2004.

31. Johanna Neuman, "Embattled HUD Secretary Jackson Takes Exit Ramp: FBI Probes Allegation of Contract Favoritism," *Chicago Tribune*, 1 April 2008.

32. Interview with Mel Martinez, 7 March 2005.

33. Phillips, *American Dynasty*, 148.

34. Steve Bousquet and Bill Adair, "Martinez: Refugee, Lawyer, Politician," *St. Petersburg Times*, 18 July 2004.

35. Mike Allen, "HUD Files Detail Martinez's Florida Trips," *Washington Post*, 17 March 2004.

36. Mike Allen, "HUD Secretary Martinez Resigns Cabinet Post," *Washington Post*, 10 December 2003.

Chapter 8. Candidate

1. Interview with Matt Schlapp, 9 May 2006; all quotation of him in this chapter comes from that interview.

2. Interview with Mel Martinez, 19 April 2006; all quotation of him in this chapter comes from that interview.

3. Interview with Ralph Martinez, 2 May 2006; all quotation of him in this chapter comes from that interview.

4. Interviews with Cesar Calvet, 26 January 2005 (he put the number at 21), and Bertica Cabrera, 19 September 2005 (she said 23); but see Bush, "Remarks at a Bush-Cheney Luncheon" (which names Mel 9 times).

5. Interview with Marcos Marchena, 11 March 2005; all quotation of him in this chapter comes from that interview.

6. Interview with Bill McCollum, 19 April 2005; all quotation of him in this chapter comes from that interview.

7. Bill Adair, "Martinez Called Florida 170 Times on Government Cell Phone," *St. Petersburg Times*, 2 April 2004.

8. Interview with John Sowinski, 4 May 2006; all quotation of him in this chapter comes from that interview.

9. "McCollum Near $2-Million in Funds; Byrd Closing Gap," *St. Petersburg Times*, 7 January 2004.

10. Brendan Farrington, "Martinez Leads '04 Cash Race," *Tallahassee Democrat*, 1 April 2004.

11. See note 9.

12. William March, "Martinez Support Limited for Now," *Tampa Tribune*, 27 January 2004.

13. Tamara Lytle, "Martinez Courts Conservatives," *Orlando Sentinel*, 12 February 2004.

14. Marc Caputo, "Martinez Gambling on Cuba Stand," *Miami Herald*, 18 July 2004.

15. Interview with Julio Rubell Jr., 11 May 2006; all quotation of him in this chapter comes from that interview.

16. Lesley Clark, "Mayor's Race May Aid Martinez," *Miami Herald*, 10 April 2004.

17. Mormino, *Land of Sunshine, State of Dreams*, 11–12.

18. Frank Cerabino, "Martinez a Compelling Tale," *Palm Beach Post*, 20 June 2004.

19. John Kennedy, "Martinez Isn't Hand-Picked," *Orlando Sentinel*, 18 December 2003.

20. In early April 2004, a poll conducted for the *Orlando Sentinel* and WESH television news channel showed the Republican contest shaping up as a two-man race between McCollum, who was getting 27 percent support, and Martinez, who had support from 18 percent of those surveyed. About one-third of likely GOP voters remained undecided.

21. Adam C. Smith, "Martinez Opposition Picks Up the Phone," *St. Petersburg Times*, 10 June 2004.

22. Steve Bousquet, "Martinez Backer Rescinds Support," *St. Petersburg Times*, 18 May 2004.

23. Adam C. Smith, "McCollum Attack May Boomerang," *St. Petersburg Times*, 7 April 2004.

24. Scott Maxwell, "Candidates Act Up; She Speaks Out," *Orlando Sentinel*, 13 June 2004.

25. Editorial, "Bring 'Em On," *St. Petersburg Times*, 9 January 2004.

26. "Stem Cell Research Becomes a Wedge Issue for GOP Moderates," *USA Today*, 19 October 2004.

27. Marc Caputo, "Gay Issues Become Focus of GOP Primary Battle," *Miami Herald*, 29 August 2004.

28. William March and Mark Holan, "Public Stage," *Tampa Tribune*, 29 August 2004.

29. Interview with Tomás Bilbao, 21 June 2006.

30. See note 28.

31. Marc Caputo, "Martinez, McCollum 'Get Nasty,'" *Miami Herald*, 28 August 2004.

32. Editorial, "McCollum for GOP," *St. Petersburg Times*, 20 August 2004.

33. Adam C. Smith, "Parties Court the Ultimate Swing Voter: Florida's Hispanics," *St. Petersburg Times*, 3 May 2004.

34. Keith Epstein, "Democrats the Key to Unlock Hispanic Votes," *Tampa Tribune*, 9 May 2004.

35. Interview with Samuel Bell III, 10 April 2006; all quotation of him in this chapter comes from that interview.

36. During World War II the Jewish Refugee Committee set up Kindertransport, or Children's Transport, which carried 10,000 Jewish children from danger in Germany, Austria, Czechoslovakia, and Poland to sanctuary in England. Tragically, 9,000 of these children never saw their parents again. See Conde, *Operation Pedro Pan*, 3.

37. Fine and White, "Mobilizing the Jewish Vote."

38. Federal Elections Commission, "2003–04."

39. Crew, Fine, and MacManus, "BCRA," 11–12.

40. Ibid.

41. Joe Follick and Lloyd Dunkelberger, "Martinez, Castor Ad War," *Sarasota Tribune*, 21 October 2004.

42. Hill Research Associates memorandum to Martinez for Senate campaign, 15 November 2004.

43. CNN exit poll, Florida, at www.cnn.com/Election/2004 (accessed 30 June 2005).

44. Crew, Fine, and MacManus, "BCRA," 9.

45. Colburn, "Florida Politics," 344.

46. See note 14.

Chapter 9. Senator

1. Portes and Stepick, *City on the Edge*, 18.

2. Interview with Mel Martinez, 7 March 2005.

3. Judy Holland, "Lawmaker Makes History: Speaking Spanish in Senate," Hearst Newspapers, 3 February 2005.

4. Henry Waxman, quoted in Stern and Perine, "Schiavo Case Puts Lawmakers at Odds."

5. Media release, Office of U.S. Senator Mel Martinez, 6 April 2005.

6. Tamara Lytle, "Memo Shadows Martinez," *Orlando Sentinel*, 13 April 2005.

7. Interview with Mel Martinez, 26 April 2005.

8. Anne E. Kornblut, "Schiavo Autopsy Renews Debate on G.O.P. Actions," *New York Times*, 16 June 2005.

9. Tamara Lytle, "Martinez Rapped for Schiavo Memo," *Orlando Sentinel*, 4 April 2005.

10. Interview with Skip Dalton, 13 March 2006.

11. Interview with Nilda Pedrosa, 12 August 2006.

12. Interview with Mel Martinez, 23 August 2007.

13. Interview with Laura Reiff, 29 June 2006.

14. Interviews with Bryan Walsh, 30 July 2007, 12 March 2010; all quotation of him in this chapter comes from those interviews.

15. Interview with Steve Taylor, 19 July 2006.

16. Interview with Tamar Jacoby, 28 June 2006; all quotation of her in this chapter comes from that interview.

17. Shailagh Murray and Charles Babington, "Splits over Immigration Reform on Display from Coast to Coast," *Washington Post*, 6 July 2006.

18. Fred Barnes, "Why Republicans Got Shellacked in the Midterms," *Weekly Standard*, 8 November 2006.

19. James O'Toole, "Santorum Bets on Immigration in Re-election Race," *Pittsburgh Post-Gazette*, 9 July 2006.

20. Danielle Knight, "Santorum and Casey Battle Over Immigration," *U.S. News & World Report*, 6 October 2006.

21. Interview with Mel Martinez, 23 August 2007.

23. Darryl Fears, "Republicans Lost Ground with Latinos in Midterms," *Washington Post*, 18 November 2006.

24. Bush, "Remarks of the President."

25. Anita Kumar, "Mel Martinez Talks About His New Job," *St. Petersburg Times*, 19 January 2007.

26. CQpolitics.com/2007/01/opposition_to_martinez_for_top.html, accessed 20 January 2007.

27. Ralph Z. Hallow, "RNC Elects Martinez as Head," *Washington Times*, 20 January 2007.

28. See note 26.

Chapter 10. Retreat

1. Interview with Mel Martinez, 23 August 2007.

2. John Kennedy, "Martinez Kicks Into High Gear," *Orlando Sentinel*, 19 May 2004.

3. Carl Hulse, "Kennedy Plea Was Last Gasp for Immigration Bill," *New York Times*, 9 June 2007.

4. Tamara Lytle, "Martinez Is Key in Deal," *Orlando Sentinel*, 18 May 2007.

5. Susan Milligan, "Immigration Bill Dies in Senate," *Boston Globe*, 29 June 2007.

6. Alan Greenblatt, "Immigration Debate," *CQ Researcher*, 1 February 2008, 120.

7. Interview with Mel Martinez, 15 December 2008.

8. Mel Martinez, address to National Association of Latino Elected Officials, Orlando, 29 June 2007.

9. Interview with Mel Martinez, 23 August 2007.

10. Interview with Mel Martinez, 23 August 2007.

11. Lesley Clark, "Martinez Defends Immigration Measure," *Miami Herald*, 21 May 2007.

12. Federal Elections Commission, "FEC Summarizes January–June 2007 Political Party Fundraising Figures."

13. Stephen Dinan, "Troubles Mount at RNC," *Washington Times*, 11 September 2007.

14. Lesley Clark, "Martinez: RNC Job Is on Track," *Miami Herald*, 22 April 2007.

15. Gingrich, "Enough Is Enough."

16. Interview with Mel Martinez, 23 August 2007.

17. Interview with Matthew Hunter, 24 January 2006.

18. Julie Hirschfeld Davis, "McCain Retools Immigration Stance," *Boston Globe*, 27 February 2008.

19. Interview with Mel Martinez, 15 December 2008.

20. Editorial, "Mel: I Told You So," *Orlando Sentinel*, 8 November 2007.

21. Transcript, *Meet the Press*, 7 November 2008.

22. Adam C. Smith et al., "Martinez to Step Aside," *St. Petersburg Times*, 3 December 2008.

23. Scott Maxwell, "Martinez Couldn't Say No to Bush and Paid the Price," *Orlando Sentinel*, 13 December 2008.

24. Interview with Mel Martinez, 15 December 2008.

25. CREW, "FEC Fines Martinez Senate Campaign $99k."

26. Beth Reinhard, "Would Be Successors Line Up as Martinez Rules out Second Term," *Miami Herald*, 3 December 2008.

27. See note 23.

28. Wes Allison, "Senator at Times, Colliding; at Times, Collegial," *Tampa Tribune*, 3 December 2008.

29. Editorial, "Mel's Legacy—We Think: Bipartisan Approach Served Mel Martinez Best in the U.S. Senate," *Orlando Sentinel*, 3 December 2008.

30. Editorial, "Mel's Farewell," *Tampa Tribune*, 3 December 2008.

31. Press release, Office of U.S. Sen. Mel Martinez, 8 February 2006.

32. Quinnipiac University Poll, 19 August 2009.

33. Interview with Mel Martinez, 19 October 2009.

Chapter 11. Conclusion

1. Mohl and Pozzatta, "A History of Florida Immigration," 406.

2. Martinez, *A Sense of Belonging*, 199.

3. Kochhar, Gonzalez-Barrera, and Dockterman, "Through Boom and Bust."

4. PBS *News Hour*, 15 June 2007.

5. Fine and White, "Mobilizing the Jewish Vote."

6. Karen DeYoung, "Lugar Urges Obama to Open Talks with Cuba," *Washington Post*, 2 April 2009.

7. 2008 Cuba/U.S. Transition Poll, Institute for Public Opinion Research, Florida International University, December 2008.

8. Machiavelli, *The Prince*, trans. Bull, 131.

BIBLIOGRAPHY

Interviews

Adams, Tom. 23 June 2005.

Aglio, Thomas. 24 June 2005.

Anderson, Oscar. 5 January 2006.

Arneberg, Marianne. 11 November 2005.

Auffant, James. 27 September 2005.

Bell, Samuel, III. 10 April 2006.

Bilbao, Tomás. 21 June 2006.

Billings, Jerry. 4 August 2005.

Buckley, Ann. 16 June 2005.

Cabrera, Bertica. 19 September 2005.

Calvet, Cesar. 26 January 2005, 5 July 2005, 5 March 2006.

Cassidy, Sean. 19 January 2006.

Chavez, Ernesto. *See* Gonzalez-Chavez, Ernesto.

Connor, Ken. 13 June 2005.

Corrigan, James. 20 June 2005.

Coto, Dr. Manuel. 8 September 2005.

Cowles, Bill. 3 February 2006.

Dalton, Skip. 16 September 2005, 13 March 2006.

Dunn, William. 16 June 2005.

Eagan, Joe. 1 February 2005.

Edwards, Ron. 17 June 2005.

Evers, Tre'. 19 April 2005.

Fernandez, Jose. 3 October 2005.

Fletcher, Rick. 19 September 2005.

Frederick, Bill. 9 December 2004, 1 August 2005

Frist, Bill. 19 April 2006.

Gonzalez-Chavez, Ernesto. 4 February 2005.

Gray, Charles. 6 May 2005.

Gray, Richard. 23 June 2005.

Hoenstine, Clarence. 3 November 2005.

Honeywell, Dan. 10 August 2005.

Hunter, Matthew. 24 January 2006.

Jackson, Alphonso. 7 March 2006.

Jacoby, Tamar. 28 June 2006.

Jimenez, Frank. 23 February 2006.

Johnson, Mary. 10 November 2005.

Kaufman, Ron. 13 February 2006.

Lalchandani, Agit. 25 October 2005.

Leonhardt, Fred. 13 October 2005.

Mandell, Robert. 7 November 2005.

Marchena, Marcos. 11 March 2005.

Martinez, Becky. 4 August 2005.

Martinez, Gladys. 28 June 2005.

Martinez, Kitty. 23 June 2005, 31 October 2005.

Martinez, Mel. 7 March 2005, 26 April 2005, 20 June 2005, 3 August 2005, 19 April 2006,
23 August 2007, 15 December 2008, 19 October 2009.

Martinez, Ralph. 21 March 2005, 2 May 2006.

McClendon, Bruce. 31 October 2005.

McCollum, Bill. 19 April 2005.

McCormick, Father John. 21 September 2005.

Moye, Jim. 2 October 2005.

Murphy, Dan. 28 October 2005, 27 November 2006.

Musser, Phil. 26 January 2006.

Oliver, Lew. 16 December 2004.

Orizundo, Dr. Hermino. 23 June 2005.

Pagan, Miguel. 19 October 2005.

Payas, Armando. 5 October 2005.

Pedrosa, Nilda. 12 August 2006.

Pignone, Fran. 18 January 2005.

Prado, Cesar. 16 June 2005.

Preisser, Gary. 22 June 2005.

Quinby, Lee. 16 June 2005.

Reiff, Laura. 29 June 2006.

Rey, Tony. 25 April 2005.

Rivera, Evelyn. 14 October 2005.

Rodon, George. 25 November 2004.

Rooks, Linda. 10 August 2005.

Rubell, Julio, Jr. 11 May 2006.

Schlapp, Matt. 9 May 2006.

Sindler, Bob. 20 October 2005.

Smealey, Sean. 2 February 2006.

Sowinski, John. 28 March 2005, 4 May 2006.

Steinke, Rick. 27 June 2005.

Stuart, Holly, 20 October 2005.

Stuart, Jacob. 18 April 2005.

Tart, Tom. 26 September 2005.

Taylor, Steve. 19 July 2006.

Thrasher, John. 1 August 2005.

Tomb, Diane. 27 February 2006.

Trovillion, Alan. 8 August 2005.

VanDercreek, Bill. 21 June 2005.

Walsh, Bryan. 30 July 2007, 12 March 2010.

Warden, Bill. 4 August 2005.

Weicher, John. 17 January 2006.

Weinberg, Thomas. 21 November 2004.

Wilkes, Tom. 18 October 2005.

Young, Dennis. 5 July 2005.

Books and Articles

Bacon, Eve. *Orlando: A Centennial History*. 2 vols. Chuluota, Fla.: Mickler House, 1975–77.

Barnes, Fred. "Why Republicans Got Shellacked in the Midterms." *Weekly Standard*, 8 November 2006.

Black, Earl, and Merle Black. *The Rise of Southern Republicans*. Cambridge, Mass.: Harvard University Press, 2002.

Bush, George W. "Remarks at a Bush-Cheney Luncheon in Orlando, Florida, November 13, 2003." In *Public Papers of the Presidents of the United States: George W. Bush, 2003*, 2: 1517–22. Washington, D.C.: Government Printing Office, 2006. www.gpoaccess.gov/pubpapers/index.html.

———. "Remarks of the President After a Meeting with the New Leaders of the Republican National Committee." In *Weekly Compilation of Presidential Documents*, week ending Friday, November 17, 2006. www.gpoaccess.gov/wcomp/index.html.

Business Week. "Cuban Refugees Write a U.S. Success Story." 11 January 1969, 84–86.

———. "To Miami, Refugees Spell Prosperity." 3 November 1962, 92–94.

Colburn, David R. "Florida Politics in the Twentieth Century." In Gannon, *New History of Florida*, 344–72.

Conde, Yvonne M. *Operation Pedro Pan: The Untold Exodus of 14,048 Cuban Children*. London: Routledge, 1999.

CREW. "FEC Fines Martinez Senate Campaign $99k for 2004 Campaign Finance Violations—Fails to Acknowledge CREW's May 2007 Complaint." 28 October 2008. www.citizensforethics.org/node/34974.

Crew, Robert, Teri Fine, and Susan MacManus. "BCRA and the 2004 Presidential and Senate Races in Florida." Paper presented at the meeting of the Southern Political Science Association, New Orleans, 6–8 January 2005. www.docstoc.com/docs/6534742/BCRA-and-the.

De La Torre, Miguel A. *La Lucha for Cuba: Religion and Politics on the Streets of Miami*. Berkeley: University of California Press, 2003.

Eire, Carlos. *Waiting for Snow in Havana: Confessions of a Cuban Boy*. New York: Free Press, 2003.

Federal Election Commission. "2003–04 US House and US Senate Candidate Info for State of Florida." www.fecinfo.com/cgi-win/x_statedis.exe?DoFn&rb2004&StateFL.

———. "FEC Summarizes January–June 2007 Political Party Fundraising Figures." 14 August 2007. www.fec.gov/press/press2007/20070813party/20070813party.shtml.

Fine, Terri, and Daniel White. "Mobilizing the Jewish Vote in the 2004 Presidential Election in Florida." Paper presented at the annual meeting of the Florida Political Science Association, Gainesville, 8 April 2006.

Gannon, Michael, ed. *The New History of Florida*. Gainesville: University Press of Florida, 1996.

García, María Cristina. *Havana USA: Cuban Exiles and Cuban Americans in South Florida, 1959–1994*. Berkeley: University of California Press, 1996.

Gingrich, Newt. "'Enough Is Enough': While Washington Vacations, a War Rages Here at Home." *Human Events*, 14 August 2007. www.humanevents.com/article.php?id=21938.

Goleman, Daniel. *Emotional Intelligence*. New York: Bantam, 1995.

Goodwin, Doris Kearns. *Team of Rivals: The Political Genius of Abraham Lincoln*. New York: Simon & Schuster, 2005.

Graves, Karen L. *And They Were Wonderful Teachers: Florida's Purge of Gay and Lesbian Teachers*. Urbana: University of Illinois Press, 2009.

Greenblatt, Alan. "Immigration Debate." *CQ Researcher*, 1 February 2008, 97–120.

Ignatieff, Michael. *The Lesser Evil: Political Ethics in an Age of Terror*. Princeton, N.J.: Princeton University Press, 2004.

Knight, Danielle. "Santorum and Casey Battle Over Immigration." *U.S. News & World Report*, 6 October 2006.

Kochhar, Rakesh, Ana Gonzalez-Barrera, and Daniel Dockterman. "Through Boom and Bust: Minorities, Immigrants and Homeownership." Pew Hispanic Center, 12 May 2009. pewhispanic.org/reports/report.php?ReportID=109.

Kochhar, Rakesh, Roberto Suro, and Sonya Tafoya. "The New Latino South: The Context and Consequences of Rapid Population Growth." Pew Hispanic Center, 26 July 2005. pewhispanic.org/files/reports/50.1.pdf.

Kohut, Andrew, John C. Green, Scott Keeter, and Robert C. Toth. *The Diminishing Divide: Religion's Changing Role in American Politics*. Washington, D.C.: Brookings Institution Press, 2000.

Levine, Robert M., and Moisés Asís. *Cuban Miami*. New Brunswick: Rutgers University Press, 2000.

Lublin, David. *The Republican South: Democratization and Partisan Change*. Princeton, N.J.: Princeton University Press, 2004.

Machiavelli, Niccolò. *The Prince*. Translated by George Bull. New York: Penguin, 1961.

———. *The Prince*. Translated by Luigi Ricci, revised by E. R. P. Vincent. In *"The Prince" and "The Discourses,"* 2–98. New York: Modern Library, 1940.

Martinez, Mel. *A Sense of Belonging*. With Ed Breslin. New York: Crown, 2008.

Martinez for Senate. *Mel Martinez: An American Story*. Campaign DVD, 2004.

Micklethwait, John, and Adrian Wooldridge. *The Right Nation: Conservative Power in America*. New York: Penguin, 2004.

Mohl, Raymond A., and George E. Pozzatta. "A History of Florida Immigration." In Gannon, *New History of Florida*, 391–417.

Mormino, Gary R. *Land of Sunshine, State of Dreams: A Social History of Modern Florida*. Gainesville: University Press of Florida, 2005.

Newsweek. "Latino Power: L.A.'s New Mayor—And How Hispanics Will Change American Politics." 30 May 2005, 25–35.

Orange County Planning Department. *Orange County Statistical Abstract, 1981*. Orlando, 1981.

Pérez, Louis A., Jr. *On Becoming Cuban: Identity, Nationality, and Culture*. Chapel Hill: University of North Carolina Press, 1999.

Pew Forum on Religion & Public Life. "Religion and Public Life: A Faith-Based Partisan Divide." January 2005. pewresearch.org/assets/files/trends2005-religion.pdf.

Pew Hispanic Center. "The Hispanic Electorate in 2004." 27 June 2005. pewhispanic.org/files/factsheets/8.pdf.

Phillips, Kevin. *American Dynasty: Aristocracy, Fortune, and the Politics of Deceit in the House of Bush*. New York: Viking, 2004.

Portes, Alejandro, and Alex Stepick. *City on the Edge: The Transformation of Miami*. Berkeley: University of California Press, 1993.

Rodríguez, Juan Carlos. *The Bay of Pigs and the CIA*. Translated by Mary Todd. Melbourne, Australia: Ocean Press, 1999.

Sharansky, Natan. *The Case for Democracy: The Power of Freedom to Overcome Tyranny and Terror*. With Ron Dermer. New York: Public Affairs, 2004.

Stern, Seth, and Keith Perine. "Schiavo Case Puts Lawmakers at Odds." *Congressional Quarterly Weekly Online*, 1 March 2005, 728.

Suro, Roberto, Richard Fry, and Jeffrey Passel. "Hispanics and the 2004 Election: Population, Electorate and Voters." Pew Hispanic Center, 27 June 2005. pewhispanic.org/reports/report.php?ReportID=48.

Time. "The 25 Most Influential Hispanics in America." 22 August 2005, 42–56.

Torres, María de los Angeles. *The Lost Apple: Operation Pedro Pan, the Cuban Children in the U.S., and the Promise of a Better Future*. Boston: Beacon, 2003.

Triay, Victor Andres. *Fleeing Castro: Operation Pedro Pan and the Cuban Children's Program*. Gainesville: University Press of Florida, 1998.

U.S. Bureau of the Census. *1970 Census of Population: General Social and Economic Characteristics, Florida*. Washington, D.C.: Government Printing Office, 1972.

U.S. Congress. House. Committee on Financial Services. *Reforming the Real Estate Settlement Procedure: Review of HUD's Proposed Respa Rule*. 107th Cong., 2nd sess., 3 October 2002. commdocs.house.gov/committees/bank/hba84631.000/hba84631_0f.htm.

U.S. Congress. Senate. Committee on Banking, Housing, and Urban Affairs. *HUD's Proposed Rule on the Real Estate Settlement Procedures Act: Hearings . . .* 108th Cong., 1st sess., 20 March and 8 April 2003. frwebgate.access.gpo.gov/cgi-bin/getdoc.cgi?dbname=108_senate_hearings&docid=f:93708.pdf.

———. *Nomination of Mel Martinez: Hearings . . .* 107th Cong., 1st sess., 17 January 2001. frwebgate.access.gpo.gov/cgi-bin/getdoc.cgi?dbname=107_senate_hearings&docid=f:77196.pdf.

U.S. Congress. Senate. Subcommittee of the Committee on Appropriations. *Departments of Veterans Affairs, Housing and Urban Development, and Independent Agencies Appropriations for Fiscal Year 2004*. HUD testimony. 108th Cong., 1st sess., 6 March 2003. frwebgate.access.gpo.gov/cgi-bin/getdoc.cgi?dbname=2004_sapp_va_5&docid=f:1910415.pdf

Weber, Max. "Politics as a Vocation." In *From Max Weber: Essays in Sociology*, translated and edited by H. H. Gerth and C. Wright Mills, 77–128. New York: Oxford University Press, 1946.

INDEX

Martinez, Mel—*continued*
National Committee general chairman, 195–96; retirement of, 215; rightward tilt of, 161; RNC chair, failure with, 210; running for county chairman, 103; ruthlessness of, 225; on Schiavo, Terri, 183; Senate Banking Committee meetings, 128; Senate campaign of, 154, 171; Senate consideration, 151; Senate election of, 174; Senate pressure of, 149; Senate race (2004), xviii; soft spoken nature of, 43; sports and, 48; taking oath of office, 176; tight budget of, 72; on 2010 election, 214–15; two worlds of, 228–29; visibility, rise of, 2; wife's family, 66
Martinez, Melquiades Rafael, Jr. ("Ralph"), 1, 15; polio vaccine pill and, 34–35
Martinez Doctrine, 118
Mas Canosa, Jorge, 88, 89
Matanzas, province of, 56
Matthews, Chris, 121
Maxwell, Scott, 217
McCain, John, 220
McCausland, Liz, 196
McCollum, Bill, xxi, 50, 69, 152, 183; political attacks of, 159–60
McConnell, Mitch, 155, 203, 221
McCormick, John, 77
McDaniell, Ray, 85
McEvoy, John T., 137
Media sortie, 179
Medicaid, 10
Medina's Marketplace, 87
Mehlman, Ken, 195
Menendez, Bob, 207
Menéndez, Pedro, 18
Mertoff, Michael, 199
Miami: Cuban assistance of, 44, 45; Cubans in, 45; Spanish spoken in, 44–45
Miami-Dade County, 2004 election of, 174–75
Miami Herald, 21, 211
Mica, John, 104, 112
Micklethwait, John, 9
Milton, George, 60, 62
Minority home ownership, 137
Moms for Life, 95
Moot court, 69
Moral clarity, 14
Moral issues, 13
Mormino, Gary, 21, 157
Mortgage Bankers Association, 144
Murphy, Dan, 101, 111, 112, 125

Muskie, Edmund, 81
Musser, Phil, 130, 132, 139

Nader, Ralph, 126
NALEO. *See* National Association of Latino Elected Officials
National Association of Latino Elected Officials (NALEO), 204
National Journal, 126
National Republican Senatorial Committee, 171
Nelson, Bill, 129, 152, 219
Neurofibromatosis, 75
Nike, xix
9/11 attack, 7, 147; security concerns after, 234–37
Nixon, Richard, 118
No Child Left Behind, 123, 134
No-fault insurance, 90
North Florida, xiii, 174–75
El Nuevo, 22

Obama, Barack, 177, 187
On Becoming Cuban (Pérez), 29
Operation Pedro Pan (Conde), 21
Operation Peter Pan (Pedro Pan operation), xv, 6, 15, 19–25, 37–41, 45–47, 53–55, 58–59, 221, 223, 225, 227; accommodations of, 22; age of participants, 244n10; beginning of, 15; Castro on, 21; Catholic Church and, 43; chores in, 55; conclusion of, 20; development of, 17–18; end of, 16, 22; espionage on, 21; experience, 121; funding of, 6; military origins of, 18; network, 32; secrecy of, 18; trustworthiness and, 33
Opinion Street, xix
Optimist Club, 56
Orange County: commissioner, 91; lame duck period of, 110; Puerto Rican presence in, 10
Orange County chairman, election procedure, 106; Martinez, Mel, race for, 105–10
Orange County Commission, on light rail, 114–15
Orange County Convention Center, 125
Orange County Democratic Executive Committee, 109
Orange County Democrats, 109
Orange County Emergency Operations Center, 119
Orange County Homeowners Associations, 117
Orange County Medical Society, 82
Orange TV, 119

Richard E. Fogelsong is George and Harriett Cornell Professor of Politics at Rollins College and is the author of *Married to the Mouse: Walt Disney World and Orlando*.

Florida has emerged today as a microcosm of the nation and has become a political bellwether in national elections. The impact of Florida on the presidential elections of 2000, 2004, and 2008 suggests the magnitude of the state's influence. Of the four most populous states in the nation, Florida is the only one that has moved from one political column to the other in the last three national elections. These developments suggest the vital need to explore the politics of the Sunshine State in greater detail. Books in this series will explore the myriad aspects of politics, political science, public policy, history, and government in Florida.

The 57 Club: My Four Decades in Florida Politics, by Frederick B. Karl (2010)
The Political Education of Buddy MacKay, by Buddy MacKay, with Rick Edmonds (2010)
Reubin O'D. Askew and the Golden Age of Florida Politics, by Martin A. Dyckman (2011)
Immigrant Prince: Mel Martinez and the American Dream, by Richard E. Foglesong (2011)